3    The Rise and Fall of the Second Empire, 1852–1871

# The Rise and Fall of the Second Empire, 1852–1871

ALAIN PLESSIS

*Professor, University of Paris VIII*

Translated by
JONATHAN MANDELBAUM

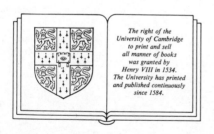

The right of the
University of Cambridge
to print and sell
all manner of books
was granted by
Henry VIII in 1534.
The University has printed
and published continuously
since 1584.

CAMBRIDGE UNIVERSITY PRESS

Cambridge
London   New York   New Rochelle   Melbourne   Sydney

EDITIONS DE
LA MAISON DES SCIENCES DE L'HOMME

Paris

Published by the Press Syndicate of the University of Cambridge
The Pitt Building, Trumpington Street, Cambridge CB2 1RP
32 East 57th Street, New York, NY 10022, USA
10 Stamford Road, Oakleigh, Melbourne 3166, Australia
and Editions de la Maison des Sciences de l'Homme
54 Boulevard Raspail, 75270 Paris Cedex 06

Originally published in French as *De la fête impériale au mur des fédérés, 1852–1871*
by Editions du Seuil, Paris, 1979
and © Editions du Seuil, 1979

First published in English by Editions de la Maison des Sciences de
l'Homme and Cambridge University Press 1985 as *The Rise and Fall of
the Second Empire, 1852–1871*

English translation © Maison des Sciences de l'Homme and
Cambridge University Press 1985

Printed in Great Britain by the University Press, Cambridge

Library of Congress catalogue card number: 84–11412

*British Library Cataloguing in Publication Data*

Plessis, Alain
The rise and fall of the Second Empire, 1852–1871.
—(Cambridge history of modern France)
1. France—History—Second Empire, 1852–1870
I. Title   II. De la fête impériale au mur des fédérés (1852–1871). *English*
944.07   DC276

ISBN 0 521 25242 3
ISBN 2 7351 0075 8 (France only)

# Contents

# Chronology

**1852**

| | |
|---|---|
| *14 January* | Constitution promulgated. |
| *2 February* | Organic decree on elections. |
| *17 February* | Decree on the press. |
| *29 February* | Election of Legislative Body. |
| *25 March* | Charter for prefectoral administration. Decree banning gatherings of more than twenty persons. |
| *7 November* | Senatus consultum calling for restoration of the Empire. |
| *21–22 November* | Second plebiscite. |
| *2 December* | Empire proclaimed. |
| *25 December* | Senatus consultum increasing emperor's powers. |
| *30 December* | Decree reinstating theatre censorship. |

**1853**

| | |
|---|---|
| *20 January* | Napoleon III marries. |
| *1 June* | Law on industrial tribunals. |
| *2 June* | Fleet sent to Dardanelles. |
| *9 June* | Law setting up pension fund for civil servants. |
| *1 July* | Haussmann becomes prefect of the Seine. |
| *5 July* | Opéra Comique plot. |

Victor Hugo writes *Les Châtiments*.

**1854**

| | |
|---|---|
| *27 March* | War declared on Russia. |
| *14 June* | Education law. |
| *22 June* | Law renewing obligation for workers to carry employment record (*livret de travail*). |
| *26 June* | Franco–British force occupies Greece. |
| *8 July* | Vienna Protocol between allies and Austria. |
| *20 September* | Battle of the Alma. |
| *5 November* | Battle of Inkerman. |
| *14 November* | Morny becomes president of Legislative Body. |

First publicly-floated government loan.
Viollet-le-Duc begins *Dictionnaire raisonné de l'architecture française*.

## 1855

| | |
|---|---|
| *26 January* | Alliance between France, Britain and Sardinia. |
| *April* | Allies defeated outside Sebastopol. |
| | Napoleon III contemplates leaving for the Crimea. |
| *26 April* | 'Exemption' system replaces military service by proxy. |
| *28 April* | Pianori assassination attempt. |
| *2 May* | Laws on public works in Paris and patent rights. |
| *May–November* | World Fair in Paris. |
| *27 August* | Slate-quarry workers' rising at Trélazé. |
| *10 September* | Sebastopol captured. |

Year of poor harvests.

## 1856

| | |
|---|---|
| *26 February–30 March* | Congress of Paris. |
| *16 March* | Birth of imperial prince. |
| *17 July* | Senatus consultum on regency. |
| *26 July* | Legislation on business companies reformed. |
| *October* | Flaubert publishes *Madame Bovary*. |

## 1857

| | |
|---|---|
| *19 January* | Law on the Landes region. |
| *April* | Baudelaire's *Les Fleurs du Mal* published. |
| *29 April* | Legislative Body dissolved. |
| *9 June* | Law extending special charter of Banque de France. |
| *21–22 June* | Election of Legislative Body. |
| *6 August* | Tibaldi and Ledru-Rollin sentenced. |
| *September* | Napoleon III and the tsar meet in Stuttgart. |
| *December* | Franco–British intervention begins in China. |

## 1858

| | |
|---|---|
| *14 January* | Orsini assassination attempt. |
| *1 February* | Decree setting up Privy Council. |
| *7 February* | General Espinasse appointed Minister of the Interior and of General Security. |
| *19 February* | Law on general security. |
| *13 March* | Orsini executed. |
| *25 April* | Legislative by-elections in Paris. |
| *11 June* | Espinasse leaves Ministry of the Interior. |
| *24 June* | Ministry for Algeria created. |
| *21 July* | Napoleon III and Cavour meet at Plombières. |
| *Summer* | Paris Conference on Rumanian principalities. |
| *15–19 August* | Napoleon III visits Brittany. |

Proudhon, *La Justice dans la Révolution et l'Eglise*.

## 1859

| | |
|---|---|
| *23 January* | Franco–Sardinian alliance. |
| *9 February* | Pamphlet on *L'Empereur Napoléon III et l'Italie.* |
| *18 February* | French occupy Saigon. |
| *25 April* | Work begins on Suez Canal. |
| *3 May* | War on Austria declared. |
| *4 June* | Battle of Magenta. |
| *11 June* | Law establishing co-operation between railway companies and the State, the latter guaranteeing interest on future bonds. |
| *24 June* | Battle of Solferino. |
| *12 July* | Villafranca conversation. |
| *15 August* | Amnesty decreed. |
| *10 November* | Treaty of Zurich. |
| *22 November* | *Le Pape et le Congrès* pamphlet. |
| *31 December* | Letter from Napoleon III to Pius IX. |
| | Société Générale founded. |
| | Mistral, *Mireille*; Ingres, *Bain turc.* |

## 1860

| | |
|---|---|
| *1 January* | Paris city limits extended. |
| | Pius IX's speech on France's Italian policy. |
| *4 January* | Thouvenel, an italophile, replaces Walewski as Foreign Minister. |
| *23 January* | Commercial treaty with Britain. |
| *30 January* | Veuillot's *L'Univers* banned. |
| *10 February* | Return to military rule (*gouvernement général*) in Algeria. |
| *24 March* | Treaty handing over Nice and Savoy to France. |
| *Summer* | France occupies Syria. |
| *18 September* | Italian troops rout Papal zouaves at Castelfidardo. |
| *24 November* | Decree granting assemblies right of address. |
| | Bessemer converter tried out for first time in France. |

## 1861

| | |
|---|---|
| *13 January* | Speech by Keller to Legislative Body. |
| *14 January* | Ollivier offers to rally to Empire. |
| *1 March* | Anti-clerical speech by Prince Napoleon before the Senate. |
| *25 April* | *Le Temps* founded. |
| *21 July* | Franco–Spanish agreement on Mexican debts. |
| *16 October* | Circular from Persigny directed against Saint-Vincent-de-Paul charity. |
| *17 October* | Letter from Tolain concerning scheme to send workers' delegation to London. |
| *14 November* | Fould appointed Finance Minister. |
| *31 December* | Senatus consultum increases Legislative Body's powers in financial matters. |
| | Building of Paris Opéra commences under supervision of Garnier. |

## 1862

| | |
|---|---|
| *23 February* | Inaugural lecture by Renan at Collège de France. |
| *29 March* | Franco–Prussian commercial treaty. |
| *5 May* | Defeat at Puebla (Mexico). |
| *5 June* | Annam hands Cochin-China over to France. |
| *July–October* | Workers' delegation at London Exhibition. |
| *15 October* | Cabinet crisis. Drouyn de Lhuys replaces Thouvenel. |
| *30 October* | Napoleon III proposes a common mediator in American Civil War. |
| *November* | Napoleon III pardons striking typographers. |

Victor Hugo, *Les Misérables*.

## 1863

| | |
|---|---|
| *11 April* | France imposes protectorate on Cambodia. |
| *23 May* | Law authorizing limited liability companies. |
| *30–31 May* | Legislative elections. |
| *23 June* | Persigny withdraws. V. Duruy becomes Education Minister. |
| *13 October* | Death of Billault, Minister of State. |
| *18 October* | Rouher appointed Minister of State. |

Crédit Lyonnais founded.
Salon des Refusés set up. Manet, *Le Déjeuner sur l'herbe*.

## 1864

| | |
|---|---|
| *11 January* | Speech by Thiers on necessary freedoms. |
| *17 February* | Manifesto of the Sixty. |
| *25 May* | Law on unions (right to strike). |
| *15 September* | Franco–Italian convention stipulating evacuation of Rome. |
| *28 September* | First International Working Men's Association founded. |
| *8 December* | *Quanta Cura* encyclical and *Syllabus* published. |

## 1865

| | |
|---|---|
| *26 January* | Death of Proudhon. |
| *10 March* | Death of Morny. |
| *15 May* | Speech by Prince Napoleon at Ajaccio. |
| *1 September* | Walewski president of the Legislative Body. |
| *October* | Student congress in Liège. |
| *October* | United States demands withdrawal of French troops from Mexico. |
| *October* | Napoleon III and Bismarck meet in Biarritz. |

Law recognizing value of cheques.
Claude Bernard, *Introduction à la médecine expérimentale*.
Manet, *Olympia*.

## 1866

| | |
|---|---|
| *7 and 11 March* | Privy Council and ministers condemn liberal reforms. |
| *19 March* | Liberal amendment of the Forty-Five rejected. |
| *12 June* | Franco–Austrian convention on Venetia. |
| *3 July* | Sadowa. |
| *18 July* | Senatus consultum on the right of amendment. |
| *5 August* | Napoleon III demands left bank of the Rhine as compensation. |
| *20 August* | Napoleon III demands Luxemburg and Belgium. |
| *3–8 September* | Congress of International in Geneva. |
| *12 December* | *Le Moniteur* announces army reform. |
| *13 December* | Evacuation of Rome completed. |

Crédit Mobilier collapses.
Offenbach, *La Vie Parisienne*.

## 1867

| | |
|---|---|
| *10–13 January* | Talks between Napoleon III and Ollivier. |
| *19 January* | Letter from Napoleon III announcing liberal reforms. |
| *20 January* | Niel becomes Minister of War. |
| *February* | French troops leave Mexico. |
| *14 March* | Senatus consultum increases Senate's powers. |
| *April–November* | World Fair in Paris. |
| *19 June* | Maximilian, emperor of Mexico, executed. |
| *12 July* | Ollivier attacks Rouher in Legislative Body. |
| *26 July* | Law exempting limited companies from government authorization. |
| *10 August* | Law on primary education. |
| *2–7 September* | Second congress of International in Lausanne. |
| *October* | Secondary education extended to girls. |
| *3 November* | French rout Garibaldians at Mentana. |
| *5 December* | Speech by Rouher on occupation of Rome. |
| *19 December* | Army reform bill discussed. |

## 1868

| | |
|---|---|
| *14 January* | Niel law voted. |
| *31 January* | Speech by Cassagnac on freedom of the press. |
| *March* | Senate debate on materialist courses at Faculty of Medicine. |
| *20 March* | French section of International sentenced on appeal. |
| *11 May* | Press law. |
| *30 May* | First issue of Rochefort's *La Lanterne*. |
| *6 June* | Law on public meetings. |
| *18 June* | International sentenced a second time. |
| *31 July* | Ecole Pratique des Hautes Etudes founded. |
| *14 August* | Rochefort sentenced. |
| *6–17 September* | Third congress of International in Brussels. |
| *13 November* | Gambetta plea in Baudin affair. |

## 1869

| | |
|---|---|
| *23–24 May* | Legislative elections. |
| *June* | Disturbances after second round of elections. |
| *16 June* | Strike at Ricamarie works. Troops open fire (14 dead). |
| *12 July* | Message from emperor announcing reforms. Rouher resigns. |
| *6–12 September* | Fourth congress of International in Basle. |
| *8 September* | Senatus consultum on liberal reforms. |
| *September* | Negotiations between France, Austria and Italy. |
| *30 September* | Emperor host to Ollivier at Compiègne. |
| *16 November* | Suez Canal inaugurated. |
| *29 November* | Legislative Body reconvenes. |
| *8 December* | Vatican council opens. |
| *27 December* | Napoleon III appoints Ollivier premier. |

## 1870

| | |
|---|---|
| *2 January* | Ollivier government. |
| *5 January* | Haussmann dismissed. |
| *10 January* | Victor Noir murdered. |
| *7 February* | Rochefort arrested. |
| *21 March* | Napoleon III announces constitutional reform. New strike at Le Creusot. |
| *5 April* | Draft of liberal senatus consultum discussed. |
| *8–9 April* | Buffet and Daru resign. |
| *20 April* | Senatus consultum on emperor's powers. |
| *8 May* | Plebiscite, followed by demonstrations. |
| *21 May* | Senatus consultum establishes liberal Empire. |
| *5 July* | International sentenced a third time. |
| *12 July* | Leopold of Hohenzollern renounces Spanish throne. |
| *13 July* | Ems telegram. |
| *19 July* | War declared on Prussia. |
| *4 August* | Battle of Wissemburg. |
| *6 August* | Battles of Froeschwiller and Forbach. |
| *9 August* | Fall of Ollivier. |
| *14–19 August* | Fighting around Metz. |
| *30 August–2 September* | Battle of Sedan. |
| *4 September* | Empire overthrown. Republic proclaimed. |
| *19 September* | Siege of Paris begins. |
| *27 October* | Metz capitulates. |

## 1871

| | |
|---|---|
| *28 January* | Armistice and capitulation of Paris. |
| *12 February* | National Assembly convenes in Bordeaux. |
| *17 February* | Thiers becomes premier. |
| *26 February* | Preliminary peace talks. |
| *3 March* | Central Committee of National Guard set up in Paris. |
| *10 March* | Bordeaux Pact. |

| | |
|---|---|
| *18 March* | Paris revolt: Commune begins. |
| *26 March* | Municipal council elected. |
| *5 April* | Decree on hostages. |
| *10 May* | Treaty of Frankfurt. |
| *21–28 May* | 'Week of bloodshed' (*Semaine sanglante*). |

# Foreword

Every period presents its own particular difficulties for anyone seeking to understand it. This is perhaps truer of the Second Empire than of any other period, and it is no accident that a recent conference on historiography should have chosen it as its special theme.[1]

The history of the Second Empire is undergoing rapid change. For a long time it was written by the Empire's adversaries, and it suffered from its tragic ending (Sedan, the Commune). Today, it is being almost totally revised. While the myths that encumbered its 'black legend' have been debunked one by one, new interpretations are revealing a period astonishingly rich in contrasts. I shall endeavour to describe it in all its complexity, even at the cost of sacrificing somewhat the narrative of important but already familiar events.

# 1

## The regime of Napoleon III

### 1. Late 1852

The preceding volume* recounted the final stages of the rapid march that in 1852 led the Prince-President Louis Napoleon to assume the title of Napoleon III: the senatus consultum of 7 November, the overwhelming 'yes' of the French people in the plebiscite of 21 and 22 November and, finally, the issuing, on 2 December, of a decree promulgating the earlier senatus consultum and proclaiming the Empire.

The transformation of a president of the Republic, even if elected for a ten-year term, into a hereditary emperor not only conferred a more prestigious title on Louis Napoleon but was also to be accompanied by a strengthening of his prerogatives, which were increased by the end of the year. Furthermore, it introduced an innovation into the Constitution that made it potentially more difficult to apply, since there was an apparent contradiction between the principle of the responsibility of the head of State and the hereditary character of the imperial dignity. Yet 2 December 1852 is a date that had very little impact on public opinion; the emperor's opponents regarded it as a pure farce, and historians have generally treated it as a 'mere constitutional formality'. True, the proclamation of the Empire may not have been the logical and ineluctable outcome of the principate, for the prince-president seems to have hesitated before deciding to change his title. But, as the proclamation entailed no major change in the arrangements of the constitutional edifice, it did not represent a decisive break. The foundations of the regime had been laid down as early as the morning of 2 December 1851, in the presidential proclamation posted on the walls of Paris. Thus, when opponents described the Second Empire as 'the regime of 2 December', their purpose was to emphasize that, as a product of the *coup d'état*, the regime bore what they considered the stigma of original sin.

---

* Maurice Agulhon, *The Republican Experiment, 1848–1852*, trans. by Janet Lloyd (Cambridge, 1983). (Trans.)

1

*A restoration?*

But the son of Hortense de Beauharnais and Louis Bonaparte, king of Holland, invoked a more distant and far more glorious origin for his regime. Despite his 'equivocal filiation', he regarded himself, ever since the death of the Duc de Reichstadt (1832), as the heir to Napoleon I, destined to succeed his uncle one day and so to revive the great Napoleonic tradition. Thus, immediately after taking control, he solemnly declared (proclamation of 14 January 1852):

> I have taken as models the political institutions that once before, at the turn of the century, in similar circumstances, gave new strength to a shaken society and raised France to the height of prosperity and grandeur. I have taken as models the institutions that, instead of vanishing at the first outbreak of popular disturbances, were toppled only by the coalition of all of Europe against us. In short, I asked myself: since France has been functioning for the past fifty years only thanks to the administrative, military, judiciary, religious and financial organization of the Consulate and the Empire, why should we not also adopt the political institutions of that period? As the creation of the same mind, they must surely embody the same national character and the same practical usefulness.

And it is indeed as a faithful and scrupulous imitator that he strove to revive the institutions of the First Empire (with the exception of the Tribunate) under the same names and with apparently similar powers. The senatus consultum of 7 November 1852 merely put the final touches on this resurrection, by stating in Article 1: 'The imperial dignity is *re-established*. Louis Napoleon Bonaparte is *emperor of the French*, under the name of Napoleon III.' (Emphasis added.)

Thus Napoleon I's very title was revived, and if the new emperor proclaimed himself to be the third to use the name, it was in order to underscore the regularity of his succession, for he regarded his cousin Napoleon II as having effectively reigned, however briefly, in June 1815. The last symbolic proof of this mimesis is Napoleon III's choice of 2 December for a solemn proclamation of the re-establishment of the Empire. He regarded this date as the anniversary not of the *coup d'état*, which had left him with a bad conscience, but of the coronation of Napoleon I and the glorious victory of Austerlitz. In short, Napoleon III's aim was to carry out a restoration.

It is of course possible that he may have deliberately built up his image as faithful heir in order to appear in the eyes of the French as the full embodiment of the 'Napoleonic myth' from which he had benefited so in the 1848 election. Hence the accusation of being a mere 'plagiarist' that was levelled against him by several of his contemporaries, most notably Karl Marx. But can one consider his attempt to copy the First Empire sheer bluff? Why not believe the sincerity of proclamations of faith made well prior to his coming to power?

*New times*

The question is ultimately a secondary one. Whether or not Napoleon III was sincere, was he not deceiving himself as to the possibility of reproducing intact a regime that was half a century old? There had been a sea-change since, and contemporaries were fully aware of the fact. Thus, in *L'Homme à l'oreille cassée* (1861), the journalist Edmond About told the story of a colonel of the First Empire desiccated by a German scientist and brought back to life under Napoleon III after being re-hydrated. Finding himself suddenly plunged into a France that is entirely new to him, the colonel feels totally out of place; he is incongruous. This novel has the merit of emphasizing that the Second Empire, whatever its appearances, was in no way a reproduction of the First, a resuscitated and anachronistic fossil.

The subjects of Napoleon III even felt they were living through a period that, to be sure, was far removed from the First Empire, but also very different from the more recent world that many of them had known in Guizot's day. The Second Empire was marked by a change so thorough-going that many contemporaries had difficulty finding their bearings. One can imagine the reactions of ordinary folk, of peasants seeing trains for the first time, or of workers – who had often only just left the peasant state – making contact with monstrous machines. Others, wealthier and better educated, left descriptions of their surprise. Among them, the travellers, tourists, poets or plain bourgeois who discovered that Paris was no longer Paris. Or the honourable members of the governing board of the Banque de France, who, faced with the changing dimension of their concern and the expansion of its activities, had to resolve week after week a host of problems previously unknown to them, the most pressing of which was to find an effective foil to the photographic forgery of bank notes. Some of these men, accustomed to relying in their decision-making on hitherto proven and now worthless precedents, wistfully observed: 'One cannot be guided by past conduct.' Finally, certain politicians who once belonged to what the Bonapartists pejoratively called the 'old parties' were no less bewildered. One of the most perspicacious among them, Rémusat, following the legislative elections of 1852 – whose results he 'could not imagine' – admitted having lost his last 'illusions' and, in his disenchant-ment, wondered 'how to believe that thirty-eight years of national opinions and habits could vanish in a few days'.[1] These were no doubt over-reactions, for there was both a continuity and a break between the age of Guizot and the Second Empire.

*The unity of the Second Empire*

But did the Second Empire itself constitute a homogeneous whole? If we limit ourselves for the moment to the political aspect, was the regime that existed in 1852 truly 'the' regime of the Second Empire, or was it characteristic only of its first phase? The question is a valid one, for Napoleon III's reign has traditionally been divided roughly in two, the 'authoritarian' Empire contrasting with the 'liberal' Empire. This presentation is especially striking in the two volumes of Lavisse's *Histoire de France contemporaine*, in which Seignobos links the first phase of the Empire to the revolution of 1848 (vol. VI) and the second to the founding of the Third Republic (vol. VII). It then becomes difficult to agree on the moment that marked the turning-point. Seignobos dates the caesura to about 1859, while the tendency in present-day research has been instead to reduce the truly liberal phase to the last year of Napoleon's reign, and at the same time to regard him as always having been a liberal! For others, who share the same impressions as many contemporaries of the period, the history of the Second Empire appears as a succession of contradictory images in a confused and incessant flow. Thus the British historian J. M. Thompson, who sees Napoleon III as a sort of Hamlet of French history, concludes that 'in fact the character of the imperial regime was changing all the time'.*

Such interpretations are not without value, for, in eighteen years of imperial reign, a considerable number of changes did take place. The period will therefore have to be studied here in an evolutionary perspective. But was not change itself foreseeable from the outset and, to a certain extent, foreseen, since the emperor always presented his Constitution as adaptable? And, if there were contradictions, were they not present more or less potentially from the outset, as inherent in the regime and in its head? One must be careful not to neglect the permanent features that made for the continuity of the Second Empire: first, the persistence of the institutions already established in 1852, since, despite policy changes, these institutions underwent only minor alterations until 1867 and even 1869; second, the remarkable stability of the governing personnel until approximately the same dates. The same men, by and large, served as ministers, as members of the assemblies and often as prefects; finally, the same sovereign ruled throughout the period.

## 2. *Napoleon III*

Although heir to the Napoleonic legend, and thus the perpetuator of a family tradition, the new emperor had no intention of sharing his authority with the other members of his clan. He adamantly refused to allow his uncle Jérôme, the sixty-eight-year-old former King of Westphalia, to take part in the council of ministers. As for Jérôme's son, Prince Napoleon, his personality hardly inspired the emperor's trust, and the latter never

* J. M. Thompson, *Louis Napoleon and the Second Empire* (Oxford, 1954), p. 225. (Trans.)

assigned him anything but ephemeral or minor tasks. After the emperor's marriage in 1853, Empress Eugénie, while not a visibly inconsequential figure, exerted only a weak direct influence on her august husband, except perhaps during the last years. As for Napoleon III's numerous mistresses, they never played a decisive political role.

Thus Napoleon was determined to exercise personal power – in every sense of the word – alone. He created a regime in which, in the last resort, every major domestic or foreign decision depended on him, and he intended to avail himself constantly of the right to modify the role of every institution and the responsibilities of every one of his followers.

### The sphinx

One can see, therefore, how valuable it would be if one could define the emperor's personality, which proves to be almost impossible to grasp. 'How,' asks Theodore Zeldin, 'can one understand a man who spoke so little and wrote even less?'[2] Made secretive by his experience of conspiracies, he seems to have done his utmost to make the investigator's task a difficult one: he left very little indeed in the way of personal evidence, and in his official speeches it is hard to isolate what is pure propaganda. As he was not in the habit of speaking his mind openly and unambiguously, even to his close relations, his contemporaries have left only very superficial portraits of him, at first accompanied by the extravagant praise of courtiers, and soon after submerged by an onslaught of judgements warped by blind and often unfair hatred. One can retain from all this a series of images of the emperor (his official portrait by Flandrin, or a classic photograph taken by Nadar towards 1865), and a catalogue of his faults and qualities: it has been said that he was a sexual maniac, that he was curiously devoid of moral sense, that he had no respect for the law and was no doubt full of contempt for men; but much has also been made of his peculiar charm, his good-heartedness, his generous loyalty to his old friends and his absence of cruelty.

But what was his worth as a statesman? It is certain that the caricatured portrait drawn by his first biographers can no longer be accepted, even though it continues to exert a widespread influence on opinions concerning Napoleon and on discussions about him.[3] Today, historians are generally agreed that Napoleon III deserves greater credit. Far from having been an insignificant puppet, he had the makings of an innovative politician far superior to the members of his entourage and to most of his opponents. He also comes across as a far more complex figure than has hitherto been imagined, since Adrien Dansette, speaking of the man whom Hugo saw as a tyrant, states that 'his ideology inclined him towards liberty'.[4] Thus one can no longer be content with the cliché of an incredibly fortunate adventurer or a crowned mafioso.

But it is not enough to rehabilitate Napoleon. It would be desirable to understand his personality in all its richness. However, the emperor still remains 'the enigma, the sphinx', as Zola put it in the special note that he compiled on Napoleon in the early days of the Third Republic, when he was working on his political novel *Son Excellence Eugène Rougon* – a note that is in a way a digest of opinions then prevailing.[5]

In order to solve this riddle, it is tempting to proceed by comparisons, to draw a parallel between the Second Empire and its master and other regimes and their leaders. Napoleon III then becomes an enlightened despot or a 'man of the twentieth century', in particular a precursor of fascism. Admittedly, one can discover a 'fascistic' aspect of him, and the resemblance is striking between his historical role and that of Mussolini:

> Both men, in the wake of a social crisis that set proletarian expectations aflame in a wild and disorderly fashion, frightened the bourgeoisie and laid the groundwork for the exercise of personal rule, took advantage of the impotence of elected assemblies to acquire – with the extensive connivance of military, financial and certain aristocratic circles – the acquiescence of the majority in a *coup d'état* dressed up as a 'return to order'. Both men, in order to consolidate their usurped authority, were obliged to pursue a glamorous foreign policy and, at first, scored a series of military and diplomatic successes; they promoted industry and agriculture, thus augmenting private wealth; they showed themselves to be well disposed towards the Church and obtained its support; they surrounded themselves with a camarilla of regime profiteers, many of whom, incidentally, proved to be excellent ministers or administrators; both men, however, overestimated their strength in an ill-prepared and ill-waged war in which all their glory collapsed.[6]

The list of these comparisons is not closed, and surely there is also room on it for a 'Gaullian' Napoleon III?

Each of these comparisons can undoubtedly shed more light on a given aspect of this complex figure, but at the risk of producing a series of different and more or less distorted Napoleon IIIs. One must resist the temptation of facile analogies that in various ways fail to take into account the factors essential to an explanation and an understanding of the man, his environment and his times.

### The antithesis of the 'men of stature'

Without adding yet another portrait to a perhaps overstocked gallery, let us try to put Napoleon III back in his historical context by drawing on contemporary accounts, particularly those left by the men who belonged to the élites, to the political class or to the intelligentsia – men who were often close to business circles, who were part of *la société*: at the time, they called themselves, in Thiers's words, the 'men of stature [*hommes considérables*] who spoke out for respectable folk [*honnêtes gens*]'. Leaving aside the opinions of those 'men of stature' who rallied to the regime and were impressed by Napoleon III primarily for the simple reason that he was the emperor, special attention will be paid here to the judgements of some of his opponents, not in order to side with them, but in order to perceive, through their criticisms, what separated them from Napoleon III, what they found objectionable about him – his personality, his methods and, finally, his ideas.

These men reacted, in the first place, to the gaps in the emperor's training. They regarded this old conspirator, who had long lived at odds with established authority, as a man with little education, in the classical sense that they gave to the word. Little did it matter that he possessed some technical knowledge in military affairs and was unusually well acquainted with scientific fields, foreign languages and even history, or that he had had an enriching series of experiences. These qualities did not really count, and this self-taught man would have had to be keener on the humanities, well versed in those ancients with whom one had to be conversant in order to possess the art of discourse, to partake of Truth, Good and Beauty – and to be admitted to the élite. Accordingly, Napoleon had little talent for parliamentary eloquence, he was bereft of an artistic sense (at least, he did not share the sometimes doubtful tastes of the 'men of stature') and he was never able to adopt good manners except superficially, so that his court, however brilliant, never truly had *le bon genre*. In short, as Rémusat observed in his memoirs, 'Louis Napoleon Bonaparte is weak in those areas where the well-bred appear as men of discernment'.[7] Hence, Napoleon, who on his arrival in France in 1848 hardly knew *la société*, was never accepted by it unanimously. For many, he remained an intruder, always something of a parvenu. As he did not share their cast of mind, his adversaries accused him quite unfairly of lacking all intelligence. Already in 1848, Thiers was not alone in calling the prince 'a cretin'. And twenty years later, one seems to find an echo of this in the verdict of the republican Jules Favre, whom the emperor had just received following his election to the Académie Française: 'What an idiot!' Zola himself noted, somewhat contemptuously: 'An average intelligence for his day: the secret of his success. The naïve heir to a legend, he has not upset it by individuality.'

His success, therefore, could be explained only by an outrageous – because wholly undeserved – stroke of luck. Yet he regarded his good fortune as entirely natural, for he had always considered himself to be the providential man whose destiny it was to govern France. But this faith in his mission appeared to his adversaries as a ridiculous pretension: 'Idol and high priest. Heir to a misunderstood prophet, prophet himself, responsible to the people and to God, he leads us to progress and freedom by Napoleonic grace', Zola commented ironically.

The second object of criticism and astonishment was his bizarre and almost abnormal behaviour as a politician. He did not intervene in important discussions, and remained oddly 'silent, unforthcoming, impassive' (Zola). His silence seemed to betray a lack of frankness, compounded by the fact that he would later prepare his decisions in utmost secrecy, with a pathological taste for concealment. Basically, he was being reproached in this for being a solitary manœuvrer who did not seek advice from the 'men of stature' and failed to trust them as they felt they deserved to be. His attitude can be explained by his past, but it also stemmed from his very keen awareness of the opposition that his policies would arouse. If he avoided discussion, it was because he felt incapable of dealing with contradiction, and also because he knew with certainty that if he showed his hand he would have to face numerous critics.

Furthermore, in practice, his politics seemed incoherent: he was 'constancy in hesitation', said Zola. At times he behaved like a perpetual hesitator, at times he displayed amazing stubbornness and an occasional capacity for surprisingly daring moves. The contradiction was only superficial: his hesitations and retreats were the actions of a man who, lacking exceptional authority, was apprehensive about coming to grips head on with obstacles too great for him. Such behaviour was part of his convoluted but flexible – indeed skilful – tactics, and would not imply that he had abandoned the prospect of implementing his schemes. Several contemporaries saw this clearly: 'He never regarded a postponement as a definitive abandonment' (Falloux); 'he takes short cuts, circumventing difficulties', but he remained 'in obstinate pursuit of his goal' (Zola). He did indeed hold fast to certain schemes and could for a long time give the impression of having shelved them; but they lingered on in his mind, and he revived them often when public opinion no longer expected it. These schemes were in the nature of intermittent obsessions. Most of his major decisions, at least until 1867, seemed to be the fulfilment of plans that he had worked out some twenty years earlier.

Well before coming to power, he had actually set out the guidelines of his policy in pamphlets such as the short but famous *Extinction du paupérisme* (1844) and the one entitled *Les Idées napoléoniennes* (1839). But many contemporaries refused to admit that these were indeed 'ideas'. Rather, they saw them as 'Napoleonic follies', 'pipe-dreams' (Rémusat), at best the 'reveries' (E. Ollivier) of a 'mediocre visionary' (Prévost-Paradol). And Zola said of him that he had 'more imagination and reverie than judgement. He tried to live the life dreamt of by the prisoner of Ham.' It is true that the emperor too was a romantic dreamer, but why this scorn for his ideas?

First, there are some obvious contradictions between certain of his views. For example, how could his concept of a strong, authoritarian government be reconciled with his professions of faith in liberal ideas (if one admits the sincerity of such statements)? In the words of Dansette, 'he proved unable to control his diversity: he failed to produce a synthesis of his heterogeneous aspirations', and he found himself torn between motives of various origins, for 'he remained all at once Napoleon's nephew, a child of exile, a man of 1848'. Furthermore, the formulation of his schemes remained somewhat vague and imprecise, and, once he became emperor, he never presented a full and systematic programme of his objectives. The reason was that this romantic cared little about putting in order and harmonizing his disparate aims, but also perhaps that he was afraid to provoke a concert of protest.

Indeed, those determined to see in the 'Napoleonic ideas' only an amalgam of insubstantial visions condemned them primarily because they could sense very well that these notions were radically at variance with their own views. Such critics regarded the emperor's ideas as monstrous because they were disturbing. Neither Thiers nor his friend Rémusat were wrong on this score, and their diagnoses, dating from the time when Louis Napoleon was only president of the Republic, show the deep cause of the durable opposition of a section of the élites to his schemes. Thiers observed, in a conversation with his mother-in-law, Madame Dosne, that Napoleon III's views were 'the opposite of those of the men of stature'. And Rémusat, in a rough comparison between the future Napoleon III and a Thiers or a Guizot, credited the latter pair with the ability to express with particular enthusiasm the ideas of 'respectable folk', to 'enact with...talent the ideas of others, sometimes of everyone else. Many others, less gifted and less brilliant, would have done what these men have done'; but the newcomer was an original with a 'gift....This idiot is endowed with a rare and powerful faculty, that of making his own mark in human affairs... [He] brings his imagination to bear on the affairs of the world and produces or modifies events according to his whim...[this] puts him in the ranks of historical figures.'[8]

### 'Napoleonic ideas'

These guiding ideas, which were uppermost in the emperor's mind and recognizable in his policies, indeed presented an undisputably original character, and proceeded from an inspiration more coherent than is generally thought. Napoleon III was neither a reactionary, nor an advocate of immobility. Without harbouring a 'social scheme', he felt the need for a move in the direction of progress. He perceived the changes in the world around him, and sought to provide an answer to the problems of his time. His aim was to 'bring the age of revolutions to a close by satisfying the legitimate needs of the people' (proclamation of 2 December 1851). And the same argument, expressed in the same words, was repeated in connection with the Italian problem in an 'unofficial' work published in 1859, *L'Empereur Napoléon et l'Italie*: 'revolution [must] be avoided by giving legitimate satisfaction to the needs of peoples'. This was at once an anti-revolutionary, ambitious and paternalistic notion, since ultimately it was he, the predestined leader, who was to be sole judge of the legitimacy of the needs of peoples (and not only of the French people). But Napoleon III was also inspired by progressivism, in his own manner (one could even speak of a left-wing inspiration, without defining the term too precisely), for his first concern was with the 'masses'. It is no coincidence that the latter word made its appearance in the language of politics at about this time. Madame Dosne had already remarked, when Napoleon was only president of the Republic, that 'his hobby-horse is the people' – a concern that was the main source of conflict between him and the friends of Thiers. One should not, therefore, regard his attitude as a mere ploy to avert all revolutionary peril. The emperor sincerely believed that the people were his chief support, and his generosity consistently led him to care about the fate of the masses and to try to ensure their happiness.

Accordingly, on the international level, he strove to deprive revolutionary movements of the mobilizing theme of nationhood, and, in the name of the right of peoples to self-determination, he sought to build a Europe of nation-states. This reshaping of the map of Europe, which ran counter to the principle of monarchic legitimacy, could naturally lead to conflict and so be unpopular in business circles, which were strongly attached to peace; but the policy would satisfy the French people's pride, or at least the chauvinism of the urban masses, who still regarded their country as *la Grande Nation*. Were they not thus to obtain the twofold satisfaction of a revenge for the shameful treaties of 1815 – which simultaneously humiliated France and toppled the Napoleonic dynasty a first time – and a new promotion to the rank of guide for other peoples? The chief point of impact of this policy was Italy, for which Louis Napoleon had always wanted to 'do something'. Finally, this policy was not confined to Europe. Its extension to central America (Nicaragua, Mexico) had been planned for a long time, and the policy was also intended to apply to the colonial sphere. It is symptomatic that as early as November 1852 Louis Napoleon had wanted to take on, at the same time as the title of emperor of the French, that of king of Algeria – a portent of what was later called the 'Arab kingdom' policy.

In the economic and social spheres, it would be vain to try to 'classify' the emperor, to make him the disciple of any given school. He appears in turn as a man influenced by English liberals, as a 'Saint-Simonian' Caesar, or at times as a socialist. He was above all an eclectic who borrowed from every doctrine whatever in his view could better the lot of the people. For Napoleon III, their fate was contingent upon material progress, and, in order to ensure the latter, he placed his trust above all in freedom. But he pushed economic liberalism well beyond the desires of many French liberals and above all of the majority of French businessmen, who clung to protectionism. From his youth he had asserted his support for a certain measure of free trade. This is one of the best examples of a 'Napoleonic idea': he promoted it by a succession of small moves, interrupted by long silences. In December 1852, following on the heels of the proclamation of the Empire, Napoleon III claimed the right to modify tariffs on his own initiative; after his government had tabled in 1856 and 1859 a series of bills calling for a partial easing of restrictions on trade – bills that had to be withdrawn in the face of opposition from protectionist deputies – he shelved the issue; finally, in early 1860, came the sensational surprise of the commercial treaty with Britain. And one of the reasons behind the negotiation of this treaty was the emperor's hope that it would lead to a decline in the cost of living, and thus to an improvement of living conditions for the French.

Nevertheless, Napoleon III did not conceive of the State's role as neutral or harmful. In his scheme for sustained expansion, the State had to act as a stimulus by launching large-scale public works or subsidizing major ventures. Admittedly, in this area as well, the emperor wavered, and his economic policy, a blend of liberalism and State intervention, may seem contradictory. But was it any more so than a good many of the policies applied in the western world today? Furthermore, while agreeing with the Saint-Simonians (such as Pereire or Michel Chevalier) on the role of economic growth as the main prerequisite for social progress in whatever form, he felt the need to regulate some of its consequences. Even in his youth, he had protested against the *laissez-faire* of liberal economists. Later, in his manifesto of 1848, he promised 'industrial' (that is, social) laws. As emperor, he hesitated for a long time before discarding price controls on bread and granting freedom of trade to bakeries (1863). Above all, he attempted, albeit in a fairly sporadic manner, to promote labour legislation. The author of *L'Extinction du paupérisme* never ceased to conjure the means of eliminating poverty. This was what Zola called his 'humanitariousness' (*humanitairerie*).

Finally, in the domestic sphere, the emperor intended to satisfy the French people's legitimate yearning for national sovereignty by founding his regime on universal suffrage, on 'democracy'.

## 3. *The spirit of the regime*

The political edifice was set up in the weeks that followed the *coup d'état*, for the basic texts were the proclamation of 2 December 1851 and above all the Constitution of 14 January 1852, soon supplemented by a series of organic decrees (on the electoral system, on press control) and by a wide-ranging legislation that defined the guiding spirit of the regime from its inception. This framework was modified only on points of detail by the senatus consultums of 7 November and 25 December 1852.

Was the power structure actually devised by Louis Napoleon Bonaparte? The question is valid, since he did not arrange the drafting of the Constitution of 14 January in the same manner as his uncle had, presiding directly over the elaboration of the Constitution of the Year VIII. Louis Napoleon entrusted the task to a select commission, one of whose members, Rouher, played an important role, bringing all his ingenuity to bear on the text, which he finished drafting in one arduous night. But Louis Napoleon had laid down the guiding principles, the 'foundations charted in his proclamation of 2 December' and submitted to the first plebiscite. Here, already, is an example of the method that often led him to initiate a policy and then to entrust its implementation to others – a procedure that could slow down or distort his initiatives. But in the immediate wake of the *coup d'état*, the members of the commission had to comply scrupulously with the intentions of the new master. This constitution, whose preamble carefully enumerates the 'foundations submitted for acceptance to the people', thus accurately reflects Louis Napoleon's thinking.

There are two possible readings of this constitutional text. One can view it as a scrap of paper, whose only purpose was to allow the author of the *coup d'état* to seize absolute power and to hand out key posts to the members of his clique as he saw fit. More than that, however, it was the fruit of the experiences and meditations of a man who felt destined to give the French the best system of government of its time.

In the vast conflict that for sixty years had been pitting the supporters of the achievements of the French Revolution against counter-revolutionaries, 'blues' versus 'whites' – a still topical conflict, as had been recently proved, at the very beginning of 1852, by a brief skirmish between L. Veuillot's *L'Univers* and the liberal *Journal des Débats* – the new regime had made a clear-cut choice. Article 1 of the Constitution, which was at the same time the only article in Title 1 (a position that gave it particular solemnity), proclaimed with significant emphasis: 'The Constitution recognizes, confirms and guarantees the great principles proclaimed in 1789, which are the basis of the public law of the French people.' This reference to the Revolution does not concern 1793, a date often invoked by the 'reds' (that is, the socialists), but 1789, that is, public liberties, legal equality, property – all rights to which, it was correctly believed, the French remained strongly attached.

But 1789 was also the point of departure of an age of instability, of a period of continuing strife that Louis Napoleon wanted to bring to a close. In his search for a lasting achievement, he claimed to substitute evolution for revolution, and therefore presented his constitution as a document that could undergo further adaptation by means of a senatus consultum or a plebiscite. In short, he sought a way to avoid both reaction and revolution, to break out of the fatal cycle that made the country sink from one to the other, for, as he stated in Dijon on 1 June 1851: 'France wants neither to return to the *ancien régime*..., nor to try out nefarious and impractical utopias'. Presenting himself as 'the man of the golden mean',[9] he thought he had found a middle course.

The solution lay in the as yet untried fusion between democracy and personal authority, in the ingenious combination of universal suffrage and a strong, even dictatorial, government. It is not surprising that the new regime rested on a democratic foundation: this was the application of one of the basic principles of 1789, that of national sovereignty. By his proclamation of 2 December, Louis Napoleon had reinstated universal suffrage (previously abolished, after a brief experiment, by the law of 31 May 1850). On his part, this was more than a gesture to curry popular favour; it was an expression of his confidence in the virtues of the popular oracle that had already made him president of the Republic. While the conservatives and liberals were not yet ready to accept universal suffrage – they feared this monster and saw it as the negation of the role of the élites, as a revolutionary peril, as the harbinger of a 'social' republic (*la Sociale*) soon to come – Louis Napoleon placed his entire trust in it, using it as a weapon against his opponents, even against republicans and revolutionaries; he was convinced that only a government with a popular base could be solid.

Such a democracy, however, could be allowed only if it was authoritarian. For the authors of the Constitution, this meant excluding parliamentarianism, for, as Rouher put it in 1866, 'was parliamentary government compatible with the immense sovereignty of ten million voters?' A strong and personal government was called for, very much in the tradition evoked by the name of Bonaparte. In *Les Idées napoléoniennes*, Louis Napoleon already expressed the belief that 'in a democratically-based government, the head alone has the governing power'. This head derived his authority from a delegation of national sovereignty. Thus democracy found its embodiment in the man it had chosen.

The moment the imperial restoration had been completed, the functioning of such a regime was liable to encounter a difficulty: was a hereditary monarchy, in which the responsible monarch exercised full authority, compatible with the preservation of total national sovereignty? Admittedly, there were the miracles of the December 1848 election, followed by the triumphant plebiscites of 1851 and 1852. Each time there was a congruence between the popular verdict and the heir to Napoleon I, who derived his powers at once from a delegation of national sovereignty and from a hereditary mission to reign, thus enjoying a dual legitimacy.

But would these miracles be certain to recur? Napoleon III seemed to think that the destiny of the Bonapartes would always earn them the support of the masses, but that was an act of faith.

The organization of the regime involved another complex issue, that of the role assigned to liberty. Liberty, after all, was a principle of 1789. A. Dansette has pointed out that while, for Napoleon III, 'liberty did not reside in the existence and exercise of the parliamentary function', he did combine a streak of liberalism with an undeniably authoritarian temperament. It would seem that he was influenced by the liberal climate he had known in Switzerland and especially in England, and that he shared the liberal aspirations so widespread in his day. One can admit that his assertions of liberalism were not purely token concessions to the opposition, and that they expressed something other than window-dressing or a simple veneer – that is, a genuine desire to make the regime evolve. However, it is in a *Lettre à un Lord* written in England in 1872 that Napoleon III made the most clear-cut statement of these liberal views. Was this not a belated plea by the fallen emperor against his reputation as a tyrant? At all events, Dansette recognizes that Napoleon's liberalism was 'deferred' and also conditional: liberties could be granted without restrictions only if opponents would avoid using them to undermine the stability of the regime and would adopt the behaviour of 'Her Majesty's opposition' in England (but that was to forget that the British sovereign was not the chief executive of an authoritarian government: consequently, the granting of freedom was liable to postponement *sine die*). This was the meaning of statements such as the following one, by Persigny, who was very close to the emperor's thinking: 'A people must be united before they can be free, and all that delays the merger of parties into the great family of the State also delays the enjoyment of freedom.' This also explains the promises made by the emperor himself regarding a future 'crowning of the edifice' – promises he expressed in these terms as early as February 1853 in announcing his marriage before the constituent bodies of the State: 'To those who regret that a greater share has not been allotted to freedom, I reply: freedom has never helped to found a lasting edifice; it crowns it when time has consolidated it.' For the time being, therefore, freedom's share remained a miserly one – a fact that by definition should have aroused liberal hostility. But there was nothing surprising for contemporaries in this sacrifice of liberty in the name of democracy. In the legacy of the French Revolution, liberty and democracy had proved incompatible, and no regime had succeeded in making them lie side by side. From 1815 to 1848, democratic-leaning policies had been abandoned, while certain liberties had developed to the great satisfaction of the 'men of stature'. It seemed logical that, with the proclamation of democracy, liberty should in its turn be put in abeyance.

All in all, this regime was indisputably original for its time. It followed no foreign model. Although monarchical, it was the opposite of the constitutional monarchy that France had known between 1815 and 1848, since the latter regime, at once parliamentary and liberal, rested on a highly restricted suffrage. Finally, while the Constitution of 1852 bore obvious and deliberate resemblances to that of the Year VIII, a fundamental difference persisted between the government of the first Bonaparte and that of Napoleon III: universal suffrage, conjured away in the earlier regime, continued to play a part in the later one, if only through the election of deputies. Whatever the means used to influence it, the national will remained at the heart of the system.

## 4. *Institutions: authoritarian features*

### *The suspension of liberties*

The regime first displayed its authoritarian nature by the tangible restrictions it imposed on public liberties. In truth, it did not need to add any significant measures to do so (except for the reintroduction of theatre censorship on 30 December 1852). The regime could consider itself adequately armed, since it inherited an impressive arsenal of laws, decrees and regulations from all the previous regimes (ranging from the First Empire to the Second Republic) – an arsenal it had promptly supplemented in early 1852. There was enough in the statute books to allow the government to enact the legal suppression of the freedom of assembly and association, and to establish a close watch over peddling and, above all, over the press.

Press regulations were laid down in the organic decree of 17 February 1852. No 'newspaper...dealing with political matters or matters of social economy...can be founded without government permission', and this permission had to be renewed with every change of editorial manager or editor-in-chief. All newspaper owners had to 'pay caution money to the Treasury' as well as a stamp tax of 6 centimes per issue in the Paris area and 3 centimes in the rest of France. This ultimately weighed on the sale price of newspapers, and so on the number of readers. Journalists were forbidden to relate proceedings of the Legislative Body (except by reproducing session minutes) and those of trials for press offences. These were subject to trial by courts of summary jurisdiction (*correctionnelle*) and not by jury. Penalties ranged from fines to the suppression of recidivist newspapers. On balance, there was nothing very new in this, all these procedures having already been used by repressive governments. But the decree did introduce an ingenious addition in Article 32: 'A newspaper may be suspended by ministerial decision even if it has not been condemned, but after two justified warnings, and for a period not to exceed two months...'. In other words, in addition to legal prosecution, the government and its representatives could also exercise surveillance by simple administrative decision, that is, by 'warning' a newspaper as soon as it published an article they disliked. This panoply of measures was intended to muzzle the opposition press in whatever form. Little did it matter that Persigny presented the decree as only provisional: 'For freedom of the press to be a tangible good in a newly constituted country, a new political generation, young, vigorous and independent, must first take the place of the souls enfeebled by revolutions.' Under the Empire, it was the temporary measures that lasted, and the legal recognition of freedoms was long in coming.

### The emperor's powers

The regime's authoritarian character was also evident from the imbalance between the various powers. On the one hand stood the chief, the master; on the other, his 'instruments', to use L. Girard's expression in his comments on Article 3 of the Constitution, which unequivocally stated that the emperor governed *by means of* the ministers, the Conseil d'Etat, the Senate and the Legislative Body.[10] Thus the assemblies were not supposed to act as counterweights to his authority, but as simple 'means' of government. And, in accordance with Article 14 (amended by Article 16 of the senatus consultum of 25 December 1852), members of the assemblies and ministers were obliged, no less than officers, magistrates and civil servants, to take an oath worded as follows: 'I swear obedience to the Constitution and allegiance to the emperor.' This was truly the mark of a personal regime. Thus there was at once a concentration and a confusion of basic powers that worked to the emperor's advantage. The list of his prerogatives, spelled out in Title 3 of the Constitution, is impressive: as 'head of State, he commands the army and navy, declares war, concludes peace treaties, alliances and commercial treaties, makes all appointments and draws up the regulations and decrees necessary to implement laws' (Art. 6). In short, he was the master of the executive writ large. The wording is almost identical to that of Article 14 of the 1814 Charter (with the exception, however, of the right to promulgate ordinances for the security of the State).

'He alone can initiate laws' (Art. 8) and 'he approves and promulgates laws and senatus consultums' (Art. 10), with no constitutionally imposed time span in which to do so. Thus he totally controlled the starting-point and the end-point of the legislative procedure, since he could always prevent the application of, and so bury, a law voted in the normal manner. Here again the Constitution simply reproduced Articles 16 and 22 of the Charter.

'Justice is administered in his name' (Art. 7). This arrangement, apparently contrary to the independence of the judiciary, harks back to the *ancien régime*, in which the king regarded himself as the 'great dispenser of justice'. Furthermore, the emperor 'has the right to declare a state of siege in one or more *départements*' (Art. 2), and thus to suspend the normal course of justice there and hand over the administration of these areas to the military authorities.

Finally, he kept the initiative in constitutional matters, since it was his prerogative to submit to the senators or to universal suffrage the constitutional amendments he might deem desirable.

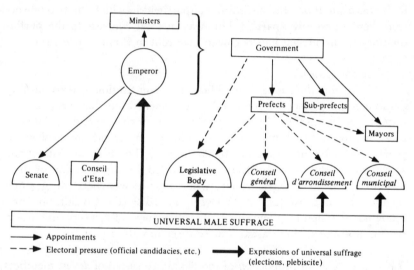

1 Diagram of the political and administrative system

These extensive powers were further reinforced by the senatus consultum of 25 December 1852, which stated that the commercial treaties the emperor was entitled to conclude 'had legal force in respect of tariff changes called for therein'; furthermore, 'all public works..., all undertakings in the public interest must be ordered or authorized by imperial decree'. No law was needed in these two areas – even though they involved State revenues and spending – for Napoleon III was determined to have a totally free hand in matters that were of special concern to him: the reduction of tariffs and the launching of large-scale projects such as railways and the transformation of Paris.

### The constitutional role of ministers

The Constitution not only reduced the emperor's 'means' to a state of utter dependency, but it separated – indeed fragmented – their prerogatives the better to prevent them from hindering the imperial will.

Accordingly, 'the ministers are dependent only on the head of State; they are responsible for the government's actions only so far as their personal sphere is concerned; they are not jointly liable'. In other words, there was no cabinet, only a set of imperial agents whom the emperor alone appointed and dismissed as he pleased. And they had no direct contact with the deputies. Not only did the Legislative Body have no say in their appointment or dismissal, but ministers were not allowed to sit in the Legislative Body and were not even obliged to defend their bills before it. It was a situation of 'constitutional apartheid in which the two powers were kept rigorously apart'.[11] This was in total contrast to the parliamentary tradition that had begun to take root in France since 1814.

### The assemblies

As for the three assemblies, the constitutional texts strictly delimited their respective roles and clearly spelled out their very uneven importance, if anything by the disproportion in the stipends granted to their members. The 'illustrious men' who sat in the Senate received 'a yearly and life-long grant of 30,000 francs', the 'men of distinction' appointed to the Conseil d'Etat were entitled for the duration of their term to a 'stipend of 25,000 francs', while deputies were belatedly granted by the senatus consultum of 25 December 1852 (the Constitution had made no provision for them) a simple 'allowance' of 2,500 per month in session, and the sessions lasted a mere three months a year.[12]

*The Senate.* A small proportion of the Senate consisted of *de jure* members (cardinals, marshals and admirals, as well as the 'French princes', that is, members of the imperial family in the line of succession); for the most part, the Senate consisted of members appointed for life by the emperor. They were therefore irremovable, which gave them a certain autonomy. But precautions were taken to limit their independence: the emperor could always pack the Senate with new appointees, provided this did not raise the total membership – initially set at 80 – to over 150. The emperor appointed the president and vice-president of the Senate, which he was also entitled to preside over in person. He convened and prorogued it at his discretion. The Senate met behind closed doors, and its decisions, the senatus consultums, were approved and promulgated by the head of State.

Despite all this, the Senate played a considerable role. As 'keeper of the fundamental compact [that is, the Constitution] and of public liberties', it had a duty to oppose 'the promulgation (1) of laws...that would violate the Constitution, religion, morals, freedom of worship, individual freedom, the equality of citizens before the law, the inviolability of property and the principle of the irremovability of the magistracy, (2) of laws that could jeopardize territorial defence'. For the same reasons, the Senate could also challenge administrative decisions and annul 'all acts referred to it as unconstitutional by the government, or denounced on the same grounds by citizens' petitions'.

Furthermore, it was up to the Senate to complete the Constitution (with regard to the colonies, and also to 'whatever has not been provided for by [it] and is needed to make it function'), to interpret the meaning of its articles and, finally, to propose changes in it. But although the Senate was entitled to 'lay the groundwork for bills of major importance', and although no law could be promulgated before having been examined by it, it did not actually participate in law-making, a task the emperor shared with the Conseil d'Etat and the Legislative Body.

*The Conseil d'Etat.* The Conseil d'Etat was composed of between forty and fifty ordinary members, who were appointed, and could be removed, by the emperor. The emperor could preside over the Conseil, and he appointed a chairman to preside in his absence. The head of State was thus entitled to rely on the Conseil to express his will, and the Constitution tended to make it his chief policy instrument. The Conseil was not a new institution: it had been Napoleon I's favourite, retaining important prerogatives up to the Second Empire itself. It remained the supreme administrative tribunal for settling litigation, and drafted the regulatory decrees required for the implementation of laws, a task for which it relied solely on the very broad guidelines laid down directly by the emperor. More generally, all government decisions went through the Conseil, of which ministers were *de jure* members. It had become a political body and, what was especially new, it exercised legislative functions of its own while acting as the linchpin that enabled the various institutions of State to participate in law-making. To grasp this one should examine the role of the Conseil in the complex legislative process, whose major phases were the following:[13]

(1) The emperor would propose a law.

(2) A draft bill was prepared in the appropriate ministry and submitted to the sovereign.

(3) The bill was examined first by a department of the Conseil, then by a general meeting of the Conseil, after which it became a government proposal.

(4) After examination, the head of State sent the bill to the Legislative Body.

(5) The seven departments of the Legislative Body appointed a seven-member commission to draft a report on the bill. The commission could propose amendments on its own initiative or at the suggestion of deputies who asked for a hearing.

(6) These amendments were sent back to the Conseil d'Etat for examination: 'At this stage one can observe the true importance of the Conseil, for it exercised a certain form of direct control over the nation's representatives.' It was free to accept, amend or reject the amendments, and an amendment once rejected could not be sponsored again by the deputies or submitted by them to the Conseil for further review. This rigid mechanism remained for the most part in effect until 1869.

(7) The bill was then discussed in the Legislative Body after the latter's commission had submitted its report. Deputies were not allowed to introduce new amendments; they could only pass or reject the bill. During this debate, the bill was defended by three *conseillers d'Etat* appointed by the emperor as 'government commissioners', since, at least until 1860, ministers were not allowed to appear before the Legislative Body.

(8) The Senate ruled on the constitutionality of the law once it was passed.

(9) The head of State promulgated the law if he saw fit to do so.

While the emperor was thus present at both ends of the process, the Conseil d'Etat took part in most of the intermediate stages. Maintaining continuous contact with ministers and the Legislative Body, the Conseil acted both as a screen (by preserving members of the government from contact with, and thus from criticism by, the assembly) and as a mediator (since it was the means by which members of the government could defend their bills). The idea – said to be Rouher's – of placing the Conseil between the executive and the legislative put it 'in an extremely promising position as regards the influence of the *conseillers*', who were in turn 'the censors and the defenders of ministers' bills'. But this curtailed the deputies' freedom of action.

*The Legislative Body.* The men elected by universal suffrage were confined to a minor and subordinate role. Even the words chosen to describe them are indicative of official concern to belittle them. They formed not a 'national assembly' of 'representatives' of the country's will, but a 'body' of 'deputies' sent in fairly small numbers (about 270) to help the head of State. Their national audience was diminished by the fact that the press was no longer permitted to give detailed accounts of parliamentary debates. Their president and vice-presidents were appointed from their ranks by the emperor, and ordinary sessions were intended to last only three months. Deputies could not vote the government out of office, nor did they have any say in its policy. They were even far from exercising undivided legislative power. Admittedly, the Legislative Body 'debate[d] and vote[d] bills and taxes', so that no law could be enforced and no tax levied without its consent. But the senatus consultum of 25 December 1852 restricted the very sphere of the legislature's prerogatives. Tariffs and public works were removed from its purview; as for the budget, it was voted by ministry. The allocation of funds per item and the authorizations for transfers from one item to another were handled by simple imperial decrees promulgated via the Conseil d'Etat. Faced with the difficult choice between accepting or rejecting the budget for each ministry en bloc, the deputies were unable to control public expenditure effectively.

## 5. Democratic features

### The means of expression of universal suffrage

By its resounding display of support for the man Louis Napoleon Bonaparte, the French people spawned a regime that claimed to preserve a democratic base and to remain attuned to the national will, that is, to derive from this popular base both its legitimacy and a stability that had been lacking in earlier monarchies. But in consequence universal suffrage had to be permanently allowed the possibility of expressing itself, and the Constitution provided two outlets.

The first and higher-ranking channel was the imperial one. Even as he became emperor, Louis Napoleon remained, according to the Constitution, 'responsible to the French people, to whom he *always* has the right to appeal'. The principle of the emperor's personal responsibility to the people, 'the only sovereign I recognize' (in the words of the 2 December proclamation), was consubstantial with the regime. This responsibility was called into play by the mechanism of the appeal to the people, commonly called the plebiscite – although it may be noted that these votes, which involved constitutional issues as well as the choice of a man, were rather similar to what were known under the Fifth Republic as referendums. Thus the Empire, a personal regime rooted in the popular masses, turned to them in order to seek approval for crucial decisions. It claimed to be the expression of direct democracy embodied in one man.

The second direct outlet for universal suffrage was the Legislative Body. Deputies were elected by all male citizens aged over twenty-one who could prove six months of uninterrupted residence in a single place; deputies also conducted the verification of their own powers. Yet every precaution was taken to prevent these elections from conflicting with the appeal to the people. The 'list system [,] which perverts elections', was banned out of fear that it would enable the major currents of opinion to express themselves openly. Another system was adopted, in which electors voted for candidates chiefly on the basis of their personal standing. This was the two-ballot vote by single-member constituencies, fairly similar to the present-day system. Candidates needed an absolute majority of votes on the first round in order to be elected; otherwise, a second ballot was called for (this was an innovation), in which a relative majority sufficed. Population density served as the criterion for dividing each *département* into constituencies, each corresponding to 35,000 voters. Thus, it was thought, deputies would be the elected representatives of their *arrondissements*, and elections could not be construed as accurately representing French opinion, since the latter would be reflected at best as in a broken mirror. Lastly, elections were scheduled at relatively wide intervals, since the Legislative Body came up for re-election as a whole every six years.

### Official candidacies

In practice, however, the relative importance of the two modes of expression left for universal suffrage was reversed. As the head of State turned to the people only when he so wished, nothing compelled him to make frequent use of plebiscites; indeed, elementary prudence made it inadvisable. Would it not be a major risk for the emperor to put his supreme responsibility at stake? Would not the consequences be even more momentous for his being a hereditary emperor? Any plebiscite that yielded a negative or even a middling positive result would run counter to Napoleonic legitimacy and provoke a crisis in the regime. It was better to content oneself with references to the miraculous results of earlier polls. Consequently, no plebiscite was held under the Empire, except, at the very last minute, in May 1870. For seventeen years, this essential mechanism never functioned; it simply grew rusty.

The only possibility for the government to take the temperature of the electoral body and the only opportunity left for the people to make themselves regularly heard – even if only every six years – thus assumed crucial importance. Every legislative election, and the same could be said for many local elections, became something of a plebiscite, a substitute for a vote of confidence addressed to the emperor. Besides, from the outset, was it conceivable that the results of the first legislative elections, held in February 1852, could invalidate those of the December 1851 plebiscite? Morny and Persigny did not think so. Their successors at the Ministry of the Interior were of the same opinion, and this was also one of the arguments most commonly used by prefects at every election. Invoking the principle of non-contradiction, they said in essence to the voters: since you approved the present emperor in 1851 and 1852, remain consistent by sending him today a body of deputies who are ready to help him; do not reverse your earlier vote.

But as each election turned into a plebiscite and called the regime in question, it became logical that the government should not take the risk of allowing universal suffrage to function in total freedom, and that it should do everything in its power to influence the outcome. Gerrymandering provided one instrument: as population changes made it necessary to redraw constituency boundaries at each election, ministers of the Interior took care to carve up hostile urban areas and drown hotbeds of opposition in safe *cantons*. They practised an 'active and dynamic electoral geography'.[14]

But above all, the government openly took part in election campaigns. Until 1869, it resorted to 'official candidacies', which, while not provided for in constitutional law, became a permanent and organic institution of the regime. The novel features of the official candidacy were precisely that it was official, that it was used in an undisguised and cynical manner and also that an attempt was made to adapt rather unoriginal practices to the dimensions of universal suffrage. In actual fact, such procedures, which came into more widespread use under the Second Empire, had already been applied between 1815 and 1848 on the restricted scale of a franchise-based electoral system. Moreover, it would be rash to assert that they totally disappeared in 1870.

Invoking as a justification the predicament of as yet highly inexperienced voters, at a loss for a choice when faced with several candidates, the authorities indicated which candidate was committed to supporting the government. To that extent, it was a fairly normal procedure. But the authorities also spared no effort to influence the voters' choice, to help the emperor's candidate by every possible means and to place innumerable obstacles across his opponents' path. The 'good' candidate was entitled to a white poster (the same colour as that of official proclamations), which was put up by officials in legally authorized locations and could not be torn under pain of prosecution. The coloured posters stuck up by opponents at their own expense and without any help were often torn up by local officials themselves or simply mislaid at the post office. All these officials – the rural policeman no less than the magistrate, the priest no less than the schoolteacher or the roadman – were mobilized to conduct the official candidate's election campaign, orchestrated by the prefect. Whoever attempted to make propaganda for the other candidates was exposed to moral or even physical threats, to harassment, punishment or even arrest. Often the 'right' ballot would be issued along with the voting card, and sometimes it would even be put into the hands of those who were about to vote. Many forms of pressure were employed, and those who voted 'properly' were promised subsidies and favours, a railway line or decorations. This is not to speak of various frauds (irregularities in voting, rigged results, stuffed ballot boxes) whose incidence was no doubt exaggerated by opponents: in most cases there was no need to cheat.

The authorities' efforts are understandable. But by treating the electorate as a minor who still had to be kept under guardianship, was the regime not depriving the people of their sovereign role in order to turn them into an instrument of imperial policy? The regime's democratic principle, contradicted by its officials' behaviour, was in danger of appearing to be a mere fiction.

## 2

# The political personnel and political life of the Second Empire

The advent of the new regime was characterized not only by the introduction of new constitutional rules, but by the accession of a group of men to positions of power. The worth of these institutions, and their very functioning, depended on the personality of these men and on the relations established between them.

## 1. The governing personnel

In addition to ministers, we shall deal here with all those whom the emperor appointed to positions of trust, such as the presidency of an assembly, the chairmanship of a department of the Conseil d'Etat and even major ambassadorships or the governorship of the Banque de France. The emperor shifted his appointees at will from one post to another, but they remained his favourite 'means' of government. As head of a deliberately personal regime, Napoleon III kept a free hand even in respect of these men. In order to have a private domain defined as he saw fit, this solitary ruler often relied on his cabinet alone. This private secretariat, which played an important but obscure role, was composed of unobtrusive but not undistinguished subordinates such as Mocquard, principal civilian private secretary. For special and often secret assignments, conducted without his ministers' knowledge, Napoleon often called on unofficial agents whom he picked among his handful of intimates (such as his chief physician, Dr Conneau). A number of diplomatic missions were carried out in such a manner.

### The position of ministers

While Napoleon could not do without ministers, who constituted 'the system of gears by means of which the imperial will exerted itself on the administrative machine',[1] he was determined to leave no autonomy or initiative to those whom he regarded as mere agents. He admitted to Prince Albert in 1854 that he did not allow them 'to discuss policy matters', and he reminded them in October 1862 that 'in our Constitution, ministers do not have a policy of their own, but are the instruments of that of the emperor'. In another statement, Napoleon called them 'great cogwheels' who were 'not to act without his consent'. Consequently, no more than he tolerated the emergence of the slightest bonds of solidarity among them, did he countenance any claims on their part to act in accordance with concepts of their own: they were not to espouse any political options other than the emperor's. Ministers who disagreed with policies being carried out were not even entitled to resign. Rouher was reminded of this in April 1864, when he disapproved the line adopted in the Danish affair: 'I cannot accept that the Minister of State should have wished to impose a policy of his own'; the emperor advised him instead to imitate Billault, who defended 'opinions that he made his own out of devotion to me and out of love for the country'. Thus Rouher had no right to resign; all he could do was to submit. Similarly, the emperor was always inclined to consider that a change in policy did not entail the replacement of the men responsible for its implementation, and he asked the ministers associated with highly authoritarian practices to enforce liberal measures.

The conduct of cabinet meetings was particularly revealing in this respect. The term 'cabinet', however, does not refer to an institution, but simply to the *de facto* meeting of ministers that the emperor generally convened twice a week. In *Son Excellence Eugène Rougon*, Zola reconstructed the atmosphere of one of these meetings, held at the Tuileries under the emperor's chairmanship in 'a drawing-room adjacent to his study'. Every point on the agenda – drawn up by the sovereign – called for a report. The Finance Minister spoke of the budget, the Justice Minister read his report on the creation of a new nobility, and so on. The emperor then asked each minister: 'What do you think of this scheme, Gentlemen?' When a discussion arose, he listened and briefed himself, but the cabinet did not take decisions. The emperor himself avoided on-the-spot arbitration (except when he made up his mind to issue a warning to the newspaper *Le Siècle*). He contented himself with settling each question by a 'We shall see' or a 'This will be looked at later', for even on minor matters, it was later – alone, or in a private meeting with the minister concerned – that he would take a decision that the other ministers would usually learn about only in the pages of *Le Moniteur*! Their task would then be to carry out the decision and defend it before public opinion. In short, they were reduced to the twofold technical role of providers of information or documentation and of executors.

Moreover, as if the better to secure their loyalty, he paid them exceedingly well. A minister's stipend was set at 40,000 francs. Very often this was supplemented by remuneration for other services performed for the emperor. For example, the many ministers who were at the same time senators or *conseillers d'Etat* enjoyed the corresponding allowance or stipend. It has been calculated that Rouher, perhaps the best rewarded minister, managed to accumulate a total income of up to 260,000 francs a year. Furthermore, the emperor, who always displayed extreme generosity, often rewarded his servants with sumptuous gifts. He gave a townhouse apiece to Billault and Magne as well as two vast estates in the Landes to Walewski, and, in 1860, sent Baroche the diamond-studded insignia of the Grand Cross of the Legion of Honour. For he naturally showered them with decorations: as early as 11 December 1852, a decree listing newly-promoted commanders of the Legion of Honour included Fould, Abbatucci, Ducos, Persigny and Fortoul (in that order), all of whom were ministers, and Billault and Rouher, who were to become ministers. Ministers were also in a position to get their friends and relatives set up in choice jobs. Not only did ministers take them on in their own cabinet, but, with the emperor's approval, they could also obtain key posts for them in the civil service, have them appointed to the Conseil d'Etat or, by means of official candidacies, secure their election to the Legislative Body. Three of Fould's sons were elected in turn to the Legislative Body, where they soon sat together. Among the *maîtres des requêtes* appointed to the Conseil d'Etat, one finds the son of Abbatucci and the son of Baroche – the latter 'at the indecent age of twenty-four'; Rouher's nephew was promoted in 1860 to the rank of *auditeur de première classe*, ahead of other colleagues with greater seniority; and, for each vacant post of *conseiller*, each minister defended his protégés. Zola deployed his great talent to portray the creatures who hovered around the minister Eugène Rougon the better to scramble for lucrative jobs and remunerative favours. In actual fact, while favouritism and nepotism existed under the Second Empire as under other regimes, they were no doubt regarded as all the more objectionable for being practised by ministers who remained in office for very long spells.

These ministers, kept under tight control by the emperor and handsomely paid, frequently declared, following Billault's example, that Napoleon III had no subjects more loyal or more devoted. But did they always confine themselves to the role of scrupulous executors of imperial decisions? The very fact that the emperor was obliged several times to remind them of the limits of their prerogatives shows that they naturally tended to transgress them. Ideally, the emperor would also have had to be capable of taking every decision and exercising total control. In actual fact, however, he has not generally been credited with an unusual capacity for work – comparable to that of his uncle – and it has often been stressed that he did not like to deal with administrative details. Admittedly, recent studies have shown that he was much more concerned with such details than has generally been thought, and that he displayed a finicky taste for paying close attention even to very minor questions. For example, in 1854, he took an interest in the various candidates in an election to the *conseil général* of the Seine-et-Oise. In 1856, he enquired as to the membership of the commission on book-peddling. These instances show that he often left precious little initiative to his Minister of the Interior. However, as he could not be omniscient – and this became even more the case when he was enfeebled by illness during the second half of the Empire – he was obliged to leave his ministers a certain freedom of action. Besides, were these men willing to be the mere instruments of the emperor's will? One might have said so had they been unprincipled careerists, henchmen ready to fulfil the emperor's whims out of greed. But they were often men of worth.

### The key men of the regime

First, one should mention three men who were close to the emperor by blood, through 'family ties' in the broadest sense. They were not Napoleon III's chosen men, and no doubt they did not enjoy his complete trust, but he did appoint them to important posts.

> PRINCE NAPOLEON (1822–1891). Son of Prince Jérôme, and so cousin of Louis Napoleon, whom be befriended during the years of exile. He sat on the far Left in the assemblies of the Second Republic. Under the Empire, was senator *de jure*. Transient Minister for Algeria and the Colonies in 1858. Self-styled representative of a left-wing Bonapartism; very anti-clerical.
> MORNY (1811–1865), natural son of General de Flahaut and Queen Hortense, and so Louis Napoleon's half-brother. Deputy for the Puy-de-Dôme from 1842, supported Guizot's policies. Met his half-brother only in 1849. Minister of the Interior at the time of the *coup d'état*, resigned in order to avoid endorsing the confiscation of the d'Orléans' property. Was obliged to wait until 1854 to obtain the presidency of the Legislative Body, which he kept until his death. Often considered the foremost member of the imperial personnel, he seems in fact to have had very little influence on the emperor, who was somewhat wary of him. Widely regarded as a symbol of his times, as one of the stars of *la fête impériale*,* and as a dynamic and rather unscrupulous businessman.
> WALEWSKI (1810–1868), son of Napoleon I and Maria Walewska. A diplomat, was ambassador to London from 1851. Minister of Foreign Affairs from 1855 to 1860, Minister of State from 1860 to 1863, president of the Legislative Body from 1865 to 1867.

Next come the ministers already in office when the Empire was proclaimed. Excluding Maupas, put in charge of a short-lived Ministry of General Police and dismissed as early as 1853, and Marshal de Saint-Arnaud, who left the War Ministry in 1854 to command the troops in the

---

* Lit. 'the imperial celebration' or 'festival' – a phrase used by the regime's admirers as well as its detractors to refer to the general prosperity (or extravagance) and intense (or frivolous) social life of the period. (Trans.)

Crimea, where he died of cholera (these two men were among the chief organizers of the *coup d'état*), we find:

ACHILLE FOULD (1800–1867), Minister of State and of the Emperor's Household. Born into a family of Jewish bankers, himself a convert to Protestantism, he remained a sleeping partner in the family banking concern; during the July Monarchy, was a deputy for the Hautes-Pyrénées loyal to Guizot. Under the Empire, remained Minister of State until 1860 – a more important post than it seemed, for its incumbent was in close contact with the emperor and was responsible for cultural affairs. Lastly, was Minister of Finance from 1861 until his death.

ABBATUCCI (1791–1857), Minister of Justice. Descended from a Corsican family friendly with the Bonapartes; deputy for the island since 1830. Presided over the 'reformist banquet' of January 1848. A magistrate – and senator from 1852 – he remained Minister of Justice until his death. A valued adviser of the emperor.

PERSIGNY (1808–1872), Minister of the Interior. A faithful companion in exile of Louis Napoleon and one of the chief conspirators of 2 December, he was forced to give up his post as early as 1854, but returned to it from 1860 to 1863 after a spell as ambassador to London. Later, was kept somewhat in the background, but remained a senator.

DROUYN DE LHUYS (1805–1881), Minister of Foreign Affairs. This career diplomat had been one of Guizot's deputies-cum-civil-servants from 1842. Twice Foreign Minister under the Second Republic, he occupied the post under the Second Empire from 1852 to 1855, and from 1862 to 1866.

BINEAU (1805–1855), Finance Minister. Graduate of the Ecole Polytechnique. Deputy for Angers as early as 1841. A specialist in railways, he was chosen as Minister of Public Works by the prince-president in 1849; after the *coup d'état*, appointed Finance Minister, which he remained until his death.

MAGNE (1806–1879), Public Works Minister (and, beginning in 1853, Minister of Agriculture, Commerce and Public Works). A native of the Périgord, son of an artisan wool manufacturer and dyer, he became a lawyer and was elected deputy in 1843 as a protégé of Bugeaud. Supported Guizot, who appointed him Under-secretary of State for War in 1847. A senator under the Empire, he changed posts several times, switching from his first ministry to the Finance Ministry (1855–1860), afterwards minister without portfolio from 1860 to 1863; finally, after serving as member of the Privy Council with ministerial rank (1863–1867), returned to the Finance Ministry until January 1870. A fine example of ministerial longevity.

HIPPOLYTE FORTOUL (1811–1856), Minister of Education and Religion. Professor of literature at the Faculty of Toulouse, then at Aix, elected to the Legislative Body as deputy for the Basses-Alpes; remained in office until his death.

THEODORE DUCOS (1801–1855), Minister for the Navy and Colonial Affairs. A nephew of Napoleon Bonaparte's consul Roger Ducos, he came from a distinguished family of Bordeaux shippers and merchants. A deputy for Bordeaux under the July Monarchy, he sat on the centre Left, and was regarded at the time as a friend of Thiers. Ran this ministry until his death.

From 1852 to 1869, only about twenty other men held office as ministers of the Second Empire. I shall leave aside those who were in office only briefly – not all of whom were minor figures – as well as those experts who, having entered officialdom well before the Empire, became either war ministers (in the case of staff officers), colonial ministers (admirals) or foreign ministers (diplomats).

Most of these promotions to ministerial office did not concern new-comers (with the exception of Victor Duruy, of whom more later) but men who, for the most part, already held important posts when the Empire was founded. The three exceptions are:

> FORCADE LA ROQUETTE (1820–1874), the uterine brother of Saint-Arnaud, served successively as Minister of Finance (1860–1861), of Agriculture and Commerce (1867) and of the Interior (1868–1869).
>
> CHASSELOUP-LAUBAT (1805–1873), former *conseiller d'Etat* and deputy for the Charente-Inférieure under the July Monarchy (he then belonged to the conservative majority), was in 1852 one of the members of the Legislative Body who took the liberty of criticizing the first budget (they were called *les budgétaires*). He became a remarkable Minister for the Navy and Colonial Affairs from 1859 to 1867, then president of the Conseil d'Etat at the very end of the Empire.
>
> BEHIC (1809–1891) was a businessman (manager of the Forges de Vierzon and chairman of the board of the Messageries Maritimes) and was said to be on the best of terms with the Rothschild–Talabot group. He too had served in Parliament under the July Monarchy, and, being suspected of Orleanism, he was not called to the government until 1863. He then served until 1867 as a distinguished Minister of Agriculture, Commerce and Public Works, but he remains a little-known figure.

Next one can mention two men whose careers intersected:

> ROULAND (1806–1878), first a lawyer, then a magistrate, elected deputy in 1846, appointed chief prosecutor at the Paris Court in 1853, then Minister of Education and Religion from 1856 to 1863. Later served as vice-president of the Senate, president of the Conseil d'Etat and finally governor of the Banque de France from 1864 to the early years of the Third Republic.
>
> VUITRY (1813–1885), born in Sens into an educated and wealthy bourgeois family; son of a deputy of Louis Philippe; graduate of the Ecole Polytechnique. After a brief career as a lawyer, he was appointed *conseiller d'Etat* under the July Monarchy; from 1857 to 1863, he headed the finance department of the Conseil d'Etat; after serving briefly as governor of the Banque de France, he was appointed in 1864 minister presiding over the Conseil d'Etat – a fine political career for a man always suspected, not without reason, of being an Orleanist at heart. In 1869, his daughter married Henri Germain, founder of the Crédit Lyonnais; Shortly thereafter, Vuitry himself became chairman of the Paris–Lyons–Marseilles railway company (the 'PLM').

Finally, three future ministers stand out for their very special importance:

> BAROCHE (1802–1870) came from a lower middle-class family in Paris. He became a lawyer and, after three unsuccessful attempts, was

elected deputy as a candidate for the 'dynastic Left' in 1847. Twice
minister under the Second Republic, he was vice-president of the
Conseil d'Etat at the time the Empire was proclaimed; he served as
president of the Conseil from 1853 to 1860 – a crucial post, which
entailed his acting in most cases as the government's commissioner before
the Legislative Body. He was later minister without portfolio presiding
over the Conseil d'Etat (1861–1863) and finally Justice Minister
(1863–1869). A man who liked order, he was 'a liberal on economic
issues, a conservative in politics and a Gallican in religious matters'.

BILLAULT (1805–1863). The son of a customs collector, he had a
brilliant success as a lawyer in Nantes; having become a provincial
notable, he was elected deputy as early as 1837. Under-secretary of State
in Thiers's cabinet in 1840, he later emerged as the 'opposition orator'
of the 'dynastic Left', which included his friends Abbatucci, Drouyn de
Lhuys, Bineau and others. President of the Legislative Body from 1852,
he was appointed Interior Minister (1854), minister without portfolio
(1860) and finally Minister of State (from 1863 until his death) responsible for defending the government's bills before the deputies.

ROUHER (1814–1884). An Auvergnat, son of a solicitor and himself
a solicitor, he entered politics as an unsuccessful candidate sponsored by
Guizot in 1846. Elected to the Constituent Assembly, he soon sided with
Louis Napoleon (who appointed him for a brief spell as Justice Minister),
but remained an unreliable friend, since he was prepared to drop Louis
Napoleon on 2 December if the plot failed. Vice-president of the Conseil
d'Etat in December 1852, he became Minister of Agriculture, Commerce
and Public Works in February 1855, then Minister of State in 1863.
Until his resignation in July 1869, he was regarded as a *de facto* 'vice-
emperor'.

All in all, these ministers, who constituted a fairly homogeneous group,
scarcely match their unflattering reputation as uneducated misfits of
dubious origin, 'barefoot' adventurers 'in patent-leather boots' (d'Haussonville) concerned only with making a fast fortune. In the first place,
they often came from good bourgeois families. Those of more modest
extraction had achieved social promotion before entering the emperor's
service. The emperor's choice was a glorious consecration of their status;
it did not create it. Baroche, for example, had already raised himself
'thanks to his ambition, talent and tenacity to become one of the great
servants of the State'.

Furthermore, without being intellectuals (except Duruy) and without
pretending to play the ideologues (this distinguished them from the leading
figures of the July Monarchy, who were often outstanding journalists or
learned professors of history or philosophy), they had nearly all received a
solid education. However, those who had gone as far as university had
shied away from the humanities and often turned to the law, sometimes to
science. These choices perhaps facilitated their success in business or
public administration.

Some of these men, such as Fould, Béhic and Ducos, belonged to the economic élite of banking, industry and large-scale trade; others, with legal training, either went into public administration, specializing in financial and commercial questions (Vuitry, for example), or became solicitors or lawyers – particularly business lawyers well connected in the world of finance and industry. Their recruitment as ministers corresponded to a period when business and politics were closely interrelated, and when it proved necessary to harmonize law and legislation with economic change. Indeed, legislation passed during the Second Empire often concerned economic matters. On the whole, Napoleon III 'recruited from a milieu primarily composed of *grands bourgeois* and of committed servants of the upper bourgeoisie...The change concerned not the governing class, but the governing team.'[2]

As for these ministers' private lives, one ought to distinguish between the socialites, who took part in all the glamorous pastimes of *la fête impériale* without – in most cases – being debauchees, and those who, like Baroche and Rouher, tried to keep somewhat away from that social life and remained faithful to a family-centred, traditional 'bourgeois' way of life. In short, many of them corresponded to the definition given by J. Maurain of Baroche as a 'Second Empire bourgeois' who had 'the strong traditions and great qualities of his class' while also displaying its prejudice and frequent narrow-mindedness.[3]

Without being outstanding politicians – a trait that the emperor would, in any case, have refused to accept – they had all it took to make 'good' ministers: they were well prepared, often competent and almost always hard-working. Indeed, these industrious men showed an indefatigable zeal. Moreover, their importance grew – even in relation to the emperor – all the more as there were still few ministerial departments (ten or so on average) and as their incumbents remained a long time in office. Feeling, perhaps, that he could count on only a handful of reliable men, the emperor was loath to replace his ministers and sought to keep the same incumbents as long as possible. If one sets aside the transient changes brought about in the imperial personnel by the storm of 1858, it was not until 1863 that the emperor carried out his first major cabinet reshuffle. As if he could trust only some twenty-odd men whom he had singled out from the beginning, he always hesitated to deprive himself of one of them by inflicting a lasting disgrace on him. When the death of a minister created a vacancy, Napoleon III naturally chose a replacement from among those he kept in his dwindling reserve. The failure to inject new blood into the governing personnel was undoubtedly one of the regime's basic weaknesses, for in the long run 'ministerial substance [was] becoming scarce', as the emperor's principal private secretary noted; also, ministers grew older: their average age, which was only forty-eight in 1852, reached a very advanced fifty-nine in 1867.

A last major observation: few of these ministers had begun as Bona-partists, and few had no political past at all. Napoleon III recruited these men from the ranks of previous regimes, and particularly of the July Monarchy. While it was out of the question to call on Louis Philippe's leading ministers, the emperor mainly chose men who, although impeded in their progress by those celebrities and still far from having achieved a great notoriety, had already held civil service positions or parliamentary office during the 1840s. Even if acting perhaps out of necessity, he undeniably demonstrated in his choice of men a great tolerance for their political past, welcoming into his government both former mem-bers of the conservative majority that had supported Guizot (Fould, Morny) and – in greater numbers – representatives of the 'dynastic Left'. After living in opposition, the latter, frightened by the upheavals of the Second Republic, came out in favour of a highly concentrated form of power – they had become authoritarian. All of these converts were genuinely devoted to the new master and often remained faithful to him after 1870.

But they also entered the government with their habits and personal views. The emperor's determination notwithstanding, they did represent political currents. The Fould–Baroche–Rouher trio, for example, some-times joined by Magne, repeatedly spoke out in favour of preserving an authoritarian order against the advice of some of their colleagues and against the emperor's own wishes. The rivalries that divided the imperial personnel and were often abetted by Napoleon III did not result only from the intrigues of coteries. It was not only the choice of men that was at issue; policy courses too were challenged. Finally, in October 1862, when a full-scale crisis broke out among his ministers, Napoleon III was obliged to concede a political role to each of them, in terms related by Baroche:

> In response to Fould's remarks, the emperor eventually admitted that, in any government, men who have a sense of dignity cannot sit on the sovereign's councils when, on a crucial issue, policy takes a course that their conscience condemns. The public cannot believe that each of them isolates himself and confines his activity to his particular sphere. They are all bound by a *de facto*, if not *de jure*, solidarity.[4]

This was a grave admission, for few of these ministers indeed seem to have shared the 'Napoleonic ideas'. Of one of them – Vuitry – it has even been written that he was 'in no way a Bonapartist; he disliked the over-democratic and vaguely socialist aspects of the doctrine', an aversion that did not prevent him from being 'perfectly loyal'.[5]

Thus, even at the governmental level, the imperial will could be hampered (the 'instruments' could become brakes) or distorted. This was an initial obstacle to the exercise of absolute personal power.

## 2. The membership of the assemblies

The membership of the assemblies displayed in varying degrees the same eclectic choice made by the sovereign, and his concern to keep the same men.

### The senators

In the Senate, stability could be taken for granted, since senators were irremovable. The first contingent (seventy-two men, not counting *de jure* members) had been appointed by January 1852. The only later changes in the make-up of the assembly occurred when the emperor made *en masse* appointments (as on 4 March 1853) – an exceptional procedure – or, as was fairly frequently the case, when he filled individual vacancies. But the Senate did not change significantly despite these appointments, for the newcomers often belonged to the same categories as the original members. From the outset, it was the army, regarded as the pillar of the regime, that provided the largest share of these dignitaries (over a quarter). This was a way of rewarding military chiefs for having rallied to the Empire. Next came the ministers, high-ranking civil servants and magistrates, such as Troplong, president of the Cour de Cassation, who served as president of the Senate until his death in 1869. The Institut de France too was heavily represented (by seventeen of its members in 1856). But these worthies also included eminent representatives of banking and industry: in addition to Fould, we find the Comte d'Argout, governor of the Banque de France from 1834 to 1857, and former minister of Louis Philippe, Gautier and Lebeuf, respectively deputy governor and board member (*régent*) of the Banque de France, Mimerel, one of the leading textile manufacturers of the Nord, the Marquis d'Audiffret and others.

The Senate was undoubtedly the place where the greatest number of genuine Bonapartists were to be found. Apart from the two princes (who were *de jure* members), appointees included relatives of the Bonapartes (a Clary and a Murat), members of the upper imperial nobility (more numerous than the descendants of the *ancien-régime* nobility), and several of the emperor's loyal friends, such as Vieillard. Yet a considerable number of servants of earlier regimes still sat in the Senate. In particular, in 1852, it numbered some twenty former deputies and twelve peers created by the July Monarchy. And this latter group, which was forty-six strong in 1856, included Troplong himself.

### The ' conseillers d'Etat'

While the Conseil d'Etat was an old institution, Louis Napoleon reappointed to the new Conseil in January 1852 only nine of the forty *conseillers* in office before the *coup d'état*. As he never exercised his right of removal during the Empire, these *conseillers* enjoyed long tenure. Once again, this made for an increase in the average age of members, which rose from fifty in 1852 to fifty-five in 1860 and fifty-eight in 1871. In order to fill vacancies, the emperor tended to appoint outsiders during the first half of the Empire and later preferred to promote *maîtres des requêtes*. These choices, however, did not alter the character of the Conseil's membership. Wright's analysis provides a fairly precise picture of this assembly, all the more interesting as it can be applied by and large to the imperial personnel as a whole.[6]

The *conseillers*, four-fifths of whom were jurists, came from families that 'were generally of high – but not necessarily of the highest – social standing, were not without financial means and often had a tradition of State service'. In other words, these were families of the middle bourgeoisie, composed of lawyers, solicitors, notaries and sometimes doctors – 'educated men who occupied a position adjacent to polite society [*la bonne société*] and who harboured greater ambitions for their children than for themselves'. They often had family ties with other sectors of officialdom (the army, the diplomatic corps, the magistrature and the *corps préfectoral*). Their personal incomes varied considerably, but often did not exceed a level of moderate financial ease. However, they all had fairly high educational qualifications. A successful career in public administration required outstanding university degrees. Even men from the provinces came to seek them in Paris, which by 'this time had acquired a virtual monopoly over the training of future élites'.

From the political point of view, the Conseil, after the sweeping changes of 1852, comprised twenty-four members (out of forty) who had already served in a parliamentary capacity in various assemblies. They too were not new men. A great variety of political views prevailed among them, but the staunch Bonapartists represented only 'a small nucleus: less than a tenth [of the *conseillers*] can be regarded as "sons of the regime", as men whose career and experience were entirely shaped by the Second Empire'. To these may be added a few converts, such as La Guéronnière, appointed in 1854, who later served as the general director of the office in charge of the book-trade and the press, and was also employed by Napoleon III as a go-between propagandist to disseminate the emperor's views on the Italian question. Far more numerous were the *conseillers* who, out of personal inclination no less than caution, behaved as 'apolitical men' or opportunists. Most of them can no doubt be classified as Orleanists, not that they were loyal to the d'Orléans family, but they remained attached to certain liberal concepts in political matters and certain conservative ideas in the economic and social realm (hence their opposition to Haussmann's ventures). The Bonapartist *conseiller d'Etat* J.-A. Abbatucci (son of the first Minister of Justice of the Second Empire) noted in his diary in 1858:

The emperor's government has to protect itself from two things: from Orleanists and Orleanism, that is, from civil servants who are outspokenly Orleanist, who aspire to the restoration of this dynasty, and from the civil servants who, even as they loyally serve the emperor, strive with all their might to implement Orleanism, namely, parliamentary and bourgeois government.

The second danger, often latent and insidious, was undoubtedly greater. The emperor must have been aware of this, since he remained ever suspicious of the 'spirit of the law faculty', the 'defenders of dangerous liberties', the 'Orleanists' who seemed to set the 'tone' in the Conseil. It was a grave handicap for him to be unable to trust an institution that he had envisaged as an essential 'instrument' of his government.

### The deputies

The deputies too can be said to have owed their appointment to the government, since, until – and excluding – the 1869 elections, the electors voted by and large for official candidates. Furthermore, the government readily put up outgoing deputies on the very strength of their incumbency. In 1857, all the incumbents, with nine exceptions (one of whom was Montalembert), were once again entitled to the white poster. The opposition having won five seats, some 250 deputies were re-elected. In 1863 there was a greater turnover, since the fiery Persigny deprived forty-eight incumbents of his support and the opposition won thirty-two seats – not what one could call a landslide. To be sure, there were also by-elections held to replace deceased deputies, but the profile of the new official candidates seldom differed from that of their predecessors. Lastly, a good number of constituencies were uninterruptedly represented by the same deputy from 1852 to 1869. An obvious proof of a remarkable stability, this phenomenon also made for an ageing assembly.

The composition of the Legislative Body in 1852 can therefore be used to draw conclusions that remain valid until 1869, at least for the government majority. The assembly included few, if any, intellectuals and journalists, and virtually no representatives of the 'new strata' (doctors, for example). Professionally speaking, deputies fell into four major categories. First, some 19 per cent were 'property-owners', men of independent means, living particularly off income from their landed properties; but some of these men had no doubt once exercised an occupation that would allow them to be classified under one of the three other headings. The second category comprised a sizeable number of former civil servants (26 per cent) and former military men (8 per cent): while civil servants were no longer allowed to stand for election as deputies (a ban designed to prevent the sort of abuses that had proliferated under the July Monarchy), there was nothing to stop a civil servant who had retired or who had resigned on purpose from being elected. Third, 7 per cent of the deputies were in the professions and 13 per cent were *hommes de loi*, a percentage indicative of the importance of jurists in this institution as well. Finally, industrialists, merchants and financiers made up nearly a quarter of the Legislative Body (24 per cent). They included Charles de Wendel, the iron manufacturer from Hayange, Eugène Schneider, co-manager of the Creusot works, mayor and – it could be said – master of the town, already a deputy in 1845, the banker Koenigswarter and several directors of railway companies.[7] On the whole, the Legislative Body, just like the assemblies under Louis Philippe, was composed of extremely wealthy individuals representative of the governing classes. Persigny, a champion of a popular Bonapartism, observed this with regret: 'We, whose only friends are below, have handed over the Legislative Body to the upper classes.' Among these notables, there was a rather high proportion of businessmen, a presence that Morny, Minister of the Interior at the time of the 1852 elections, had called for in a famous circular.[8] But Morny also wanted the deputies to be picked from outside the political class, and, as far as this demand was concerned, the prefects, having failed to find genuine newcomers, often had to make do with those who had rallied.

This explains the particular political make-up of this assembly of official candidates, from which the opposition was absent. Only about a third of the pro-government deputies of 1852 were true Bonapartists – either Bonapartists from the beginning, many of whom, it so happens, had gone through an Orleanist phase (we encounter here the descendants of illustrious figures of the First Empire such as Caulaincourt, Suchet, Macdonald and Cambacérès), or friends of Napoleon III (such as Dr Conneau, Véron and Granier de Cassagnac), or relatives of his ministers (Maupas's son, Fortoul's brother). Next came some forty men with no previous political experience, in fulfilment of Morny's wish. But on the whole the turnover in parliamentary personnel was less extensive than one would expect.

In actual fact, the majority of the assembly was composed of conservatives who, although they had admittedly rallied to the new regime, had served the earlier ones as civil servants, parliamentary deputies, or, at the regional level, as *conseillers généraux*, mayors, members of chambers of commerce and so forth. Only the leaders of the former parties were excluded from the Legislative Body. The assembly included at least thirty erstwhile legitimists, but it was the men of the July Monarchy who supplied the largest contingent. In their search for candidates, the prefects displayed a preference for those who had belonged to the opposition to Guizot, to the 'dynastic Left' from whose ranks Louis Napoleon had recruited several of his ministers. But there were also seventeen Orleanists who had been members of Guizot's majority. One can also count separately a few deputies – most notably Montalembert – whose primary affiliation was Catholicism.

Ultimately, what united the vast majority of these deputies, regardless of their past, was – no less than their devotion to the emperor's person – their attachment to order and the fear of the revolutionary peril. These men were offshoots of the 'party of order' that had come into being during the Second Republic. Consequently, it is legitimate to assume that in the Legislative Body as well there were few convinced supporters of 'Napoleonic ideas'. Moves to implement certain of these ideas were liable to provoke criticisms and even defections.

### 3. The role of the three assemblies

#### The Senate's lethargy

The hierarchical order that the Constitution had intended to establish among the three assemblies was upset in practice, first because of the Senate's self-effacement. The senators failed to carry out their duties. They passed only a few senatus consultums (about thirty between 1852 and 1856) and, while occasionally tempted to debate legislation – an activity that lay outside their prerogatives – they abstained from availing themselves of their right to lay the groundwork for bills of major public interest. Indeed, in January 1856, an article in *Le Moniteur*, no doubt inspired by the emperor, reminded the senators of their obligations and advised them to visit the *départements* in order to conduct inquiries and later submit vast reform schemes to the government. But this was of no avail. The senators' inertia – their dereliction of duty – can be explained, in the first place, by the secrecy of their proceedings (which was hardly likely to stimulate their zeal) and, even more, by their very personality. Having been appointed as *illustrations*, they were by definition elderly men who had reached the end of their political careers and were seeking the undisturbed enjoyment, at long last, of what they considered a lucrative post and an honorific reward.

Yet, however acute the deficiency of this cogwheel in the ingenious law-making mechanism, it did not endanger the functioning of the whole.

#### The myth of the Conseil d'Etat

The 'distinguished' – and therefore competent – men appointed to the Conseil d'Etat cannot be accused of indolence. Did they not, between 1852 and 1860, in addition to their other tasks, examine one thousand eight hundred and four bills? In their own day, their omnipotence was proclaimed by Rouher ('the Conseil d'Etat sees everything and examines everything', he declared in 1866) and criticized by disgruntled parliamentary deputies and by liberal observers. Later, it was recognized by the republican university. In the words of a *conseiller d'Etat* of the Third Republic (Gaillard), speaking in 1873, it was admitted that 'the Empire was *par excellence* the regime of the Conseil d'Etat'. Wright, however, would revise this traditional view, which he regards as a myth.

First, the relations that were supposed to exist between the Conseil d'Etat and the ministers were not clearly established by the constitutional texts themselves. Even under the Second Empire, two schools of thought voiced divergent interpretations of the matter: the one, which included in particular the journalist Cucheval-Clarigny, emphasized the pivotal role of the Conseil, while the other stressed its character as an instrument subordinated to the executive branch. But, in practice, was it free to impose its will on the ministers, to rein them in? The ministers, who would have thought it degrading to make concessions to this 'group of scheming and irresponsible magistrates', were to make sure that the *conseillers* remained docile. It was not the *conseillers* who controlled the members of the government; it was the ministers who had numerous means at their disposal to reduce the Conseil to the rank of a subordinate body. In their unrelenting effort to avoid discussions in the Conseil that could diminish their credit, the ministers could rely on secret relations in the place, resort to various pressures to restrain recalcitrant *conseillers*, invoke imperial patronage and brandish the threat of the right of removal. Thus, since 'he was supported by the emperor, the president of the Conseil, his protégés and his friends and relatives in the Conseil's departments, and could if necessary mobilize a bloc of colleagues and *conseillers* outside the departments when the Conseil met in general session, a minister rarely had any problems getting his bill approved'.

Is it accurate, however, to speak of the Conseil's 'basic impotence'? Certain evidence suggests that even the emperor had difficulty in imposing his will on the *conseillers*. If one is to believe the republican deputy Darimon:

> [I]n the Conseil d'Etat, Napoleon III was viewed as a great utopian. Whenever a bill bearing the stamp of the emperor's cabinet reached the great cause list, it was whittled down, cut, amputated and arranged in such a way that it was doomed to rejection. How many bills remained dead letter!

And, also according to Darimon, the emperor at the end of his reign complained of the Conseil in these terms:

> I am not a jurisconsult. The Conseil d'Etat comprises a host of high-minded men, but it is frightened of reforms. It always has some legislation to quote against me. I would have done more than I did for the working class if I had found strong support in the Conseil d'Etat.

No doubt the emperor was invoking somewhat easy excuses, for the government always had the means to secure approval for its bills. But it had to put those means into practice, or threaten to do so. The Conseil could, if not halt, at least obstruct government initiatives, and this brake could be effective if applied in conjunction with others, in the Legislative Body or even in the government itself.

With respect to the deputies, the *conseillers d'Etat* at least maintained the supremacy symbolized for all observers by the difference in the dress prescribed for members of the two assemblies. Victor Hugo, in *Napoléon le Petit*, gleefully contrasted the Conseil, 'cheerful, well paid, sprightly, red-eared, outspoken, sporting its sword, paunch and gold embroidery', with the Legislative Body, 'pale, thin, sad, embroidered in silver':

> The Legislative Body walks on tiptoe, turns its hat over in its hands, puts its finger to its lips, smiles humbly, sits on the edge of its chair and speaks only when spoken to. Thus, in the shop where laws and budgets are made, there is a master, the Conseil d'Etat, and a servant, the Legislative Body.

It is true that the *conseillers* were often poorly thought of by the deputies, who envied and criticized them, and that inevitable tensions, or even open hostility, arose between the two groups. But in practice their relationship was in no way a 'master–servant' one, and this is true at the two levels at which they established contact.

First, the Conseil ruled on the amendments proposed by the commission of the Legislative Body. Admittedly, at least during the first half of the Empire, many amendments were harshly treated. Thus, between 1853 and 1861, of 262 amendments proposed by the commission to the budget laws alone, the Conseil adopted a mere 92, rejected 135 and modified 35. But it was the ministers who effectively decided on the fate of amendments, sometimes even after direct, secret and unconstitutional contacts with the deputies. In this area, the Conseil d'Etat served primarily as a scapegoat.

Furthermore, as defenders of legislative bills before the Legislative Body, the *conseillers* had to exercise what was in theory a crucially important function, but in practice a difficult one for them to carry out properly. These unfortunate jurists were not always very favourable to the ministerial proposals they had to defend; having been kept in the dark as to the reasons behind these texts and as to their specific implications, they were incapable of answering the questions put to them. Furthermore, they often lacked experience as public speakers and did not necessarily possess the eloquence and calm required to impress the deputies, whom they were fearful of challenging. At the slightest revival of parliamentary life, the *conseillers* were overwhelmed by the situation. Indeed, the ministers, who found that their bills were poorly interpreted and poorly defended, felt that they could do a better job themselves: even in the very first years of the Empire, certain ministers gave explanations directly to groups of deputies whom they contrived to meet.

Eventually, ministers and deputies, by a concerted effort, undermined the *conseillers'* authority far more rapidly than certain historians have thought. The *conseillers'* position, while apparently privileged, was actually uncomfortable. They were, so to speak, 'sandwiched' between the government and the Legislative Body. In this respect, one can truly speak of their impotence. On their own initiative, the *conseillers* gradually withdrew into their traditional role as administrative judges. This failure of the Conseil d'Etat, its incapacity to play its assigned part in the law-making process, was a serious one, for it meant the disappearance of the screen that was supposed to stand between the government and the deputies. Consequently, the measures taken between 1860 and 1869, which reduced the Conseil's constitutional powers and increased the presence of ministers before the Legislative Body, can indeed be interpreted as liberal concessions granted by the emperor or wrested by the opposition. However, they were just as much a *de jure* recognition of practices that had tended from the very outset to substitute for the legislative procedure originally devised.

### The revenge of the Legislative Body

The Legislative Body was thus gradually freed from the tutelage of the Conseil d'Etat, and all circumstances worked towards a revival of an assembly that had come into being as a humble body with only a minor role. In truth, from the very outset, the deputies, even the most submissive, were never the 'reptiles' castigated by Montalembert or the 'servants' mocked by Hugo. The fact that they had been invested by the government did not cause them to regard themselves as its lackeys. Were not most of them notables, aware of their importance and independent of the regime on account of their personal situation? While devoted to the emperor, they were strongly inclined to exercise their powers seriously – however limited these may have been. The government, obliged even in the heyday of the authoritarian phase of the Empire to depend on a parliamentary majority, was constantly required to handle the deputies with care and pay some attention to their views. Above all, whatever the precautions taken to make each of them appear exclusively as the representative of his *arrondissement*, they were the men elected by universal suffrage. This status gave them a moral legitimacy and a special authority; it also introduced into the system the fatal seed of evolution. Furthermore, the significance assumed by the legislative elections conferred an even greater prestige on the men whom it was becoming so important to choose.

Eventually, the 'instruments' to whom the Constitution granted the least independence – the ministers on the one hand and the deputies on the other – came to play a decisive role. As it happens, they embodied the two typical institutions of a parliamentary system that was in contradiction with the founding spirit of the regime.

### 4. The administration

#### Civil servants

In a regime in which political life and its partisan divisions had to give way to administrative life, the administration was vested with a crucial role. All civil servants, in addition to their official duties, were entrusted with political missions. For a strong regime, civil servants were the guardians of order and the agents of official propaganda responsible for watching over, and directing, public opinion. And in a regime that claimed to be democratic, they were meant not only to guide electors in their choice, but also to keep the government informed of changes in public opinion. The emperor was in danger of being cut off from the aspirations and complaints of his subjects, who could not express themselves freely either in the press or at the polls. His civil servants were therefore to serve as his eyes and ears. Napoleon III indeed paid special attention to their reports – the copious ones prepared two to four times a year by the 28 public prosecutors (*procureurs généraux*) concerning the material and moral condition of the inhabitants under their jurisdiction, the more concise and more frequent reports from the prefects and the information passed on by the gendarmerie or the police.

However, it did not prove necessary to overhaul the earlier administrative system, the essential features of which had come into being under the First Empire. It was enough for the new regime to keep the system well under control. The alterations made in central and local administrative bodies were aimed only at reinforcing government control over the administrative machine.

The number of public employees at the State and local level nevertheless swelled from 477,000 in 1851 to 628,000 in 1866 and nearly 700,000 at the end of the Empire (not counting members of the clergy on the State payroll). Setting aside the fairly stable figures for the military (some 360,000 men), the number of civilian State employees more than doubled, from 122,000 to 265,000. Law enforcement officials accounted for a major share of this figure. While there was a slight decrease in the numerical strength of the gendarmerie (from 24,500 to 23,000), that of the police soared from 5,000 to 12,150, and three-quarters of the 36,000 communes employed a rural policeman. In 1866, the sum total for this category was 67,000. It is tempting to use these figures to emphasize the police-centred character of the regime. But the increase in police personnel can also be explained by the growth of large towns, and it was not specific to the Empire, since it continued under the Third Republic. As for the increasingly ill-paid rural police (their average salary was 211 francs a year around 1855 and only 140 a decade or so later), it would be exaggerated to regard as efficient civil servants these poor wretches without uniforms, who were more often a nuisance than a help for the gendarmes.[9] Lastly, the personnel of other administrative services expanded at an often no less – if not more – massive rate: this was true of public education (65,000 civil servants in 1866), the postal service and the administration of the *départements*.

Recruitment presented no difficulties in an age when the civil service enjoyed a certain esteem, offered the prospect of social promotion to many and promised the then exceptional security of a guaranteed pension at the age of sixty and after thirty years' service (law of 9 June 1853 reorganizing and harmonizing the civil service pension system).

The government had many ways to stimulate the zeal of its civil servants and incite them to carry out the full scope of the political tasks assigned to them. In a regime where the agents of the State spied on one another and were all under constant surveillance by prefects, public prosecutors and police, their advancement depended on their devotion. If they did not give satisfaction, the ministers could always transfer, demote or remove them (except for magistrates or field officers). In practice, civil servants seem to have displayed a wide variety of attitudes. A good number of lower-ranking civil servants were loyal to the Empire, which had bettered their condition; police commissioners were usually dedicated and diligent; justices of the peace, who were removable, were far from adamantly refusing to act as electoral agents. Others, however, including even humble rural policemen, behaved with appalling indiscipline at election time. The prefect of the Tarn-et-Garonne was not alone in observing, in 1853, that 'the agents of the State, by and large, are neither submissive nor devoted'. The situation hardly improved, since a confidential circular of 12 April 1866 from the Minister of the Interior deplored 'the inadquate assistance' provided by civil servants to the prefects 'from the political point of view'.

Yet the government apparently hesitated to make sweeping use of its arbitrary powers. Even the very establishment of the regime did not entail massive purges. Admittedly, 132 irremovable magistrates were put into enforced retirement (on the strength of a decree of March 1852) and certain civil servants were sanctioned. But apparently not many were affected, and (with the exception of schoolteachers) far more were transferred than were dismissed. Ultimately, therefore, a wide variety of political opinions prevailed even in the early days of the Empire among civil servants, even and perhaps especially among the higher-ranking. Many of the magistrates who remained in office cultivated a nostalgia for previous regimes and did not hesitate to criticize the prefects for their excessive political zeal. The prefects often questioned the loyalty of the public servants with whom they had to work: the prefects of the Vienne and the Hérault complained in 1854 that the leading civil servants in their *départements* were legitimists.[10] The prefect of the Haute-Garonne calculated with a curious precision that, in 1852, his 983 civil servants comprised 629 legitimists, 241 Orleanists, 53 republicans and only as many Bonapartists.[11] At the same time, in order to regain control of the situation, he requested the transfer of five top-ranking officials (two field officers, the public prosecutor, the rector and the chief tax collector); he was to obtain only three.

Thus the administration, some of whose staff had been chosen by earlier regimes, did not behave as a monolithic corps, ready to obey every order from Paris with slavish obedience. For example, many high-ranking officials who, when asked to track down republican agitation, applied their instructions from Paris with zeal and sometimes anticipated on them were – to say the least – unenthusiastic when ordered to act against certain notables. In the ranks of the administration itself there existed invisible brakes, elusive obstacles that thwarted the government's action. Napoleon III's awareness of them prompted him to comment to Emile Ollivier: 'It's well to govern, but one must administer.'

### The prefects

The structure of local administration, which the Second Empire did not even feel the need to revamp, was a striking replica of the central power structure: in keeping with the Napoleonic principle, each echelon comprised an official responsible for implementing policy and vested with authority, who was assisted by a council exercising an essentially consultative role. Thus, at the level of the *département*, one found the prefect and the *conseil général*, then the sub-prefect and the *conseil d'arrondissement* and finally – except in Paris and Lyons, as the two largest cities in France were denied all specific representation – the mayor and his municipal council. The mayors, whom the Second Republic had turned into elected officials, once again became civil servants; indeed, they could even be appointed from outside the ranks of their town council. But in this authoritarian administrative system, whose structures were reinforced yet further, there was only one key man, responsible for the unhindered transmission of power all the way down the hierarchy: the prefect. The sub-prefects, who were placed under his close supervision and knew that their advancement depended on their submissiveness, were simply his direct collaborators; the mayors, whom the prefect chose personally in towns of less than

3,000 inhabitants, and whom he was free to suspend or dismiss, were merely his delegates.

Even more so than under the First Empire, the prefect was a 'poor man's emperor', the emperor's presence in the *département*. His already far-ranging powers were increased by the decree of 25 March 1852, a true charter of prefectoral administration that remained in force until 1964. The prefect remained the delegate of the central authority, responsible for order and for enforcing laws and regulations; he was in charge of the police and had the exclusive right – among others – to authorize the opening of cafés and taverns as well as to order their closure. Furthermore, whereas he had previously been a mere executor of ministerial directives, he now became 'the representative in his *département* of the governmental unit'.[12] In order to administer his *département*, he was vested with decision-making powers in numerous areas hitherto reserved for the various ministries. He ruled by proxy on all matters concerning food provisioning, agricultural development, public works, minor road maintenance, fairs, poor relief and so on. One hundred and twelve areas, described at length in five tables, fell within his purview. Not only did the prefect strictly supervise local communities (from 1855, he appointed even deputy mayors), but he controlled most of the lower-ranking civil service jobs, and henceforth picked public employees in twenty-six categories, ranging from *départemental* architects to humble rural policemen. A law of 1854 gave him the additional right to appoint and fire schoolteachers – hitherto the rector's prerogative. And it was the prefect who sent reports to Paris concerning all government officials. Lastly, the regime was determined that the prefects should not neglect their basic task as political organizers.

However, the decree of 25 March 1852 – which called for a form of devolution rather than fully-fledged administrative decentralization, quite to the contrary – simultaneously increased the central authorities' control over the prefects and made them subject to ministerial jurisdiction. Prefects were henceforth obliged to account for all their actions and the government was empowered to annul all their decisions. Furthermore, the development of new means of communication helped to accentuate both the local role of the prefect and his submission to the government. He could make more frequent visits to the various localities of the *département*, particularly when recruiting boards met, and thus make his presence better felt; but the ministers could contact him rapidly thanks to the electric telegraph and summon him to Paris if needed. With some bitterness, a former prefect observed in 1860 that his colleagues had become mere instruments of ministers and even of the ministerial bureaucracy.

In order to allow him to carry out his numerous tasks, the prefect, who already had all the public services of the *département* at his disposal, was provided with a personal and more numerous administrative staff, comprising a prefectoral council, a principal private secretary and a 'secretary general' – a post revived in 1865. In addition, as a demonstrable token of the high esteem in which it held these senior civil servants, the regime showered favours on them. First, they were rewarded with honorific distinctions, such as prestigious promotions in the Legion of Honour, to which were added decorations in many foreign orders. Second, if they left the prefectoral career, they could obtain the most sought-after posts in the central administration, a seat on the Conseil d'Etat or even one in the Senate, which eventually included twenty-one former prefects. Lastly, they were exceedingly well paid: their salaries were the highest in the civil service (if one excepts the incomes of chief tax collectors). Whereas prefects earned between 10,000 and 30,000 francs under the Second Republic, by the very beginning of the Empire the eight first-ranking prefects each earned 40,000 francs, the eighteen second-ranking prefects 30,000 and the others 20,000. Moreover, the number of prefects in the top two ranks increased considerably during Napoleon III's reign. These bountiful stipends, violently denounced by the opposition, were offset by heavy expenses, barely covered by special funds and occasional allowances. For prefects were asked to live in style – their advancement was even partly dependent on it. To the cost of settling into veritable palaces was added the expense of lavish receptions. All in all, the prefectoral function was not a source of wealth; it only allowed incumbents to maintain their rank.

The men who were vested with such powers and endowed with such prestige – the men whose imaginative authority the Bonapartists praised so highly – were only the detestable agents of tyranny in the eyes of the republicans, who accordingly depicted them in an unflattering light. Zola, for example, left cruel portraits of a number of them in *Les Rougon-Macquart*: in *La Curée*, Hupel de la Noue, the worldly prefect who dabbles in literature and spends eight months a year in Paris; in *Son Excellence Eugène Rougon*, some passing references to an 'imbecile' called Campenon – who owes his prefecture to the protection of Marsy (Morny?) – and to Langlade, a dissolute prefect who sends bothersome husbands to the Legislative Body. But above all, this last volume contains Zola's archetypal prefect of the Second Empire, Léopold du Poizat. The son of a former bailiff of Coulonges who made a fortune through usury and died mysteriously, this young careerist with shady connections is appointed prefect of the Deux-Sèvres less on the strength of his (highly undistinguished) legal training than as the protégé of the powerful Rougon (Rouher?), who thus rewards 'the most determined member of the gang'. The new prefect soon wields his arbitrary power to the point of ordering the odious and fatal arrest of the notary Martineau. And by way of a general verdict on the prefectoral establishment, Zola adds this confidential comment by Rougon: 'I've been dealing with prefects for a month...What a collection! Some are stupid. Well, at least they're obedient.'[13] All in all, Zola regards the prefects of the Empire as *déclassés*, promoted out of favouritism, often mediocrities, always slavish. But on this point Zola, far from giving us 'historical novels', lapses into fiction.

Thanks to the researches of Le Clère and Wright,[14] we now have a more accurate view of the 220 officials who administered the *départements* during the Empire. Some of them had been appointed by earlier regimes. Having already been purged to a certain extent after Louis Napoleon's election as president of the Republic, the prefectoral establishment by and large welcomed the *coup d'état*. Consequently, a holocaust of prefects proved unnecessary: as eight had resigned and six had been removed, it was enough to replace fourteen out of eighty-seven. In the early days of the Empire, some fairly sweeping reshuffles were carried out, when Persigny was Minister of the Interior (until 1854). Napoleon III would no doubt have wanted to keep on the same men at the head of the various prefectures, for reasons he described to Persigny in 1862 in these words: 'I attach the utmost importance to the stability of the prefects in their *départements*. A mediocre prefect, but one who has a long acquaintance with the area, is better than a distinguished and transient prefect.' As it happened, twenty-four prefects remained in office for over ten years, the prefects of the Ardennes and of the Seine-Inférieure for the duration of the Empire; Haussmann served as prefect of the Seine from 1853 to 1870, Vaisse as prefect of the Rhône from 1853 to 1863. Here again the stability of the personnel led to an ageing of the prefectoral establishment, whose average age rose from forty-four and a half years in 1852 to forty-nine in 1860. This stability, however, was only a relative one: while prefects remained in office longer than their successors during the early Third Republic, their tenure was shorter than that of the *conseillers de préfecture*, mayors and most civil servants – not to speak of the *conseillers généraux* – for successive ministers were not lenient towards the prefects: between 1854 and the end of the Empire, they removed fifty-two of them. Furthermore, if only to satisfy the desire for advancement, several reshuffles had to be carried out, which gave some contemporaries the impression of watching a 'lancers' quadrille'.

The appointment of these top-ranking officials, far from being left to the ephemeral preferences of a protector, resulted from a decree prepared by the Minister of the Interior and submitted by him to the emperor, who examined it attentively. Napoleon III exhibited an abiding interest in prefectoral changes at least until 1860, since he always had the final say in the matter so long as Billault was at the Rue de Grenelle ministry. Admittedly, at the beginning of his reign, the emperor used prefectures as worthy rewards for influential men who had served him loyally when he was president, whereas in later years fewer outsiders were appointed. Throughout the period, however, the choice of prefects was conducted with care and evidenced a definite consistency.

An analysis of the birthplaces of the 220 imperial prefects reveals, first, the already great predominance of the Paris area, since 55 prefects were born in the Seine and the Seine-et-Oise; next, but far behind, come the prefects of Corsican origin (7) and those from the Dordogne (8) and the Puy-de-Dôme (6). The last two cases point to the undoubted, but ultimately somewhat limited, influence of Magne on the one hand, of Rouher and Morny on the other; more generally, they testify to the importance of the south-west and the Auvergne in the administrative system as well as the political life of the Second Empire.

In social terms, the prefects came either from the aristocracy or – in a majority of cases – from a very solid bourgeoisie, the most modest being of middle-ranking bourgeois families. Most of them were sons of civil servants or military men, and thus seemed destined by family tradition to serve the State. Thus they often had relatives who occupied important positions in other branches of the administration, the army, the Conseil d'Etat or even already in the prefectoral establishment. Certain dynasties were now providing their third generation of prefects.

These men had acquired solid, and in some cases brilliant, educational credentials. Except for the rather small number who had attended the *grandes écoles* (Polytechnique, Saint-Cyr, Navale), they had studied law at university, particularly in Paris. Before joining the prefectoral establishment, they had started out in the civil service or the professions, but very rarely in journalism. Their family, training and profession made them notables 'already established in social and political life before their appointment', enjoying, if not a large fortune, at least relative financial ease (their private incomes averaged between 10,000 and 20,000 francs of *rentes* a year). Even Janvier de la Motte, depicted as the archetypal prefect of the new breed, conformed to the general pattern: born into a family of magistrates and parliamentary deputies, he practised as a lawyer before becoming sub-prefect of Dinan in 1847; after serving in several sub-prefectures during the Second Republic, he was appointed prefect of the Lozère in 1853 and prefect of the Eure in 1856, a post he occupied for twelve years. His was a very classic career, progressing through the successive regimes.

Indeed, many of these prefects had embarked on their careers under Louis Philippe or Cavaignac, and even in 1870 only a third were 'sons of the regime' who had started out under the Second Empire. Not only did they come from fairly diverse backgrounds, but they also represented a wide spectrum of political views. Not all of them were even genuine

Bonapartists, since some still had legitimist sympathies, others were both staunch anti-legitimists and Orleanists, others still were republicans who had rallied to the emperor's person. Even among the Bonapartists, the imperialists of long standing were far fewer in number than the converts who seemed to have belatedly discovered their political ideal in the Empire. On the whole, one can distinguish four major trends among the prefects:[15] the 'traditional conservatives', hostile to all social innovation; the 'right-wing democrats', such as Janvier de la Motte, who believed that the emperor should draw his strength directly from the people; the 'supporters of an authoritarian democracy' that would impose social reforms; lastly, the 'left-wing democrats', who were concerned about freedom and favoured closer ties with the working class. These diverging opinions did not compromise corporate unity or prevent all these prefects from proving extremely loyal to the emperor. Moreover, most of them were good, hard-working and diligent officials, who shouldered their social obligations 'with selflessness and dignity'.

Were they also those 'firm-handed prefects' whose arbitrary rule was so often denounced? M. Blanchard has already put forward the hypothesis that it was perhaps 'the republicans of 1871 who created the legend of the firm-handed prefects of the Empire, veritable miniature despots wielding ferocious authority over civil servants and mayors, ruthless and merciless practitioners of the official candidacy, incomparable at hunting down opponents and rigging elections';[16] Le Clère and Wright have debunked this 'myth of prefectoral omnipotence'. At the very most, the traditional image can apply to the early days of Empire, when certain prefects, turning into champions of authoritarian democracy, spared no effort to win over the masses and destroy the notables' influence. It can also apply to a few isolated cases such as Janvier de la Motte, who administered his *département* of the Eure with energy, wasting no time over legalistic procedures and displaying a blatant partiality and an undeniable political flair. This wily and corrupt administrator eventually had to resign when, on account of his debts, he was involved in a spectacular trial. However, he was so successful in winning the approval of the masses in the *département* that they elected him as a Bonapartist deputy at the beginning of the Third Republic. Flaubert intended to use Janvier de la Motte as the hero of a political novel that he was planning to write about the Second Empire. Was it, as some say, because Flaubert saw him as a symbol of the regime? It is far more likely that the novelist was taken with the prefect's extraordinary personality.

In reality, the prefects of the Empire wielded less extensive powers than the statute books would suggest. They also became increasingly depoliticized, turning into plain 'functionaries'. While they still played a role in elections, they renounced their claims to constant hegemony over political life. Instead, they preferred to behave as cautious civil servants and sensible bureaucrats – a very understandable change.

First of all, the prefects were overburdened with administrative duties, as they had to make their *département* participate in the economic modernzation of the country and had to resolve all the new problems this created. They proved competent administrators and efficient organizers of economic life. Furthermore, the moment he sought to become 'the master of the *département*', in the words of Seignobos,[17] the prefect had to contend with a general conspiracy: he was poorly aided by his own civil servants and by independent – and consequently unsubmissive – magistrates. Above all, he had to reckon with the notables. No doubt he had been ordered to undermine their influence and, in principle, had a formidable weapon at his disposal for the task: patronage. Whoever in the *département* wanted to solicit the government for a favour – whether a job, a subsidy or a scholarship – had to turn to the prefecture, and nowhere else, in order to have any chance of success. In actual fact, the prefect never managed to retain exclusive patronage: the notables, at least if they were not in the opposition, could also influence decision-making in Paris, where their connections reached into the governing circles. The ministers and the emperor himself, the better to win over a local personage, would hand out favours directly, ignoring the prefect's advice and thus whittling down his power. And the prefect, faced with the uselessness of his efforts, practically gave up the open struggle against the notables, all the more easily as he himself belonged to the 'enlightened' classes. Self-interest also led him to handle with care the influential figures of the *département* whose interventions could affect his advancement. Indeed, close connections were doubtless established between prefects and ruling economic circles. It was no accident if, after 1870, several prefects had no difficulty shifting to a business career.

Among those who did their utmost to erode the prefect's patronage were the deputies themselves, despite – or in order to make people forget – the fact that they were elected thanks to the official candidacy. Their local and national influence grew to a point where Persigny observed in 1866 that 'the deputy is becoming an inordinately important figure in his province, for he controls the very source of all favours and of State patronage over all the administration'. Some deputies were well aware of this. Granier de Cassagnac, for example, did not hesitate to assert before his electors in the Gers in 1869: 'There are no prefects, there is no emperor. I am the emperor.' The prefect had also to contend with the *conseillers généraux*.

### The *conseillers généraux and local notables*

Every precaution had been taken to ensure that the *conseil général* remained an assembly under the prefect's authority and incapable of exercising control over him. Its powers were severely curtailed by the decree of 25 March 1852. Its main tasks were to vote the budget for the *département* that was submitted to it and apportion direct taxation among the *arrondissements*, adding on local taxes. Every one of its decisions had to be approved, according to its nature, either by the emperor, by a minister or by the prefect. Its meetings were confidential; the executive fixed the calendar of its sessions and appointed its president. Finally, the *conseil* was forbidden to issue proclamations or petitions or to consult other local assemblies.

But the *conseillers généraux* wielded a considerable influence that was unconnected with the powers officially vested in the *conseil général*. Their primary source of strength was their permanence. After the *coup d'état*, which prompted the more spectacular than large-scale withdrawal of a few liberals, the *conseils* were put up for re-election, but the change of regime and the application of universal suffrage did not, in the end, lead to more than a very partial turnover: 66 per cent were re-elected, and most *conseillers* 'leaped over the breach of 1848'.[18] The assemblies came up for re-election, only by thirds, every three years. During the Empire, the *conseillers* served an average of two consecutive terms, thus remaining eighteen years in office. Here again, stability meant ageing (the *conseillers* in 1870 were on average ten years older than their predecessors had been in 1848).

Furthermore, as Victor de Broglie noted in his *Vues sur le gouvernement de la France* half-way into the Empire, these assemblies enjoyed 'the two-fold advantage of a thoroughly popular origin and a thoroughly aristocratic composition': their members were elected by universal suffrage, which was indicative of their enduring audience in the country and at the same time increased their influence; more importantly, nearly all of them were still solidly entrenched notables. Even when the membership changed on account of demographic renewal, the *conseillers* still belonged to the same social type and their recruitment evidenced an undeniable sociological stability. The same categories of notables remained in office: notables by virtue of their occupation or fortune, their reputation ranging from the *cantonal* to the *départemental* or national level, they were all 'men of the same circles', of the 'best circles'. A striking persistence can also be observed in the representation of the various socio-professional categories in the *conseils généraux* between 1840 and 1870: landowners and land rentiers invariably made up a third of the membership; professional men, particularly notaries and lawyers, represented 30 per cent, and civil servants 21 per cent – an increasing proportion of whom were from the upper echelons; lastly, businessmen accounted for slightly over 15 per cent, among whom merchants seem to have gradually gained ground on industrialists.

The *conseillers* included a fair number of politicians. Imperialist deputies, even when elected in Paris, took to standing in *départemental* contests so as to strengthen their ties with their electorate. Four-fifths of the deputies, as well as three-fifths of the *conseillers d'Etat* and two-thirds of the ministers, stood successfully for election to the *conseils généraux*. Often these men served as presidents of the *conseils* – presidents more stable than the prefects and, because of their connections in government circles, better able to get a hearing there. One can understand why the brutal Janvier de la Motte had to display boundless respect towards the president of his *conseil général*, Troplong, who was also president of the Senate! All in all, the local assemblies were composed of individuals 'both important and imbued with a sense of their own importance', scarcely inclined to treat the prefect as a local emperor. How could the prefect of the Saône-et-Loire – assuming he had the slightest wish to do so – take a stand against E. Schneider, member of his *conseil général*, but also deputy, vice-president and later president of the Legislative Body, head of Le Creusot, *régent* of the Banque de France, a man whose annual income at the end of the Empire totalled 1,500,000 francs? When serious unrest broke out at Le Creusot, Schneider dealt directly with Paris. This was no doubt an exceptional case, although there were at least ten *départements* that notables regarded as their fiefs. And, in many instances, prefects had to compromise with *conseillers généraux* and avoid giving them offence. Admittedly, the Empire used administrative pressure against traditional social influences, in an attempt to 'substitute administrative rule for the rule of notables'. However, the administration could not dispense with the latter's aid.

Now in 1870, and quite probably all during the Empire, the majority of *conseillers généraux* were far from displaying genuinely Bonapartist feelings. It is true that the prefects regarded only 16 per cent of the notables as declared opponents or simply as 'doubtful' men on whom they could not rely – a percentage they could not but find satisfactory. But the others were not necessarily unconditional supporters. A vast majority of notables remained 'apolitical': 60 per cent of them, who professed no political opinion, willingly co-operated with the imperial administration, but would have done so with another one. Their collaboration was indicative of concordant interests rather than heartfelt Bonapartism. The notables' apolitical stance, primarily determined by the desire to maintain public order, helped to preserve the status quo and was conditional on the respect of their ascendancy. Finally, there remained 24 per cent of notables who 'had rallied' – *conseillers* who, having belonged to various political families, remained at most sentimentally faithful to a particular ideal, but behaved with as much devotion as the preceding categories.

Thus, by their overwhelming stability – better, by their inertia – the *conseils généraux*, which went unchanged through the political vicissitudes of the 1840–1870 period, were the image of the governing classes; despite their diversity, their disagreements and their hierarchies, these classes were assured of their collective right to run the country.[19]

Hence the complexity of local politics, in which the prefect, far from being in control, was only one of several actors.

Even at more modest levels, civil servants were hard put to dictate political behaviour to members of the assemblies. Many mayors preferred to nurse their popularity rather than turn into the government's agents; those who chose the latter course were not always heeded. Thus, when the mayor of Silhac (Ardèche) invited his town councillors to vote for the official candidate in a legislative by-election in 1864, nine of them reacted immediately by sending him the following letter:

The undersigned...wish to state that they cannot accept that you should prescribe their conduct in the elections, as you did in your circular... They declare that they shall vote freely, despite your letter, for that candidate of the two who better represents their political opinions. They declare, furthermore, that they do not recognize a mayor's right to tell them that they should either vote against their conscience or resign from an office to which the voters have elected them.[20]

Admittedly, this commune was in the *canton* of Vernoux, the only one in France to have cast a majority of 'noes' in the December 1851 plebiscite. But, even in most other places, civil servants who wielded their authority too brutally and too extensively were liable to come up against such displays of pride.

## 5. Conclusions

### Political weaknesses

There was a primary weakness in the Second Empire, which was that of any personal regime: its longevity depended on that of the emperor, to whom the people had delegated their powers. If the emperor should disappear, the Empire was liable to collapse, especially if he left no direct heir fit to succeed him. This explains the haste with which his entourage went about concluding his marriage: Napoleon III married Eugénie de Montijo less than two months after becoming emperor. But their union remained sterile at first, despite the sea baths – then reputed to be aphrodisiac – taken by the imperial couple at Biarritz. At long last, in 1856, the imperial prince was bórn. For the duration of the Empire, he was only a minor, and the imperialist leaders had to live with the constant prospect of having to face the dangerous test of a regency.

Furthermore, there was no such thing as a Bonapartist team surrounding the throne, sharing the sovereign's feelings and thoughts, united around a consistent doctrine. Louis Napoleon, after his election as president of the Republic, found himself 'man without troops'. He was obliged, little by little, to recruit his governmental and administrative personnel from a wide variety of backgrounds, in particular from 'that mass of former Orleanists, former civil servants, discouraged politicians, demoralized liberals, and self-interested or slavish subordinates – the sort of conservative marsh that eventually teemed with the mass of Bonapartists for the nonce or latter-day imperialists'.[21] These *ralliés* were genuinely attached to the sovereign's person, but little inclined to regard him as a charismatic or infallible figure. Their having rallied to him did not mean that they had abandoned their own political ideas, especially as the emperor made no attempt to violate their consciences. And, as Bonapartism was a heterogeneous collection of variegated currents 'whose only common features were a penchant for authority, the cult of military glory and rather imprecise references to the principles of the Revolution',[22] and as 'it was everywhere – to the Left, to the Right, and occasionally at the centre',[23] it was tempting for everyone to interpret it in his own way, stressing those aspects that he found most attractive. Napoleon III, aware that his regime was torn between conflicting tendencies, exclaimed one day: 'What a government I have! The empress is a legitimist, Napoleon Jérôme a republican, Morny an Orleanist. I myself am a socialist. There are no Bonapartists except for Persigny, but he is insane.' For all its exaggeration and unjust cruelty towards Persigny, this quip is not inaccurate: even as head of State, Napoleon III did not achieve the fusion of parties that Napoleon I had, to a certain extent, succeeded in bringing about. Thus the emperor remained a lone man.

Finally, this regime had no 'party' to serve it, or rather, as at the time there were no parties in the modern sense of the word, it could not rely on organized political structures. Even in the early days, Morny, then Minister of the Interior, did not deem it worthwhile to prolong the existence of the committees created to win the first plebiscite. During later election campaigns as well, committees were set up here and there, but they were few and short-lived. Moreover, the formation of a Bonapartist party would have run counter to the official doctrine of the regime, which continually denounced the 'former parties' as divisive, and professed to be able to organize a great national gathering of all 'good Frenchmen': the immense majority of the French people could, by definition, only be Bonapartist. The role usually played by the party in modern dictatorships was vested here in the State apparatus; but the administration, which had been assigned in particular the task of undermining legitimist and Orleanist influence and fairly often went about doing so, was not composed exclusively of pure imperialists and could not arouse the hostility of all the notables without risk. A compromise was necessary. The regime itself needed the notables, but its need brought it face to face with social realities.

### Winning over the affluent classes

Even had he wanted to do so, Napoleon III would have been hard put indeed to recruit genuinely Bonapartist personnel and leaders. For in mid nineteenth-century France, not a 'new country' in political terms, Bonapartism was virtually extinct as an organized political force. If the name of Napoleon had become extremely popular, especially among the peasantry, it was because the Napoleonic legend had glorified the first emperor as 'the father of the people and of the soldier'.[24] But 'the Bonapartists, most of whom were veteran soldiers, remained poorly represented among the enlightened classes':[25] Armengaud's observation, which concerned the eastern part of Aquitaine, applied to the greater part of the country. In most areas, top-ranking civil servants, leading financiers and industrialists and, more generally, to use the contemporary expressions, the 'affluent', 'enlightened' or 'upper' classes – whose wealth and influence had grown over the preceding half-century – by and large espoused other monarchic ideals, particularly Orleanism, or were simply indifferent to the form of regime. Napoleon's name had only a scant appeal in such circles. This explains the relative failure of Morny, who, in 1852, having asked his prefects to find new men willing to stand as the government's candidates for the legislature, was finally obliged to fall back on the old political personnel. For lack of an adequate Bonapartist élite, the Second Empire suffered from a dearth of men. Furthermore, since it rejected social revolution (it was founded precisely in order to combat the revolutionary peril), it was condemned to rely on borrowed personnel and could not dispense with the help of established social forces, which it thus had to win over, at least partially. The emperor knew that he had to obtain the support of prominent families. If he failed, if he came up against a systematic abstention of the élites, he would be unable to remain in power. Guizot made this point in a letter of 1852:

> Risings are put down with soldiers, elections are won with peasants, but soldiers and peasants are not enough to govern; one also needs the assistance of the upper classes, who are by nature governing classes. The latter, however, are generally hostile to the president.[26]

Yet the president had some decisive arguments with which to woo them. First, a judicious distribution of posts and favours enabled him to set up a clientele of faithful followers; in addition, contrary to Guizot's claim, a large portion of the affluent classes rallied to Louis Napoleon out of fear of 'anarchy', and thus out of reason and self-interest more than out of intimate conviction and enthusiastic attachment. The president's task, however, was complicated by the firm establishment of universal suffrage. In the days of the 'property-franchise monarchy' (*monarchie censitaire*), politics concerned only the affluent classes, and the people did not participate, except to revolt. Now that the Empire had 'integrated the masses into political life',[27] the latter was conducted simultaneously on two levels: that of the indispensable élites and that of the masses – ill-educated and unsophisticated, no doubt, but now free to express a yearning for a better life that had to be satisfied to some degree. The government now needed popular support.

But the wishes of the 'labouring classes' rarely coincided with the desires of the 'affluent classes'. Hence the totally unprecedented dilemma that would henceforth unfailingly present itself for any political democracy that refused to usher in a social revolution: how could one appeal both to the traditional élites and to a majority of voters? The most lucid contemporaries understood at once that the new regime thus found itself in the predicament of having to rely on both conservative and popular elements. For example, as early as 10 December 1851, the young Prévost-Paradol wrote that Louis Napoleon could not count forever on this dual support and indefinitely reconcile 'labour and capital. He will not miraculously unburden the poor without crushing the rich. He will not be M. Thiers and M. Proudhon all in one.'[28] Louis Napoleon himself grasped the need to solve this difficult problem, since he wrote to his cousin in November 1852: 'When one bears our name and when one heads a government, there are two things to be done: *satisfy the interests of the most numerous classes and win over the upper classes.*'[29] Here too, Louis Napoleon sought the 'middle road', the narrow path that would make it possible to 'balance the influence of the higher classes with that of the masses'.[30]

Even when the Empire, thanks in particular to the fear of the 'red spectre', had successfully wooed a portion of the 'upper classes', their support remained conditional: it was the object of a sort of tacit contract, in which these classes expected the new regime to ensure order, prosperity and the preservation of the status quo. But in consequence, unless he breached this contract, the emperor could find himself unable to take any initiatives, and obliged at least to postpone the implementation of certain 'ideas' that were dear to him but anathema to 'vested interests': his social reformism and his belief in free trade. Whatever his powers, he could not impose his policies at will; he was obliged to manoeuvre.

Finally, the curious and original development of this regime has often been noted: at first dictatorial, it gradually – and unlike any other dictatorship – moved in a liberal direction. This evolution can be explained by the emperor's genuine desire to make more room for democracy and even for freedom, as well as by the advances of a political opposition that wrenched ever more momentous concessions from a weakened emperor. But in a deep sense it also reflected the influence exercised, even within the regime, by the representatives of the 'upper classes'. Disregarding the interlude of 1848, which in certain respects was but a false break, one can sense the enduring influence of certain social spheres. Often it was the same persons who remained at the head of key institutions, such as the Banque de France. And even when a changing of the guard took place, owing to the succession of generations or to the desire to replace those who had compromised themselves too deeply with earlier regimes, it was the team that changed, not its social provenance. Thus the regime could never expect more than a moderate – and often uneasy – loyalty from those who occupied positions of power. The Empire never secured the human resources needed to be truly and totally authoritarian. From the outset, a considerable gap existed between theory and reality, between statutes and their enforcement, for

> the development of society in the first half of the nineteenth century, accelerated by the advent of universal suffrage, tended to modify, *from the very moment it was set up*, the political and administrative apparatus of the Empire, all the more so when the backing of a parliamentary majority became both desirable and necessary.[31]

Ultimately, the most astonishing feature of the Second Empire is that it lasted longer than any of the regimes that had preceded it since 1789, and that it was overthrown only because of a military disaster. It is also surprising that Napoleon III managed to conduct an original policy. No doubt this success is primarily attributable to the emperor's political flair. While lacking a genius for which history usually refuses to give him credit, he demonstrated over a long period a remarkable capacity to adapt to circumstances and an undoubted skill at manoeuvring. Another explanation lies in the new vitality of the economy.

# 3

# Economic progress and change

In the economic history of France, the Second Empire is regarded as a decisive period, an age of brilliant prosperity and rapid expansion, marked by the rise of capitalism and culminating in the 'birth of modern France'.

## 1. Prosperity and expansion

### A stable population

Under the Second Empire, France's population rose from 36,000,000 to 38,500,000 inhabitants, dropping in 1872 to 36,140,000 on account of the casualties of the Franco-Prussian War and the Commune as well as the loss of Alsace-Lorraine. But the rise in the number of Napoleon III's subjects was partly due to the annexation in 1860 of Savoy and a portion of the Comté of Nice, whose population at the time stood at 700,000. Not counting border changes, France's population growth appears to have remained very weak. After the economic crisis and the ensuing political crisis in mid-century, which led to a significant demographic depression, no signs of recovery can be observed during the first years of the Empire. The perceptible upswing of 1861–1866 remained a modest trend: its rates were well below those of the end of the July Monarchy, and it came to a halt several years before the war of 1870. Throughout the Empire, the average annual growth rate was a bare 0.27 per cent, a progression twice as slow as in the age of Louis Philippe, and also considerably slower than during the first fifteen years of the Third Republic. The French population had already reached a virtually stationary state that it was not to attain again before the late nineteenth century (Table 1).

This stability contrasted with the vitality of neighbouring nations. France ceased to be the first demographic power in Europe (Russia excluded), as it was overtaken by the States that later formed Germany, whose population rose from 35,900,000 in 1850 to 41,000,000 towards 1870. This relative decline of France was a subject of concern for certain far-sighted contemporaries such as Prévost-Paradol, who, convinced that his country could not remain a great power unless it was sufficiently populated, was obsessed by the notion of French decadence; Gobineau, for his part, saw this phenomenon as a consequence of the inner weakening of the race. But the governing classes, still widely imbued with Malthusian ideas, remained indifferent to the problem.

Demographic stagnation was not due to heavy emigration. While emigration was not negligible, at least at the very beginning of the period and especially following the war of 1870, it was, at most times, more or less offset by immigration, particularly the influx of Belgians from Flanders coming to work in industry in the north. The number of foreign residents rose from 380,000 in 1851 to over 740,000 in 1872. The cause of the halt in population growth must therefore be sought in the make-up of the demographic structure.

Table 1. *Average annual growth rate of the population (with constant borders)*

| 1841–6 | 0.68 | 1861–6 | 0.36 |
|---|---|---|---|
| 1846–51 | 0.21 | 1866–72 | 0.2 |
| 1851–6 | 0.14 | 1872–6 | 0.56 |
| 1856–61 | 0.3 | 1876–81 | 0.41 |

The French birth rate under the Second Empire was considerably lower than that of neighbouring countries (35 per thousand in England, 37 per thousand in Germany). This was not due to a decrease in the number of marriages – a figure that remained fairly stable – but to the restriction in the number of births in French families. Voluntary birth control, a very early phenomenon in France, had made steady progress since the eighteenth century, and was spreading to new regions. Thus, in April 1857, the sub-prefect of Châtillon-sur-Seine (Côte-d'Or) noted in his report 'a decrease in the number of children. This moral restraint, to use Malthus's phrase, is practised today even in the countryside, and large families are unheard of.' Moreover, the example came from above: 'The rulers of the hour were not of the sort who were tempted by large families' and 'if there was a *fête impériale*, it was not a family celebration'.[1] Yet on the whole, the birth rate (just like the fertility rate) stopped declining under the Empire; interrupting its century-long decline, it even showed signs of reviving.

The curve of the general mortality rate was indicative of a demographic pattern which, in many respects, remained that of the *ancien régime*. First, its jagged profile reflected, particularly before 1860, a series of very sharp variations from one year to the next that did not really disappear until the Third Republic. Thus the number of deaths rose by a quarter between 1853 and 1854, a year in which there were almost a million deaths in France, especially on account of the Crimean War (in which a total of almost 95,000 persons were killed, most of them victims of cholera), problems of food provisioning and above all a devastating cholera epidemic that claimed 145,000 lives in 1854 alone (it was particularly lethal in the Ariège, where 4 per cent of the population died). And throughout the period, various outbreaks of smallpox, cholera and typhus took their toll on the population here and there. Furthermore, the mortality rate reached in 1854 and nearly equalled in 1859 was unprecedented – with the exception of 1849 – since the very first years of the July Monarchy, the black years of 1832 and 1834, whose memory was beginning to fade away. Conversely, the best moments of the Second Empire did not match the level reached in 1845 (21.1 per thousand). Thus the mortality rate interrupted its long downward movement, which resumed under the Third Republic: life had once again become more precarious and more threatened. This deterioration of life, this diminished resistance to death, is surprising in a period of alleged prosperity. One can attempt to explain it by a certain ageing of the population, the impact of European wars and expeditions to distant places, the rapid spread of alcoholism and the grinding poverty of an ever larger urban proletariat. However, the upturn in mortality affected both the rural areas of the Loir-et-Cher, at least until 1857, and, all during the Empire, *arrondissements* as little industrialized as those of Brioude and Yssingeaux in the Haute-Loire.

In actual fact, it was not adults who were victims of this new onslaught of death. While their mortality rate remained stable or even declined slightly, a brutal and terrible upsurge in the infant mortality rate occurred. The number of infant deaths in the first year of life (per thousand live births), after having slowly decreased to the still sizeable figure of 144 in 1845, rose again sharply, reaching peaks of 215 in 1859 and 228 in 1871 – sad records of the age of statistics. The slow progress made earlier seems to have been cancelled out, and if one adds the number of deaths of children aged from one to four, which seems to have increased rather than declined, and that of still-births (33,000 a year at the end of the July Monarchy, 48,000 at the end of the Second Empire),[2] one finds that one baby in three failed to reach his fifth year (Table 2).

This long series of infant and child deaths was part of the daily life of the French at the time, and undoubtedly affected their attitudes and behaviour. Perhaps the desire of certain families to compensate for such brief appearances in life explains why the birth rate stopped declining.

But whatever their human aspects, these massive losses of children affected the natural trend in the same way as a fall in the birth rate, and they partly explain the slowing of population growth. And a stationary demographic state is not a factor of economic expansion. As it leads to a relative stagnation of needs and an inelasticity of domestic demand, it is an incentive to reduce rather than increase production and to preserve rather than change existing structures.

Table 2. *Infant mortality in 1860*

| | | |
|---|---|---|
| Number of births in 1860 | | 1,002,000 |
| still-births | 45,000 | |
| died in their first year | 190,000 | |
| died between 1 and 4 years | 97,600 | |
| died before their fifth birthday | 333,000 | 333,000 |
| reached their fifth birthday | | 669,000 |
| Total | | 1,002,000 |

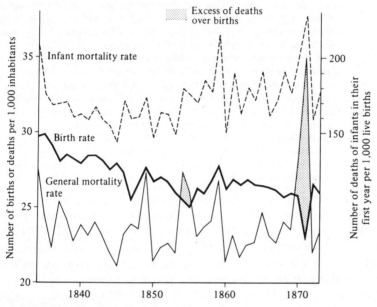

2 Population change, 1834–73

*Source:* Figures taken from the *Annuaire statistique de la France*, Paris, Imprimerie Nationale/PUF, 1961, pp. 33–5.

Yet at the start of the Second Empire the economy was helped by a favourable demographic factor, as the 'full' generations born during the Restoration – when the birth rate was still relatively high – and spared by wars reached maturity. In the words of Rondo Cameron, one is

> struck by the fact that the remarkable rise of the entrepreneurial spirit in the 1840s and 1850s coincided with a modification in the age distribution of the population, whereby the most productive age cohorts (roughly speaking, those aged between 25 and 45 years) reached a high point in their influence for the nineteenth century.[3]

But by the 1860s this advantage had disappeared.

### The role of the State

The Second Empire was the first regime in France to have given such distinct priority to economic objectives. Even as he took major initiatives in this field, Louis Napoleon defined these objectives in his speech in Bordeaux in October 1852 (see the preceding volume in this series). Once emperor, he elaborated on them, in particular in a letter addressed to his Minister of State, Fould, and published in *Le Moniteur* of 15 January 1860. In this letter he

> proclaimed the truth that the mediums of exchange must be increased in order for trade to flourish; that, without trade, industry stagnates and maintains high prices that hamper the growth of consumption; that without a prosperous industry that ensures capital growth, even agriculture remains in its infancy. Thus all these interlinked factors contritribute to the steady growth of public prosperity...As for agriculture, it must enjoy the advantages provided by credit institutions...; a sizeable sum must be devoted each year to large-scale drainage, irrigation and land clearance projects. To stimulate industrial production, [industry] must be granted special, low-interest capital loans that will enable it to upgrade its plant. One of the greatest services to be rendered to the country is to facilitate the transport of vital raw materials for agriculture and industry. In order to achieve this, the Minister of Public Works shall expedite as promptly as possible the construction of communication routes such as canals, roads and railways whose chief purpose will be to bring coal and fertilizers to places where they are needed for production.

Thus the emperor wanted to ensure prosperity by this bold development plan. He believed, with the Saint-Simonians, that economic progress would, to quote the phrase launched by Isaac Pereire back in 1831, bring about 'an improvement in the condition of the largest and poorest class', and thus the satisfaction of the masses. But, for the emperor as for the Saint-Simonians, prosperity required the modernization of the nation's equipment. Hence his feeling that his glory and the nation's greatness depended – no less than on military victory – on the success of an 'industrial revolution', in the broadest sense, that would hoist France to the level already reached by England. Only such a revolution would bring about full employment and also, by lower prices, an increase in consumption, which was the emperor's chief goal.

Furthermore, while Napoleon III sought to promote a form of progress both material and moral, just like Guizot – who in 1843 had told the French: 'Enrich yourselves, improve the material and moral condition of your country' – he replaced the simple advice of Louis Philippe's minister by more imperative expressions that committed the State: 'Our task is...' (Bordeaux speech), 'it is necessary that..., the minister...shall...' Adopting once again the arguments of Saint-Simonianism (which sought to make the government play an exclusively economic role) and the ideas of Michel Chevalier (who regarded the government, far more than as a 'policeman', as the 'manager of the national Association'), the emperor believed that the State was not a 'necessary ulcer', and that it must play a crucial role, undertake ambitious projects, 'at once construct and dazzle'.[4] The means of transport and production would not be taken over by the State (the *coup d'état* had removed the spectre of nationalization), but the State's task was to stimulate renewed expansion and foster structural change.

To begin with, the State could intervene directly by acting on the volume and nature of its spending – and the Empire is credited with having actually done so. Napoleon III had a prodigal temperament, and certain members of his entourage incited him to spend somewhat recklessly. Among these men was Persigny, who 'had accurately realized that the regime had to be extravagant, because the Empire must be a succession of miracles: the public had to be overawed by the almost uninterrupted occurrence of prodigies due to the presence of one man',[5] and brought about by massive investments to which the State's finances would contribute. And to make up the budget deficit, since new taxes were out of the question, all that the State had to do was to make extensive use of credit. Financially speaking, the practice of big budgets and heavy borrowing was justified by the very modern theory of productive expenses, advocated by Persigny and Haussmann and already defended by Louis Napoleon in *L'Extinction du paupérisme*: by stimulating economic development, investment expenses yield fabulous profits and increase income to such a point that debts that initially seem overwhelming can later easily be reimbursed.

Such a policy worried orthodox financial circles, which raised the spectre of bankruptcy. From the outset, the policy was strongly criticized by the group of deputies known as the *budgétaires*, who strove for budget cuts as far as their limited means would permit. It was even disliked by certain ministers, Magne and Fould in particular, both of whom served as Minister of Finance. Thus Magne spoke of his determination to

> wage an all-out war [against] these mistaken ideas. I am speaking of the financial schemes with which the Minister of Finance is being bombarded. The more mistaken these sophisticated projects, the more appealing and dangerous they are...They knock at every door: the civil service departments (to which they promise a wealth of resources) and the sovereign (to whom they promise the means of relieving the Empire's population and of undertaking great public works) are the auxiliaries that they are seeking to enlist. No words are too harsh against the minister who finds in his common sense and in the keen notion of his duty the strength to resist, clearly perceiving the misfortunes that threaten the nation. He must put up with constant reproaches for his stubbornness and immobility. He is narrow-minded, retrograde, outmoded and impervious to the great ideas of the day.[6]

The emperor, who was quite unfamiliar with financial matters, must have heeded such warnings and taken fright at the catastrophes announced.

Hence, in this field too, his hesitant policy. To be sure, the Second Empire ushered in the age of large-scale loans, which it issued directly to the public instead of transferring them to banking syndicates. The first of its kind was a loan of 250 million francs floated in March 1854 by Bineau at the outbreak of the Crimean War. The loan was highly successful, since 99,224 subscribers contributed a total of 468 million francs. This enabled the regime to extol in its propaganda 'the universal suffrage of capital' and 'the democratization of public credit' and to discover a convenient way of obtaining plentiful resources. The number of subscribers to later loans rose steadily to 672,000 in 1868. The volume of public debt rose accordingly (Table 3).

Table 3. *Public debt, 1853–69 (in millions of francs)*

|  | Consolidated debt (government stock, in capital) | Floating debt |
|---|---|---|
| on 1 January 1853 | 5,577 | 802 |
| on 1 January 1865 | 13,026 | 839 |
| on 1 January 1869 | 11,516 | 794 |

The debt swelled rapidly until 1865, and the increase during Napoleon III's reign was 100 per cent as against 20 per cent during the July Monarchy. One would also have to take into account the greater indebtedness of the *départements* and communes, especially the city of Paris. These loans served to fill deficits averaging 250 million francs a year from 1852 to 1865. In consequence, they enabled the State's total expenditure to increase heavily, albeit fitfully: from 1,513 million francs in 1852, a level close to that of the last years of the July Monarchy, it soared to a record 2,309 million in 1855, after which it hovered around the 2,000 million level. Thus the regime did most of its 'big spending' in its early days. Furthermore, the increase was partly due to rising prices. All in all, the ratio of the State's current expenditure to 'physical output' (value of agricultural and industrial production) did not rise significantly before the beginning of the Third Republic, since it represented the following percentages:[7]

| 1815–24 | 13.5% |
|---|---|
| 1845–54 | 12.8% |
| 1855–64 | 13.1% |
| 1865–74 | 13.5% |
| 1875–84 | 18.4% |

While less prodigal than the opposition charged, the regime inaccurately prided itself on giving priority to productive expenses. In actual fact, the greatest budgets were those of the war years, and the loans floated during these periods represented a heavy drain on capital markets, making it difficult for private enterprise to raise finance. Admittedly, orders for armaments, particularly for the navy, opened major markets for iron and steel companies, but the financing of public works in the budget was conducted with extreme parsimony. The Empire devoted fewer funds to them than had the July Monarchy, as Casimir-Perier noted in an article in the *Revue des Deux Mondes* of 1 February 1861: 'During the seven fiscal years from 1852 to 1859, only 508 million francs have been spent on special public works, whereas the last seven budgets of the July Monarchy devoted 958 million francs to them.' In 1869, the budget of the Ministry of Agriculture, Commerce and Public Works still accounted for only 4.5 per cent of the total budget. Even allowing for the projects financed by the *départements* and communes, public investment remained very low, and subsidies an exceptional occurrence (for example, in 1860, in order to help industry to modernize and to face British competition).

Nevertheless, the State's role was not negligible. First, by its very existence, this strong government inspired confidence in business circles. Furthermore, it established a close co-operation with them, particularly in the Conseil Supérieur de l'Agriculture, du Commerce et des Travaux Publics, where high-ranking civil servants, ministers (Rouher, Baroche) and economists (Michel Chevalier) exchanged views with leading industrialists and financiers such as Schneider, Lesseps and the banker d'Eichtal. The government, very well informed about their ambitions and free of all parliamentary control, did its best to facilitate their activity. It often let the new corporate firms stifle traditional small entrepreneurs, without heeding the complaints of the latter. For example, it allowed the railway companies to outclass older internal water transport companies. And under pressure from business circles, which constantly demanded greater freedom, it refrained from enforcing bothersome regulations. When a conflict arose between iron and steel manufacturers and townships or local inhabitants in ore-rich areas, the government's policy was always to avoid inflicting 'non-indispensable constraints on this industry'. It also adapted legislation to the rise of capitalism, enacting numerous laws and decrees on economic matters. Furthermore, it provided a lively stimulus for private enterprise by initiating large-scale public works and granting concessions for vast railway networks. Finally, when railway companies or the Compagnie Générale Transatlantique required assistance for raising capital, the State guaranteed the interest on their securities. In short, as the Pereires had wished, 'the "strong" State became the welfare State of large-scale capitalism'.[8]

*A favourable economic cycle*

Whatever its own merits, the Empire had the good luck of bene-
fiting at the outset from the favourable economic cycle prevailing in
western countries since the middle of the century. In France, the political
climate delayed its positive effects, but with the return to order their
impact was all the more forceful for their having been pent up. Back in
1949, Ernest Labrousse explained the reversal of the economic cycle as
follows: after the discovery of gold in California (1848) and later in
Australia, prices, which had generally been falling since 1815, rose sharply
until 1856, remaining thereafter at a high level, which provoked a sharp
increase in entrepreneurial profits and thus triggered a rapid expansion.
This classic pattern[9] remains on the whole valid, even if it seems difficult
today to explain the connections between these phenomena.

Table 4. *Available monetary resources (in millions of francs)*

|  | 1845 | 1870 |
|---|---|---|
| Gold | 500 | 5,000 |
| Silver | 3,000 | 2,000 |
| Total | 3,500 | 7,000 |
| Less reserves | 300 | 1,100 |
| Coinage in circulation | 3,200 | 5,900 |
| Paper money | 300 | 1,500 |
| Deposits | 400 | 1,200 |
| Total money supply | 3,900 | 8,600 |

*Source:* R. Cameron, *Banking in the Early Stages of Industrialization* (New York:
Oxford University Press, 1967).

The first novelty was the swelling of the money supply, which increased
at least twofold at the same time as its composition changed (Table 4).

It was gold in particular that irrigated a country hitherto accustomed
to paying with heavy silver coins. To a certain extent, gold came to be
traded against silver, in keeping with a traditional pattern of speculation in
bimetallist countries: bad currency, in this case gold, because it was
becoming relatively less scarce, chased out good currency, in this case
silver, which was at a premium towards 1856. Furthermore, the inflow
of gold can be explained by a steady surplus in the current balance of
payments, particularly in the balance of trade. The latter, which had
previously been even, ran an average annual surplus of 250 million francs
until 1866, then deteriorated during the last years of the Empire.

In addition to coin, the money supply included bank notes issued by the
Banque de France, of which the smallest denominations from 1864

onwards were the fifty-franc bills. The swelling of fiduciary circulation reflected the increase in commercial exchanges, for the issue of bank notes was linked to the discounting of the drafts that constituted the Banque's 'commercial portfolio', which itself tripled. But as the bank notes issued were still guaranteed by sizeable gold and silver reserves (which soon went over the 1,000-million mark: see the item 'reserves' in Table 4), they served to a great extent as convenient substitutes for coin. As for bank money (deposits), despite its increase, it played only a modest role, far less important than in Britain.

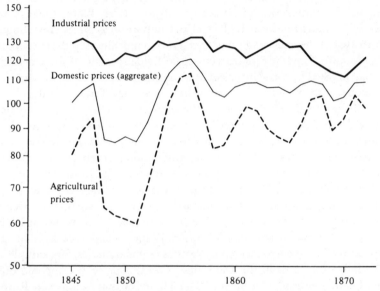

3 Domestic prices, 1845–72 (1880 = 100)

*Source:* Based on the figures in M. Lévy-Leboyer, 'L'Héritage de Simiand: prix, profit et termes de l'échange au XIXe siècle', *Revue Historique*, January–March 1970.

A doubling of the money supply in two decades corresponds to a fairly slow growth. At the time, however, such growth constituted a genuine revolution, for it followed a protracted period of stagnation. Gone were the days of 'money shortages': the economy was now adequately provided with means of payment.

Price movements were also affected. It has long been stated that prices rose steadily during the whole of the Second Empire. The indexes calculated in particular by M. Lévy-Leboyer provide us with a more detailed picture of this trend.[10] It is true that the annual domestic price index, after falling from 149 in 1812 to 85 in 1851, rose considerably (Fig. 3).

The level reached towards 1870 corresponds to an increase of 30 per cent in two decades. Such a rise, which may seem insignificant to our contemporaries, could well be perceived as revolutionary by producers previously accustomed to coping with the problems posed by falling prices. However, two observations are in order. First, there was a fundamental divergence between the movement of agricultural prices and that of industrial prices (Fig. 3). While the former increased by 66 per cent, the latter continued to drop, on account of technological progress and of the ensuing decline in costs. The prices of these products merely experienced a slowing-down in their century-long decline. Furthermore, for production as a whole, the only clear-cut and continuous rise in prices occurred prior to 1856, even reaching an annual rate of 10 per cent before 1854. Later, these prices hovered around a relatively high level, in comparison to prices prevailing in the 1840s, but they never again behaved as dynamically as in the early years of the Empire. Thus the Empire seems to be divided into two distinct periods, the first marked by a rise in prices at a rhythm comparable to present-day inflationary phenomena, the second by stagnation, if not stability.

According to Ernest Labrousse, the increase in selling prices (or their slower decline) led to a greater increase in entrepreneurial profits, since production costs included elements whose cost rose more slowly (rent, interest and – in a society where no trade-union organization existed – wages) or even declined owing to technological progress. Even if one refuses to admit that prices played this dynamic role, the fact remains that profits, which had previously seemed to be so difficult to maintain, swelled more easily, at least in the case of large companies. This is shown in the survey on 'Profits in nineteenth-century France' conducted by Bouvier, Furet and Gillet,[11] corroborated by various regional studies, for example on large industrial firms in the Dauphiné. And this profit boom could only stimulate the entrepreneurial spirit, which, according to James de Rothschild, was 'a feature of the times'.

### The various facets of imperial prosperity

The euphoria of high profits coincided with a boom in the national income, which is reckoned to have increased (in millions of francs) from 11,400 in 1815 to 15,200 in 1860 and 18,800 in 1870. Even calculated in constant francs, all the indexes show a vigorous expansion of production and trade (Table 5).

This increase was particularly striking for the building industry and above all for exports, which took off well before the signing of the commercial treaty with Britain in 1860. The share of exports in 'physical output' rose from 7 per cent in mid-century – that is, barely the percentage reached at the end of the *ancien régime* – to 17 per cent, and their dynamism gave a strong impetus to the entire economic machine.

No doubt the entrepreneurs of the period enjoyed the prosperity that the new regime boasted of having ushered in. The *fête impériale* stood in contrast to the earlier difficulties, which reappeared in the last two decades of the century. However, this prosperity was not enjoyed by all – as we shall see later – and it did not bring untroubled happiness. Napoleon III's subjects frequently complained of difficulties that no longer stemmed exclusively from bad harvests – although these were still feared – but from crises in commerce and industry, often international in scope, which they

Table 5. *Output, 1853–69 (1890 = 100)*

|  | Agricultural production | Industrial production | Building | Exports |
|---|---|---|---|---|
| 1853 | 64 | 51 | 50 | 25 |
| 1854 | 77 | 51 | 54 | 23 |
| 1855 | 66 | 55 | 57 | 26 |
| 1856 | 72 | 57 | 63 | 30 |
| 1857 | 93 | 56 | 66 | 30 |
| 1858 | 101 | 61 | 62 | 32 |
| 1859 | 80 | 59 | 62 | 36 |
| 1860 | 86 | 62 | 85 | 38 |
| 1861 | 78 | 62 | 93 | 34 |
| 1862 | 98 | 61 | 86 | 39 |
| 1863 | 102 | 67 | 94 | 46 |
| 1864 | 98 | 67 | 92 | 50 |
| 1865 | 108 | 67 | 84 | 55 |
| 1866 | 99 | 71 | 96 | 61 |
| 1867 | 81 | 68 | 97 | 57 |
| 1868 | 105 | 76 | 103 | 58 |
| 1869 | 114 | 78 | 105 | 66 |

*Source:* Lévy-Leboyer, 'La Croissance économique en France au XIXe siècle', *Annales (ESC)*, July 1968. According to the figures in J. C. Toutain's still unpublished *Le Produit intérieur brut de la France de 1789 à 1975*, growth was considerably slower.

perceived as linked to credit and to stock market speculations. The first scientific analysis of these crises was made by the French economist Clément Juglar in his book *Des crises commerciales et de leur retour périodique* (1860).[12] More generally, expansion, far from being steady, was marked by feverish spurts and by uncertainty. Producers were no longer assured of the future; everything changed abruptly, in particular the price of money, as evidenced by the discount rate of the Banque de France. After having stood unchanged at 4 per cent from 1820 to 1847, this rate, now regarded as the thermometer of the economic situation, changed no fewer than 72 times under the Empire, from as high as 10 per cent to as low as

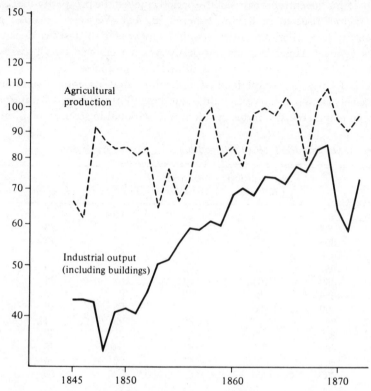

4  Output, 1845–72 (in constant prices, 1890 = 100)

*Source:* Based on the figures calculated by M. Lévy-Leboyer, 'La Croissance économique en France au XIXe siècle', *Annales (ESC)*, July 1968.

2.5 per cent. While generally favourable, the climate was none the less unstable.

Finally, if one goes beyond these accidents, one can distinguish two successive and very different rhythms in this expansion. Even if the dividing line is hard to locate, the production indexes seem to show that growth was more rapid at the beginning of the Empire, until 1858–1860, than after. The early years were also marked by steadily rising prices. Hence an undeniable euphoria among businessmen that consolidated the new political regime. Then

> the bourgeoisie suddenly ceased to be afraid of large figures, long-term plans and the financial obligations these entailed. Stirred by the joy of creating no less than by the desire for gain, consumed by an intense speculative fever, it plunged into business with the near certainty, after the troubled years, of being able to count on tomorrow, and even the

day after tomorrow. The entrepreneurial spirit of capitalism rushed headlong into the field of action.[13]

The ranks of this dynamic capitalism were also swelled by new, adventurous elements that turned towards the novel notions of world market, yield and productivity.

Later, even if the situation sometimes appeared to be returning to its earlier state – and the regime strove to bring this about – growth became more hesitant. Towards 1860 began the long 'deceleration of the French economy'.[14] Even in expanding sectors, prices tended to drop, as evidenced by this comment from the Comité des Forges on 11 March 1867: 'Owing to the low level of prices at present, the situation of the French metal industry today is to no one's advantage...The industry is growing, but industrialists are not prospering.' Production was still expanding, but profits seemed threatened. Consequently, the boldness of entrepreneurs often gave way, during the final years, to an obvious gloom. Fearful of the future, they now hesitated to forge ahead, and thus to ask for credit. This provoked what contemporaries called the 'strike of the 1,000 million' (*grève du milliard*) – of the 1,000 million francs in specie that lay idle in the vaults of the Banque de France. At the same time, business lost some of its confidence in a regime incapable of recreating the initial miracle.

## 2. Money

A considerable number of novels, plays and works by moralists of the period dealt with Money, as if all of society were obsessed by its power. Among many others, one can mention *La Question d'argent*, by Alexandre Dumas the younger, *Les Manieurs d'argent*, by the imperial prosecutor O. de Vallée and *L'Argent*, Jules Vallès's first book, commissioned by the financier Mirès. Similar themes are to be found in Jules Verne's first *Voyages extraordinaires*, in Labiche's plays and even in the Comtesse de Ségur's *La Fortune de Gaspard*.* Xavier de Montépin promptly entitled one of his serials *Sa Majesté l'Argent*. And although Zola did not devote a book to *L'Argent* before 1890 – a work that marked the culmination of his social history of a family under the Second Empire – he had emphasized the various roles of money back in his earliest novels, particularly *La Curée*.

Admittedly, the theme was not original, and it was often treated in a traditional and moralizing manner. But the authors stressed that society was under the absolute and exclusive domination of this new god, which bestowed power and fame. Money was the key to all pleasures; to own

---

* The Russian-born Comtesse de Ségur, née Sophie Rostopshin (1799–1874), was the author of numerous – and still read – edifying novels for children. Among them, *La Fortune de Gaspard* is of particular historical interest for its description of traditional rural life in Normandy. See the bibliography, **46** and **47**. (Trans.)

wealth was already to experience the enjoyment of power. As Dumas the younger observed: 'Today a man must have but one aim, that of becoming very rich.'

### The stock exchange

As it happened, new possibilities for making a quick fortune opened up for adventurers, for the like of Saccard, whom Zola shows us building up two immense fortunes in succession, first by taking advantage of Haussmann's enterprises to speculate on expropriation compensation and on buildings in Paris, then by plunging body and soul into stock market games.

The Paris 'Bourse' – just one of the country's several money markets – took on a new dimension, as shown by the increase in the number of securities quoted on it.

|  | French securities | Foreign securities | Total |
|---|---|---|---|
| Late 1850 | 90 | 28 | 118 |
| Late 1869 | 198 | 109 | 307 |

Paris had become a very important international money market. In 1869, the volume of securities traded reached 33,000 million francs. Furthermore, after the sharp rise that followed the *coup d'état* and whetted speculators' appetites, prices were continually subject to wide fluctuations. Economic and political instability had repercussions on the Bourse. Periods of euphoria were suddenly interrupted by wars or trade crises, and by the rumours surrounding these events. How many opportunities to get rich by pocketing the difference! The spurts of speculative fever over stocks in turn affected the financial market. There was even speculation on the forward market, although it did not yet have a legal existence. Every newspaper now carried a stock market column, and it was said that no novel was read more widely than the share price listings. According to Dumas the younger, 'the Bourse became for this generation what the cathedral had been in the Middle Ages'.

This speculation attracted sharp criticism from contemporaries. Proudhon, in his *Manuel du spéculateur à la Bourse* (1854), denounced the political influence of 'the new power, the feudalism of the stock market... Stock price quotations rule. The influence [of speculation] on the government has revived. Its opinion, expressed in francs and centimes, has legal force and makes up for the silence of newspapers.' Others complained, not without some exaggeration, that 'the demon of speculation' had contaminated all classes of society. In the Legislative Body, in 1856, the deputy Perret denounced the novel character of moveable wealth, whose owners 'too often indulged in the habits of speculation and agiotage...

The cause of the disorder must be ascribed to the prevailing fondness for easy gains...The Bourse has become a sort of temple for the worship of stock gambling...Speculation has assumed such proportions that, in itself and in its consequences, it is an insult to those who work.' The same year, the emperor congratulated Ponsard for having, in his play *La Bourse*, 'condemned the nefarious fashion of the day'.

### Company financing

But money was also often considered a source of the new civilization that would bring progress. Thus Jules Verne, even while denouncing the evil of gold, showed that wealth gave scientists their power and enabled them to reach the scientific and humanitarian goals they had set for themselves.[15] And Zola, after denouncing the corrupting effect of money, celebrated its civilizing power in these words:

> Madame Caroline became suddenly convinced that money was the manure in which the mankind of tomorrow would grow...Without speculation, there would be no living and fertile enterprises, no more than there would be children without lust. If down there...construction sites were being set up and buildings were rising from the ground, it was because money was raining down on Paris, corrupting everything in a frenzy of speculation. Money, poisonous and destructive, became the ferment of all social vegetation, and acted as the necessary compost for the great undertakings whose realization would bring peoples closer together and pacify the earth...Was not money alone the power capable of razing a mountain, filling in a stretch of sea, making the earth at last a fit dwelling-place for men discharged of the burden of work and henceforth simply engine-drivers? All good came from money, which was also the source of all evil.[16]

For money to become productive, however, it had to take the form of capital invested in companies. Firms often financed their growth by systematically reinvesting a portion of their profits. Thus higher profits enabled companies to self-finance their needs on a more massive scale. This was how corporate industry (mining, iron and steel) developed, but the practice was also widespread among small firms, for example in the textile branch: the family concern Méquillet-Noblot, which made cotton at Héricourt, gradually doubled its own resources during the Empire.[17]

But this mode of financing sometimes proved inadequate to meet the considerable needs of new capitalist firms. It then became necessary to bring funds together, to centralize savings. 'Business', said Dumas the younger in what became an often-quoted apophthegm at the time, 'is quite simple: it's other people's money...' The instruments for obtaining it – transferable securities – already existed, and their many virtues became widely appreciated. According to the monetary survey of 1865, security issues in France represented since 1852 an annual average of 1,500 million francs in investments.

These securities consisted chiefly of bonds. Railway debentures were the classic form: they yielded 15 francs in annual interest for a nominal capital of 500 francs, but were issued below face value at a price determined by market conditions. The advantage of such debentures was that subscribers had no say in the company; also, their reasonable price and their fixed yield made them relatively easy to place even among investors of fairly modest condition. The funds thus raised enabled companies either to carry out new projects or to buy another concern. When Morny, in 1855, purchased forges and mines belonging to the Aubin company for the railway company of the Grand Central, he raised the required capital by issuing 44,200 bonds of this kind.

Finally, the amount of initial capital needed to set up new businesses was in most cases beyond the means of an individual or a family. While general partnerships were still the most common type of company, these associations of individuals could not, barring exceptions, raise more than fairly limited funds. The solution was for a business to take the form of a joint-stock company, which alone made it possible to attract the savings of countless shareholders. Of these associations of capital, partnerships known as *sociétés en commandite par actions** were by far the most common. The much more flexible and efficient limited company (*société anonyme*), 'the cornerstone of corporate capitalism', was far less widespread. Between 1819 and 1857, only 600 limited companies were established, many of which disappeared. They consisted primarily of shipping or railway companies, insurance firms, mining concerns, a few iron and steel firms and – much more infrequently – textile firms. This low figure was due to the stringent regulations laid down by the law. A limited company could be established only by government permission – which could always be withdrawn – and its very functioning was subject to State control. The pressure from business led the government to liberalize this legislation in two stages. A law of 1863 abolished the requirement of a preliminary authorization for companies whose capital did not exceed 20 million francs. The Crédit Lyonnais set itself up at once as a limited company, and its example was followed, in Lyons alone, by the establishment of seven other 'limited liability companies' (*sociétés à responsabilité limitée*). Finally, the impediment represented by the limitation on capital was eliminated by the law of 1867, which stipulated that 'henceforth, limited companies can be set up without government permission'. This law was without doubt very liberal and very favourable to corporate capitalists. Rouher, one of its sponsors, himself provided an explanation of its purpose: 'Our

* In which the active partners had unlimited liability and the sleeping partners limited liability. (Trans.)

aim has been to open up a totally free path for all possible varieties of fair partnerships.' While presented as the foundation of financial democracy, this law ultimately established the ascendancy of boards of directors. Most of its provisions remained in force until 1966. Although it did not have time to have much effect during the Second Empire, it testified to the determination of economic leaders to be free to concentrate all the capital they needed in their hands.

### The banking revolution

Economic growth required the transformation of the earlier banking system, which proved unsuited to its needs. The old credit institutions did not, however, disappear, but engaged in a very largely successful effort to participate in the new business boom.

Thus the Banque de France, whose capital was boosted from 91 to 182 million francs and whose bank notes came into increasingly widespread use, behaved far less timidly than has been alleged. To its traditional transactions (discounting), whose volume swelled considerably, it added new forms of credit. The Banque provided crucial assistance to railway companies by automatically granting advances on their shares and bonds to all applicants (which helped to place these securities with the public), by making direct loans to the companies and by handling the sale of their new issues directly at its own counters when such sales proved difficult (from 1858 to 1861). Finally, whereas it had previously been for the most part a Paris-centred bank, it increased the number of its branches (74 in 1870) in response to government pressure and thus became the linchpin of an at last centralized credit system. The growing number of local banks and discounters turned to its branches for support. Certain local banks were set up as joint-stock companies, such as the seventy-eight offices of the Prost bank opened between 1852 and 1856. The more liberal distribution of credit reduced the need of entrepreneurs to call on the services of a usurer.

Even the family-run houses that made up the banking establishment (*la haute banque*) were more open to change than has long been believed. They were the first to become interested in railways. Working with their own resources and the deposits of a limited clientele, and so in greater security than the 'new banks', the 'old bankers' soon realized, however, that the latter afforded a means of obtaining colossal funds. Thus the members of the *haute banque* were among the first to take part in the establishment of the new banks, such as the Crédit Mobilier and the Société Générale. If James de Rothschild eventually stayed away from the new institutions – an attitude that symbolized his stubborn attachment to traditional practices – his colossal resources allowed him to do so: he held a quarter of the capital of the family concern, which stood at 553 million francs in 1863[18] and rose through self-financing to 888 million francs in 1874. To his means of action must be added the large deposits that so many wealthy families felt obliged to maintain with him. Even though he suffered a relative setback during these 'difficult years', he remained a force to be reckoned with.

The old banks evolved also because they had to face up to the competition of the new banks, whose major common feature was that they were joint-stock establishments. The most famous was the Crédit Mobilier, founded by the Pereire brothers – before the actual proclamation of Empire – with the backing of the new regime, which was wary of the Orleanist sympathies of the *haute banque*. Its founders had set their sights high.[19] The Crédit Mobilier was to be an investment bank that would finance industrial companies, help them to form their capital by channelling savings in their direction and provide them with the advances they vitally needed. As a railway bank, it set out to control the major companies in the field and to centralize their financial movements. In addition, it offered to facilitate both public and private loan issues and to lend against transferable securities and industrial shares. Finally, Isaac Pereire, as he clearly stated in his report for 1855, was determined to promote a policy of mergers involving all firms in a given branch, and thus eventually to set up a sort of holding that would control highly concentrated sectors.

In the event, the Crédit Mobilier was a creative bank whose influence made itself felt in many places. In France, it took an interest in several railway companies (Chemins de Fer du Midi, de l'Est) and in related industries (coal basin of the Loire); it launched what later became the Compagnie Générale Transatlantique, carried out the merger of the six gas companies supplying Paris and founded the Compagnie Générale des Omnibus de Paris as well as the Compagnie Immobilière, the largest of the firms engaged in the rebuilding and improvement of the capital; one can add, among other projects, the founding of two major insurance companies and the reorganisation of the salt industry. Abroad, the Crédit Mobilier participated in countless top-ranking enterprises: Austrian, Russian, Swiss and Spanish railways, credit institutions (Bank of Darmstadt, the Spanish Crédit Mobilier), the Ebro canal company, mines, public utilities and so on.

In order to cope with so many tasks, the Crédit Mobilier understandably required enormous financial means. Its capital, which amounted to a comfortable 60 million francs divided into 120,000 shares with a face value of only 500 francs (so as to attract the average saver), could not suffice much longer, even augmented by a few deposits. Its founders thus placed high hopes in short-term and, even more so, in long-term bond issues, with which they expected to boost their resources tenfold. They reckoned that these borrowed funds would provide them with the means of lending – in the long run – to every major firm, and of substituting a single 'holding' security (*omnium*) for bonds of various origins. The functioning of this free-spending bank was contingent upon its bond-issuing capacity.

The State, however, refused to allow it to issue bonds in 1853 and 1855. After the apogee of 1856 – it handed out a fabulous dividend of 200 francs per share – came the difficult years. Nevertheless, the Crédit Mobilier sprang back and continued to wage an epic struggle across Europe against its rivals, notably Rothschild. It was a duel of titans between 'Rothschild, the tough, solid and single-minded banker, who saw the railways as an opportunity for profitable issues and other financial gains', and 'Pereire, the romantic entrepreneur who saw a better world at the end of the track. Where Pereire was enthusiastic about launching, spending, building and expanding, Rothschild worked cautiously and never grew impatient...'[20]

But while Rothschild was certain of being able to work with capital of his own, the Crédit Mobilier was chronically short of funds. In 1862, the Pereires tried to obtain permission, through the intermediary of the Banque de Savoie, to issue bank notes throughout France, a solution that would have given them access to virtually unlimited credit opportunities. In the face of objections from the Banque de France the scheme fell through. Next, in 1863, the Pereires sought permission to double their capital, but the government delayed its reply. In the meantime, the Crédit Mobilier had to continue advancing funds to the firms it had established, particularly to the Compagnie Immobilière, now engaged in vast construction projects in Marseilles. Finally, in 1866–7, it found itself in acute financial trouble: the Banque de France, at Rouher's request, agreed to rescue it, but only on condition that the Pereires and their friends resigned. Although now reduced to struggling along, the Crédit Mobilier had played a decisive role, for it had practically 'forced all capital institutions to follow its example' (Persigny).

Several banking concerns of its kind were founded in its wake; they were smaller in scope and run by less honourable men. One such establishment was J. Mirès's Caisse Générale des Chemins de Fer, whose partly fictitious capital amounted to 50 million francs. Having set out to finance every new business venture, it succumbed by 1861, partly under the attacks of the Pereires.

Finally, this period saw the birth of a certain number of large credit institutions that were destined to a longer existence, since they still constitute the vital cogwheels of the present-day banking system. The Comptoir d'Escompte de Paris was followed in 1859 by the Crédit Industriel et Commercial, in 1863 by the Crédit Lyonnais and the Banque Impériale Ottomane, in 1864 by the Société Générale and the Banque des Pays-Bas and in 1869 by the Banque de Paris (the last two were to merge some time later).

These joint-stock banks, in particular the Crédit Lyonnais, began to discover that they possessed a miraculous means to attract savings into their coffers by offering to the public – through heavy advertising – a wide range of attractive deposit schemes: demand deposits (bearing interest), time deposits and current accounts. To develop their clientele, the banks provided a number of services as inducements. The law of 1865 introducing cheques in France made the banks' campaign easier. Lastly, the Crédit Lyonnais, followed on a larger scale by the Société Générale, founded their very first branches, which enabled them to obtain greater results from the new techniques for attracting customers.

Although they worked with what were often demand deposits, these banks did not hesitate to embark on bold ventures similar to those of the Crédit Mobilier. They

> were perfect 'mixed' German-style banks, Pereire-style Crédits Mobiliers hardly less enterprising and less imprudent than these 'outsiders' of the new banks. The Crédit Lyonnais, born under the star of the Pereires, imitated them in every respect...An ambitious industrial policy, controlling interests in industrial firms, medium-term credit, underwriting industrial security issues – all these constituted one of the aspects of the 'big business' activities of the larger Paris joint-stock banks. The other aspect consisted in the highly attentive handling of lucrative operations with States. During this period, only differences in organization distinguished the Crédit Lyonnais from the Banque de Paris.[21]

But these new establishments were only just embarking on their career. They had not yet developed their branch networks, and, while credit now played a more important role in the economy, France still had one of the lowest 'bank densities' among the developed countries of the time.

### Capitalist concentration

Economic expansion was accompanied by the building of colossal fortunes, as Zola observed, with some exaggeration, in an article published in *Le Rappel* on 13 May 1870: Balzac's richest heroes 'would today be fairly modest gentlemen. Nowadays, millions of francs are pocketed by the dozen...Today, one can meet Nucingen in every street; the lynx has become legion; he has lived off the Empire and he supports the Empire' – at least so long as he thought it in his interest to do so.

The formation of these big fortunes went hand in hand with the progress of large-scale enterprise. At least *in certain sectors*, a 'large-unit' capitalism[22] tended to replace the earlier system, in which no firm outclassed the others. There was an increasingly distinct tendency in these sectors for competition to lead to concentration, and the scale of capitalism seemed to be changing. Everything contributed to this decisive shift: the very workings of liberalism, technological progress, the influence of banks, the establishment of limited companies – for, as Auguste Blanqui noted in his programme of 1869–70, 'greedy and vigilant capitalism [this is one of the earliest occurrences of the word] has seized on the technique of partnership, and this magnificent instrument of progress has become a veritable rifle with which to exterminate small- and medium-scale industry'.[23] These very same sectors, now the battleground for ferocious clashes of interest, simultaneously witnessed the development of all the modern forms of what was already a highly diversified pattern of concentration: mergers, takeovers, financial controls and combines. However much securities 'became democratized', powerful financial groups were being created at the same time, with interests in banking, transport, iron and steel and engineering industry. For example, close links existed between Rothschild, the Compagnie du Nord and the Société de Construction des Batignolles; between the Crédit Mobilier, the Compagnie du Midi and the iron and steel firms of Saint-Etienne; between the Société Générale, the Paris–Lyons–Mediterranean line ('PLM'), Le Creusot and industrial firms in Marseilles.

Contemporaries became aware of the advances of concentration. Morny, who discovered them as a means of carrying out even more lucrative business deals, fully recognized the future of oligopolies and praised their role. Only a powerful railway company enjoying a high credit could 'freely attempt improvements. . .and dare to lower its rates!' As for the sovereign and the government, their hesitant attitude primarily reflected their concern to diminish costs. They thought this objective could be reached both by maintaining competition in the coal sector and by encouraging the creation of very powerful railway companies, regarded as the only sort that could bring about a fall in transport fares. On balance, although the authorities occasionally put a brake on concentration, they more often tolerated and even encouraged it.

This often resulted in a remarkable concentration of economic power in the same hands. The pamphleteer Georges Duchêne, a former associate of Proudhon, drew up a list of the great feudal lords of the times, in which he amalgamated every variety of lucrative enterprise.[24] In 1863, according to him, 'banks, credit institutions, liners, railways, large factories and firms of every size constituting a capital in shares and bonds worth 20,000 million francs were in the hands of 183 financiers'. Among these 183, ancestors of the '200 families',* he discerned a sort of super-aristocracy of some thirty names: newcomers, such as Morny and the Pereires (Emile was on 19 boards of directors, Isaac on 12, their son and nephew Eugène

* The '200 families' – originally the 200 largest shareholders of the Banque de France – came to feature prominently in the demonology of left-wing and right-wing anti-capitalists alike. For further details, see Alain Plessis (interviewed by Pierrette Crouzet), 'L'Age d'or de la Banque de France', *L'Histoire*, no. 53 (February 1983), p. 96; for the classic version of the myth, E. Beau de Loménie (**102**).

on 9; with their relatives by marriage – and allies – the Thurneyssens, they reigned over 50 companies), and also established families. The Rothschilds had 27 seats on various company boards, the Mallets 22.

In order to make their businesses profitable and to triumph over their rivals, these men – who tended to appropriate the most dynamic sectors of the economy – needed the help of officials and political leaders – the providers of concessions, markets and authorizations. In the great financial battles, the support of the sovereign, which could be decisive, was much sought after. The Pereires, for instance, who enjoyed the sympathy of Persigny and Morny, were at first supported by Napoleon III. But when, in 1862, the emperor attended a hunt organized by the Rothschilds at Ferrières, this gesture made the Pereires 'furiously' angry: it signified their disgrace. Not only did the big capitalists enter the Legislative Body (the Pereires, Schneider), but close ties (about which we still know little) were established between business and politics. Political debates often overlapped with financial rivalries. In 1856, for example, two deputies spoke out in the Legislative Body on the subject of the Pyrenean railways, accusing the government – in this particular case, Rouher – of having promised the concession for the lines to the Pereires despite the fact that the State had received more attractive offers. But the deputies' initiative seems to have been motivated less by concern for the public good than by their connections with Mirès, a rival of the Pereires.[25] The Pereires, for their part, regularly denounced the collusion between the Talabots, their rivals of the 'PLM', and the head of the civil engineering department (Ponts et Chaussées), de Franqueville. And when Mirès, in 1861, found himself with his back to the wall, he is alleged to have written a letter to Napoleon III 'in which he blamed his ruin on the bribes he had been forced to hand out to the emperor's friends' to the tune of 7 or 8 million francs. The corrupt beneficiaries are said to have included the young Baroche, son of the minister and himself a *conseiller d'Etat*.[26] A number of prominent figures of the Empire seem to have been involved in this widespread racketeering, and Morny came to symbolize these men, who skilfully exploited their political situation for the purpose of participating in all manner of *affaires*. To be sure, the opposition's accusations and insinuations must not be accepted uncritically. Napoleon III's ministers were often honest men, and the regime, on the whole, was tarnished by fewer scandals than the July Monarchy. But this was precisely because it now seemed normal for largescale business activities to be intimately connected with politics.

Lastly, the big financiers thrived on the influence they now exercised over the press, in which they had taken an interest primarily because of the opportunities they had spotted for making profitable deals. On account of the caution money requirements and especially of technological progress (the adoption of the rotary press, which made large print runs possible), newspapers demanded ever greater amounts of capital, but these investments proved extremely profitable owing to the boom in newspaper sales, particularly in railway stations as the rail network expanded. *Le Petit Journal*, an inexpensive (5 centimes) non-political daily launched in 1863 by the banker Millaud, reached 260,000 copies by 1865. Above all, financiers were quick to realize that the press provided them with a formidable weapon for directing public opinion so as to further their own interests. In Jules Vallès's *Le Peuple* of 12 February 1869, G. Duchêne showed with the aid of numerous examples that 'since 1852 the press has always been masterminded by certain financial powers'. The Rothschilds were said, not without reason, to sponsor the Orleanist-leaning *Journal des Débats*. Mirès owned *Le Constitutionnel* and *Le Pays*, two of the three leading imperialist newspapers. And

> the collusion between politics, money and newspapers was never as perfect as when 1,500 shares of the company of the two associated papers *Le Pays* and *Le Constitutionnel* – shares that had become available as a result of the liquidation of Mirès's assets – were purchased by Morny thanks to a loan of 550,000 francs from the Roman railway company.[27]

As for the many financial or stock market papers, they were all at the service of the financial groups that had launched them. As they were always closely linked with 'funds' whose main activity was the negotiation of securities, the purpose of such papers was to promote the sale of these securities by resorting to obtrusive advertising. For example, at the same time as Mirès founded the Caisse Générale des Chemins de Fer, he purchased *Le Journal des Chemins de Fer*. Having thus acquired the means of harnessing the mass of savers, financiers were able to channel at will and in their best interests the capital they tapped.

### Capital exports

According to R. Cameron,[28] French savings, which represented a considerable mass indeed at the time, fell into three roughly equal parts: one was absorbed by French government borrowing, another was invested in France in industry and especially in railways, while the last third was exported, so that total French investment abroad rose from 2,000 to 15,000 million francs between 1850 and 1870. France thus became a major lending country, exporting its capital across the Continent and particularly to Mediterranean countries. Over half the funds exported went as loans to foreign governments (Italy, Spain, Portugal, Russia, Austria and Hungary, Greece, the Balkan States, various parts of the Ottoman Empire, Mexico and even the United States). Railway construction in Europe also absorbed a considerable amount of French capital (in the Iberian peninsula, Austria, Hungary and Switzerland), and was often carried out under the supervision of French engineers. In addition, French investments abroad contributed to the building of the Suez Canal, the founding of public utility companies in a number of capitals, and the establishment of banks, mining concerns and iron and steel companies.

The Crédit Mobilier was a driving force behind the massive export of national savings. However, when Pereire was criticized for such practices at the time of the monetary survey of 1865, he defended himself by accusing Rothschild (albeit not in name): 'I am not the one responsible for the Italian loans, the Belgian loans [etc.].' Indeed, the two giants were locked in battle 'from the plateau of Castille to the Danube valley, from London to Constantinople and from Moscow to Trieste'. And all the banks participated, even the new establishments, even the Crédit Foncier, founded with the purpose of helping French agriculture!

The size of French investment abroad can be explained by the mechanism of the 'law of profit', the search for maximum returns. Morny, who was far from hostile to this, observed that 'capital comes and goes to where it is drawn by the lure of gain'. In truth, once the needs of big companies (the railways in particular) had been satisfied, domestic industry required little capital. There were various reasons for this: entrepreneurs were determined to work with their own funds, the population was stagnant and coal resources were limited. Domestic demand for capital was thus relatively weak, whereas it seemed inexhaustible in those foreign countries where governments were in dire financial straits and where the entire modern economic infrastructure was still to be built: that was where the high interest rates were. Admittedly, foreign investments did not always prove to be good deals for ordinary buyers of shares, and the railways built with their money often brought them disappointment. But the financiers who promoted capital exports secured all manner of rewarding commissions.

The effects of capital outflow on the French economy were complex. It did rather little to boost foreign sales of industrial products, but it did provide an inflow of revenue that, from 1866–7 onwards, amounted to 600 million francs, a figure now higher than that of net capital outflow. Cameron believes that, on balance, these exports helped to 'postpone the decline of France'. But, conversely, the haemorrhage of savings contributed to the slowdown in economic growth of the 1860s, which was partly due to insufficient domestic investment. The weakness of domestic capital demand is not alone to blame, for in certain regions, such as the Haute-Loire, there were chronic complaints about the lack of money – proof that unsatisfied needs did exist. Lastly, the emigration of savings has been accused, not without reason, of provoking recurrent contractions of financial and monetary markets. When the monetary survey was conducted in 1865, the governor of the Banque de France explained the surges in interest rates – of which tradesmen complained – by the

> devouring of available capital. Everywhere there is a tremendous competition to obtain capital; everyone is asking for it: States that borrow, cities that build, companies that speculate, the stock market that gambles, industry that manufactures, agriculture that produces, commerce that trades.

A period of plentiful money, the Second Empire was also, repeatedly, a period of dear money. The fact remains that the government, while moved by these criticisms, had no systematic policy in this area, and was unwilling or unable to halt the emigration of capital.

### 3. The railway revolution

The changes that marked the Second Empire were particularly spectacular in two fields: the development of the large urban centres (of which more later) and, above all, the growth of transport. France now entered into 'the age of railways'.

The building of the railway network was accomplished through the combined efforts of the government and of corporate capitalism. The State's role proved decisive. The law of 1842 had assigned priority to the construction of a certain number of main routes, dividing the task between the State, which would handle all the infrastructure, and private companies, which were required to install the superstructures (track, stations, etc.) in order to obtain concessions for running the lines. Not content with enforcing this law, the imperial government provided a variety of incentives. In early 1852, it handed out concessions for many new lines and, more importantly, it granted companies extended operating leases (usually 99 years) that made it easier for them to amortize their initial expenses and thus greatly increased the profitability of railway enterprises. At the same time, afraid that an excess of companies would cause them to hamper one another and compete, the government promoted mergers.

Once this initial network was completed towards 1858, plans called for other lines that would probably carry less traffic and would be costlier to build – at a time when the economic situation seemed less propitious. The government intervened once more to maintain the profitability of railway construction. Not only did it incite the Banque de France to help the companies place their bonds, but, as stipulated in the Franqueville conventions, it guaranteed interest payments on these bonds by pledging its own financial participation if the need arose. From 1863 on, under constant pressure from a railway-hungry public opinion and from its own deputies – who at each election were forced to promise new lines – the government had to contend with a greater 'circumspection' on the part of the major railway companies, which were hardly anxious to build less profitable lines. As a stimulus, the government tried to foster competition from smaller companies, to which prefects were empowered to grant concessions for lines 'of local interest'. More importantly, the government continued to guarantee the interest on bond issues. The practical implications of this clause were that by the end of 1870 the leading companies had already received 634 million francs from the State, which had heavily committed itself for the future.

For the great financial interests, thus relieved of part of the burden of constructing secondary lines, railways remained good and 'big' business. This was the only time in France when railways yielded high profits, not to mention the opportunities afforded for the banks to claim various commissions and grant remunerative advances to the rail companies. Revenues effectively rose in tandem with investments (Table 6).

Table 6. *Railway finances (in millions of francs)*

|  | 1852 | 1869 |
| --- | --- | --- |
| Accumulated expenses |  |  |
| of the State | 597 | 1,180 |
| of the railway companies | 1,002 | 7,030 |
| Volume of railway company revenue | 100 | 800 |

The sharing of such a plentiful cake provoked pitched battles, full-scale 'network wars' that pitted the *haute banque* – particularly Rothschild, who controlled the Compagnie du Nord and had stakes in the Paris–Orléans, Lyons–Mediterranean and Lyons–Geneva lines – against their competitors, especially the Pereires, who controlled the Compagnie du Midi (Bordeaux–Sète). Among so many tangled episodes, two stand out. The first concerned the fate of the Grand Central. Founded in January 1853 under Morny's aegis, with the assistance of many capitalists including the Pereires, the company sought to link Paris to the south of France by nudging in between the Paris–Orléans (extended to Bordeaux) and the future PLM. It was entirely in the Pereires' interest to link the lines of the Compagnie du Midi to the capital by eluding their rivals' grasp. But the first routes granted to the Grand Central served only high-altitude regions where construction was difficult and traffic not likely to be profitable in the short run. Its network was encircled by that of better-equipped rivals; its isolation brought it close to total paralysis. Eventually, Morny left the Pereire clan and in 1857 the Grand Central disappeared. The Paris–Orléans and the Lyons–Mediterranean, which joined up with the

Paris–Lyons to form the PLM, proceeded under the aegis of Rouher to share 'the scattered bones of the giant'.

This was not a very satisfactory solution for the Pereires, who in 1860 tried, on a more modest scale, to extend the Compagnie du Midi network to Marseilles by securing a concession for a 'coastal line' linking Sète and Marseilles.[29] A new conflict broke out between two coalitions of interests: on one side, the Pereire camp – supported by the groups involved in the development of the Camargue, by the Loire coal producers and by the Rhône river transport companies – counted on the backing of M. Chevalier and, above all, on imperial protection; on the other, the Talabots, masters of the PLM, and their vast empire in Marseilles – backed by the coal company of La Grand-Combe, by Bartholony (of the Paris–Orléans) and by Rothschild – could count on the benevolence of Franqueville and possibly of Rouher. Finally, the inquiry ordered by the emperor came to the conclusion that the coastal line should not be built: the Pereires had lost.

The network apportionment decided on in 1857 remained unchallenged thereafter. The forty-two small networks that existed before the *coup d'état* were replaced by six large companies (Compagnies du Nord, de l'Est, de l'Ouest, du PLM, du Paris–Orléans, du Midi), all of them dominated by the magnates of finance and industry. The first board of directors of the PLM in 1857 included members of the banking establishment (G. de Rothschild, Baring, Mallet), top industrialists (Schneider, Schaken) and former Saint-Simonians who had embarked on a business career (Enfantin and...I. Pereire!).

An impressive amount of construction was carried out in record time: very soon the tentacles of the 'railway octopus' extended from Paris to all the borders. In 1851, lines in service totalled 3,248 km and consisted of sections often impractical to operate. By 1869, 16,465 km were in use. All the main routes of the present-day network had been completed by then.

The railway revolution had decisive consequences. It brought about the sudden disappearance of one of the typical features of the old economy: the compartmentalization of space imposed by the absence of modern means of transport. For the inhabitants of the larger towns at least, a rapid, large-scale and cheap means of transport had finally been built. It used to cost 25 centimes to carry a tonne of goods by road; by rail, the cost dropped to 10 centimes, and shortly thereafter to 5. In consequence, rail traffic grew steadily.

The impact of railways was all the greater because, on the national level, rail traffic did not replace the volume handled by traditional means of transport, but was added onto it (Table 8). Railways thus created traffic.

The road network remained in heavy use, but its physiognomy changed. While trunk roads were less travelled, *départemental* roads and especially byways acquired a new-found importance by becoming the indispensable tributaries of rail lines. Road haulage (*roulage*), sometimes undertaken by large specialized firms and far more often by the peasants themselves, evolved in response to railways, and the regime concentrated its efforts on improving and building minor roads.

Table 7. *Volume of passenger traffic*

|  | 1852 | 1869 |
|---|---|---|
| Passenger traffic (in thousands of millions of travellers per km) | | |
| by road | 1.36 | 1.46 |
| by rail | 0.988 | 4.1 |
| Total | 2.348 | 5.56 |

Table 8. *Volume of freight traffic*

|  | 1852 | 1869 |
|---|---|---|
| Freight traffic (domestic transport, in thousands of millions of tonnes per km) | | |
| by road | 2.6 | 2.8 |
| on canals and waterways | 1.7 | 2.0 |
| by sea (coastal navigation) | 1.3 | 0.8 |
| by rail | 0.6 | 6.22 |
| Total | 6.2 | 11.82 |

*Source:* Toutain (**143**).

As for inland water transport, it succumbed in several areas to competition from the large railway companies, which waged a bitter price war against it. The PLM, for example, killed steam navigation on the Saône and the Rhône. But in regions where natural and economic conditions were more favourable, inland water transport adapted itself and, having managed to resist thanks to the lower cost of water transport for heavy goods, ultimately played a role in the general growth of the economy.

With railways, new social types emerged: the railwaymen, soon 137,000 strong, who earned an average annual wage of slightly over 1,000 francs for a 12-hour working day; and also the owners of railway securities, such as the naïve shareholder in Labiche's *Les Chemins de fer*, who comes up from the provinces to Paris with all his family to collect his coupons and suggest to the *messieurs* of the board of directors that umbrellas left behind in trains should be sold off to increase the dividend with which he is obsessed.

More generally, the lives of many Frenchmen, and even their outlook, were transformed by railways: their horizons suddenly broadened. Their mobility increased, since they now travelled three times more than before. They now each wrote an average of nine letters a year as against five earlier, while the electric telegraph network developed rapidly from 1852 onwards (by 1855, it was 10,000 km long and connected all the capital towns of the *départements* to Paris; it later expanded fourfold). Even the reading habits of the French were influenced by the advent of railways, since, while traditional chapbooks (*littérature de colportage*) lost ground, Louis Hachette launched his rail station bookstalls.

The material living conditions of the French were also greatly transformed. The volume of goods traffic rose twice as fast as that of industrial production and three times as fast as that of physical output. One can thus measure the growth of commercialization – a consequence of the development of a unified national market. The advent of railways spelled the end of local food shortages, a drop in certain consumer prices (the price of a tonne of coal fell in Paris even as its price at the mine bank increased) and thus larger-scale consumption. Railways also helped to improve housing and increase farming yields by enabling quality building materials and enriching agents (such as lime) indispensable for siliceous soil to be brought cheaply to areas where they were lacking. Finally, thanks to the railways, certain peasants were now able to shift from subsistence farming to cash-crop farming, and even to specialize in the most profitable crops.

But railways also claimed victims. By transforming the conditions of trade, they led to the death of fairs and the decline of peddling, while mail-order sales began to develop and the sales representative made his appearance. Keener domestic competition broke down the barriers of age-old isolation in many areas and caused the disappearance of numerous geographically protected activities. Hence the inexorable decline of certain local industries, such as the metal industry in the Haute-Saône. By revolutionizing production conditions, railways brought wealth to certain regions at the expense of others, thus modifying economic geography. They also helped big firms that could not be satisfied with a local market and now had the means to compete at long range.

Railways also played a role in opening France to the international market. The development of foreign trade owed at least as much to them as to the French merchant fleet, which expanded far too slowly (steamships accounted for only 145,000 tonnes of shipping tonnage out of a total of 1 million) despite the creation of two large shipping companies, the Compagnie Générale Transatlantique and the Messageries Maritimes.

Finally, the railways seemed to control the movements of the industrial cycle: the waves of railway investments (1853–6 and 1860–4) brought prosperity, for railways were a driving force behind the country's industrial growth. Quite apart from the expenses involved in replacing and increasing stock, the mere cost of setting up the rail companies over the decade 1855–64 represented 7.2 per cent of gross domestic product. Very massive orders were placed, particularly with iron and steel manufacturers and engineering firms: iron tracks, which needed frequent replacement (steel tracks, which were far more resistant, were not introduced until the end of the Empire), station halls, rolling-stock, iron bridges (which definitively supplanted wooden bridges from 1858 on) were all in demand. Such large-scale orders stimulated the rise of these industries, their concentration and also their modernization, for the rail companies, in their search for better products for their stock (tougher tracks, improved bands and axles) and by exerting a constant downward pressure on the prices of those products, provided powerful incentives for industrial innovation.

## 4. Industrial growth

### The rise of big industry

In several industrial sectors, decisive changes were taking place. This period saw the triumph of large-scale modern industry, characterized by the accelerated development of production (often accompanied by a decline in product prices) and by heavy outfitting in machines and looms, while at the same time the constant search for innovation led to improvements in manufacturing processes. Mechanization was helped by the development of steam engines, which often replaced hydraulic power, and by technological progress, which often owed more to empiricism than to scientific discoveries. The concentration of the technical means of production and of workers in large-size establishments and vast factories required relatively substantial investments, and thus an adequate concentration and accumulation of capital. This led to a financial concentration continually intensified by competition, which ruined the weak and made the strong prosper.

These modern features appeared for example in the mineral chemical industry, which was based at the time on sulphuric acid and sodas. Newly-built factories, the *soudières*, provided a rapidly growing output, essentially concentrated in the hands of a dozen big firms (such as Saint-Gobain and Kuhlmann). And concentration became heavier through combines and mergers.[30]

But it was in the sectors directly linked to demand from railway companies and the navy that big industry was becoming a dominant presence. These sectors were iron and steel manufacturing and the heavy engineering industry. The latter was called into being by orders from railway companies; later, it found a steadier source of business in other fields (building textile-manufacturing equipment, machines, bridges and ships). In these sectors, where prices fell rapidly while output soared (cast iron production rose by 6.7 per cent a year), the very modes of production changed. After a period of poor progress, iron- and steel-making entered into a 'phase of accelerated industrialization'[31] between 1850 and 1864, initially characterized by the spread of new techniques. Wood-fuelled iron-casting declined sharply, giving way to the rise of coke-fired blast furnaces (which contributed 44 per cent of total production in 1851 and 80 per cent in 1864).

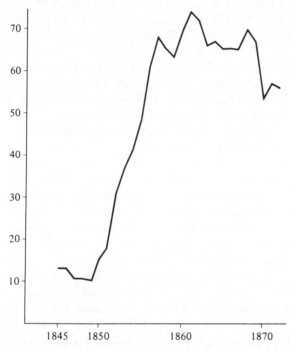

5 A measure of the impact of innovation in the French iron and steel industry: the number of workable patents taken out annually, 1845–72

Source: Figures calculated on a three-year moving average, on the basis of the annual data used by M. Pinson, 'Les Brevets dans la sidérurgie française', Cahier de l'ISEA, February 1965.

Other advances included the introduction, in 1861, of the process developed by the Englishman Bessemer, which finally made it possible, by means of a converter that transformed cast iron directly into steel, to obtain great quantities of steel far more cheaply. The number of patents involving iron and steel manufacture that were deposited during this period testify to a powerful upsurge of inventiveness.

At the same time, a deep structural evolution was taking place that gained even further speed after the commercial treaty with Britain (1860). By 1864, although the 'industrialization' of iron- and steel-making was not yet completed (some one hundred old 'Catalan forges' and 210 wood-fired blast furnaces survived), the modern mode of production had undoubtedly triumphed. Henceforth, 'only industrialized iron and steel production affected output and price trends, benefited from expansion and was in a position to precipitate it.' While the small-scale rural metal industry disappeared, 'France's big factories', as Turgan described them in 1866, made their impressive appearance. Typical examples in the engineering industry were the Fives-Lille works and the Derosne & Cail plant, which employed 2,800 workers in Paris. But Le Creusot was the epitome of the 'big factory': in 1867–8 it employed 9,950 workers and its production, chiefly destined for the railways and the navy, represented a value of 14 million francs. Its plants, as well as two mines and a colliery, were spread over 125 hectares. A bevy of steam engines powered 160 coke furnaces as well as forges and production workshops.[32]

Under the management of well-established dynasties, these big firms made steady progress: in 1869 De Wendel supplied 11 per cent of the one million tonnes of cast iron produced in France, and Schneider nearly 10 per cent. In order to obtain adequate resources of their own, some of these firms turned into associations of capital: thus Bougueret Martenot & C$^{ie}$ gave birth to Châtillon & Commentry, and Petin & Gaudet became La Marine & Les Chemins de Fer. Every form of concentration was used: horizontal integration through the purchase of competitors, vertical integration (many of these iron and steel manufacturers had their own collieries), acquisition of stakes in other firms (Schneider turns up in the new Decazeville company, founded in 1865) and combines. The entrepreneurs of the industrialized iron and steel sector established the first major French cartel, the Comité des Forges (1864), with Schneider as chairman. This institution, to which officials had given their unwritten authorization despite existing legislation, was designed to serve as an information centre, a centralized technological stimulus, a means of seeking new outlets abroad, an instrument of cohesion that would attempt to fix uniform prices and, lastly, a pressure group qualified to negotiate with the government.

The development of the coal industry was almost as rapid. Its output, increasing at an average annual rate of 6.1 per cent, rose from less than 5 million tonnes to over 13 million. Poor natural conditions, which were to contribute to slowing French growth and made it difficult to satisfy fast-increasing needs (railways and ships, iron and steel, steam engines), impeded the development of most deposits, but the coalfields of the Nord and especially of the Pas-de-Calais (the latter discovered in 1847 and worked under a concession from 1850 to 1855) were operated with a dynamism that spread to the entire region, which became the top coal-producing area by 1863. Nevertheless, technological progress remained limited, for in this primary industry the introduction of machines and improved processes affected coal transport, sorting and washing more than extraction itself. Furthermore, while capitalist magnates often sat on the boards of coal companies (the Periers at Anzin, Morny and Emile Pereire at Carmaux), concentration received only scant encouragement. It was blocked by the State, which was anxious to preserve competition in this sector in the hope that energy costs would decrease as a result. The State therefore banned the grouping of concessions without its permission (decree of 23 October 1852), broke up the Compagnie des Mines de la Loire (1846–54) – a vast consortium that controlled the Rive-de-Gier and Saint-Etienne basins – and split up the Pas-de-Calais concessions among 18 companies, frequently set up with limited resources of regional origin. Knowing that it would have to content itself with its share, each company, in order to keep a small number of shareholders, avoided raising outside capital. Thus, only self-financing could ensure modernization.

### The evolution of traditional sectors

In most other branches of industry, new features appeared, but they did not play a dominant role. The impact of technological progress was weaker than in the metal industry. Above all, old forms of production survived alongside concentrated firms. While families in the countryside apparently worked somewhat less for their own consumption, and while, in certain rural areas, 'scattered industry' organized by merchants or industrialists was gradually disappearing as looms were being grouped under one roof in urban establishments, the artisan workshop, run by a master who worked while supervising a handful of journey-men, resisted quite successfully: small-scale industry often remained dominant.

The building industry was in its golden age. But the few improvements (industrial cement-making, the introduction of iron as an adjunct to wood in frame-building) barely transformed working methods in this labour-intensive industry, which often employed migrant workers (particularly those who went up to Paris from the Creuse). Despite the emergence of the first building entrepreneurs, concentration was the exception in this highly scattered branch, which claimed 127 employees for 100 employers in 1851, and still 144 employees in 1866.

Output growth in the textile sectors was more erratic and, on the whole, more hesitant (its annual rate averaging some 2 per cent). The cotton industry – the most dynamic – was severely affected from 1860 on by the 'cotton famine' following upon the American Civil War. The wool and linen industries took their revenge, but the last years of the Empire were marked by persistent stagnation.

These difficulties, as well as the fall in prices due to the 'nationalization' of the domestic market and to British competition (especially after 1860), led to an undeniable attempt at modernization, which spread even to isolated centres such as Cholet. Spinning was transformed by improvements in the instruments of production, such as the invention of the carding machine and the substitution of self-acting jennies for mules. The Vosges, which in 1856 numbered 320,000 spindles of which 9 per cent were on self-acting jennies, had 464,000 in 1868, of which 80 per cent were automated. Nearly three-quarters of the textile machinery in this area was thus modified or replaced. Mechanized looms became widespread in the weaving sector, and hand weaving declined particularly in the west.

The geography of industry was also changing. The modernization of equipment was often accompanied by the disappearance of cottage industry and a shift of industrial activity from the countryside to the towns. For example, the hosiery looms in the Aube were eventually concentrated in Troyes. Yet, conversely, the thriving silk industry in Lyons spread to all the adjacent rural areas, even to the Bas-Dauphiné and to the Baronnies. Regional specializations gradually emerged: the jute industry settled in the Nord and the Somme, and the linen industry spread in the Nord; the wool industry, initially very scattered because of its dependence on local sources of raw materials, was increasingly concentrated around a few major centres such as Roubaix, Reims, Sedan, Elbeuf, Castres and Mazamet; calico-printing developed particularly in Alsace (Mulhouse), whereas it declined in Normandy. In short, the present-day distribution of the chief textile industries was for the most part established under the Second Empire.[33]

Some concentration gradually took place in these industries. In Lyons the number of 'manufacturers' fell from 750 in 1830 to 450 in 1860; in the Vosges, the number of spindles per mill rose from 9,800 in 1860 to 14,000 in 1868. In several regions, marginal artisan or semi-artisan industries disappeared along with the more backward forms of production. Yet, on the whole, artisan workshops continued to play a considerable role in these industries, since in 1866 the average worker-to-employer ratio was only three-to-one. The artisan sector still supplied at least 70 per cent of total production.

And while a certain amount of financial concentration was carried out to the benefit of manufacturers, brokers and bankers, 'textile capitalism' generally preserved very distinctive features. Situated outside public investment circuits (limited companies were the exception, and no textile company shares were listed on the stock exchange), it was composed of firms with a strong family tradition, their capital provided by members of a single family who formed general or limited partnerships. These businesses, making the least possible use of outside capital and bank credit, grew by systematically reinvesting part of their profits. Technical conditions specific to textile manufacture made this mode of financing attractive, since firms could replace or add to their plant year by year.

On the whole, the textile industries experienced not so much a revolution as a complex and often slow evolution. In many other branches (such as food processing or wood and furniture) changes remained even more limited and barely affected traditional structures: 'small-scale industry' still prevailed.

### General assessment

Industrial growth was in no way homogeneous. It varied in form and intensity according to region: the decline of textiles in the west contrasted with their buoyancy in the east and the north. In a single region one might find all types of industry as well as widely differing rates of growth. The Dauphiné offered a juxtaposition of branches in a deep state of decline (cloth manufacture in Virons), others surviving as relics, albeit prosperous ones (glove-making in Grenoble, drapery in Vienne) and finally branches that adapted themselves with no difficulty (silk, paper) or at the price of change, such as the metal industry, which, having been forced to abandon mass production of cast iron in the face of competition from the north and north-east, turned to more delicate products. The same applied to the Haute-Loire, where the share of artisan industry remained considerable and often declined only after 1870: some of the older industries experienced rapid growth (metals, chemicals), others grew slowly (food processing and the leading industrial activity of the *département*, lace-making) and new products and processes appeared (town gas).

On the whole, industry modernized its equipment. The economist Markovitch observes that

> it is under the Second Empire that the share of [industrial] capital formation in national income rose from 17.5 per cent to 20.5 per cent, reaching a level that was to be barely surpassed...It is not without reason that historians have taken the habit of dating the beginning of France's true industrialization to the period of the Second Empire.[34]

Mechanization was thus able to gain speed, and steam engine power soared from 71,000 to 305,000 hp. Furthermore, as this technological progress, which left relatively vast sectors virtually untouched, chiefly benefited large companies, and as the output of 'pure' industries (less the artisan sectors) grew twice as fast as industrial production as a whole, Markovitch concludes that 'the period of the Second Empire [also] marks the decisive shift of the centre of gravity from small-scale to large-scale industry'.

Nevertheless, small-scale industry did not disappear, and its importance at the outset was such that it was able to preserve its dominant position even with a weak growth rate. The ratio of employees to employers clearly demonstrates the highly dispersed character of the work force and the considerable number of employers, most of whom headed very small firms.

Industrial work force in 1866[35]

employers   1,334,000          workers   2,898,000

As for the growth of industrial production in general, four recently calculated indexes yield fairly consistent results for our period:[36] the average annual rate for these years is close to 2 per cent. This is a low figure compared with today's rates, and it is also lower than those reached during the 1840s (almost 4 per cent). Markovitch draws the conclusion that the Second Empire was 'a period marked by a slow-down of industrial growth'. Admittedly, one must bear in mind that the earlier rates concerned figures far lower in absolute terms and were consequently less significant. But, at the very least, the Empire was in no way a period of more rapid growth.

Table 9. *Average annual industrial growth rate*[37]

| 1850–54 | 3.87% | 1860–65 | 2.19% |
|---------|-------|---------|-------|
| 1855–60 | 2.36% | 1865–70 | 1.16% |

Nevertheless, there are explanations for this surprising discovery of the 'stagnant ponds amid imperial prosperity'. First, a noticeable slow-down would seem to have occurred from approximately 1856–8 onwards (Table 9).

Another explanation concerns the weight of the various branches in industry as a whole. If one considers the work force employed in each of these branches or their added value, which represents 'the specific contribution that can be ascribed to that industry', one finds that the consumer goods industries still considerably outweighed capital goods industries. Basic industries represented barely over 10 per cent of the work force and 7 per cent of added value. It was thus consumer goods industries (such as textiles, food, building) that were the truly dynamic industries and set the pace for the entire economy. But, with the exception of the building industry, these branches enjoyed only moderate growth and indeed were entering a period of stagnation. Their loss of vigour, partly connected with demographic stagnation, was not offset by the spectacular development of the metal industry and mining, which had too slight an influence on the growth of total production. Hence, too, the limited impact of technological

Table 10. *Relative sizes of industrial sectors*

Structure of the industrial work force in 1866[1]

| | Number of workers (millions) | % of total | Added value of each branch *c.* 1860[2] as % of total industrial production | |
|---|---|---|---|---|
| Energy | 64 | 1.5 | | |
| Extractive industries | 95 | 2.3 | | |
| Chemicals, tobacco | 36 | 0.8 | Basic industries | 7.3 |
| Metals (processing of base metals) | 345 | 8 | | |
| Textiles, leather, fur and clothing | 2,100 | 48 | Textiles and clothing | 39.9 |
| Food | 300 | 6.7 | Food | 16.2 |
| Building | 550 | 13.7 | Building | 23.6 |
| Miscellaneous industries (esp. timber) | 850 (approx.) | 19 (approx.) | Other industries | 13 |
| Total | 4,340 | 100 | | 100 |

*Notes*: 1. Based on the figures calculated by J. C. Toutain (**117**) and Mme Cahen (**116**). 2. Based on M. Lévy-Leboyer, 'Le Processus d'industrialisation: le cas de l'Angleterre et de la France', *Revue Historique*, April–June 1968.

progress and the restricted scope of structural changes, for it was mainly these 'star' industries that were being modernized and concentrated.

## 5. *The limits of economic change*

While industry underwent a series of uneven advances rather than a genuine 'revolution', the economy of the Second Empire appears on the whole as a mosaic of new phenomena and traditional features, with the latter heavily predominant. The commercial sector was marked by the simultaneous appearance of department stores and modern retailing methods (fixed and marked prices, narrower profit margins, advertising). Aristide Boucicaut's Bon Marché set the example in 1852, soon imitated by Le Louvre (in which, once again, the Foulds and Pereires were involved) and Le Printemps (1865). But the influence of these department stores remained limited. Most retail outlets did not even come anywhere near the size and modernity of the Quenu-Gradelle *charcuterie* depicted by Zola in *Le Ventre de Paris* complete with a sign in gold letters, a well-ordered window display and busy assistants. Tradesmen most often contented themselves with modest premises where they worked without employees, since in 1866 the commercial work force was composed of 700,000 'bosses' as against only 244,000 employees. *A fortiori*, tradition remained the hallmark – as we shall see – of the vast agrarian sector, where change was long indeed in making itself felt.

On balance, all the evidence points to the heavy persistence of the past. The first sign is the structure of the estates left behind by the French, since despite the rise of the stock market, transferable securities (*rentes*, stocks and bonds) accounted for only a minimal and barely increasing share of estates (Table 11).

The structure of the work force and its evolution between the two censuses of 1856 and 1866 are also revealing (Table 12).

Table 11. *Contents of estates*

|  | 1852 | 1868 |
|---|---|---|
| Total gross assets of estates (in millions of francs) | 2,047 | 3,455 |
| of which transferable securities | 117 | 204 |
| % of total assets held in transferable securities | 5 | 6 |

Table 12. *Distribution of the employed population by sector*

|  | 1856 | | 1866 | |
|---|---|---|---|---|
|  | (000s) | % | (000s) | % |
| Primary (agriculture, fishing) | 7,305 | 51.4 | 7,535 | 49.8 |
| Secondary (manufacturing) | 4,418 | 31.1 | 4,384 | 28.9 |
| Tertiary (services) | 2,493 | 17.5 | 3,229 | 21.3 |
| Total | 14,216 | | 15,413 | |

*Note:* Little use can be made of the 1851 census, nor of the somewhat bungled census of 1872.

Agriculture thus remained heavily preponderant, as in traditional economies. While its share declined slightly – it did continue, however, to employ nearly half the work force – it still absorbed the same number of workers. The fact that it shed only a meagre surplus of the population proves that there was no agricultural revolution. Admittedly, over a million of these agricultural workers acknowledged spending an average of 148 days a year in activities other than those connected with the land, but this is only a further sign of archaism.

Even though it was henceforth in industry that the worst crises broke out (the crises of 1857 and 1866, however, were not without agricultural antecedents), the industrial population was not only outnumbered but stagnant, which confirms the absence of wholesale industrialization.

Finally, one should not be misled by the growing share of the tertiary sector in the work force, if one bears in mind that this included over a million domestic servants, almost as many tradespeople – most of them very modest – and over 600,000 civil servants.

The Empire witnessed not a brutal structural change, but a series of remarkable inroads of new capitalism. These inroads, being limited in scope, rarely provoked the disappearance of old forms of production and trade. Hence a mixed, dualist economy, in which very modern features coexisted with vast sectors or regions that remained enclaves of tradition. All in all, the extent of modernization must not be overestimated.

It may be misleading to compare the portraits of French society provided at two generations' interval by two great novelists, but Zola's epoch did not abruptly replace Balzac's world. Not that Zola, writing mainly during the Third Republic, committed an anachronism. But his fondness for novelty and his prescience often led him to describe the more spectacular forms of innovation: the large-scale coal industry in *Germinal,* the department store in *Au Bonheur des dames,* railways in *La Bête humaine* and the stock exchange in *L'Argent.* All these phenomena made their appearance during the Empire. But the historian must be as attentive to persistence as to change. A greater number of Frenchmen of the time were living in the world described by the Comtesse de Ségur. No doubt Paris remained only in the background of that world, but the capital itself was still an artisan town: 'Professionally speaking, few if any changes occurred in Paris during these years of Empire that are said to have marked a radical economic and social turning-point. On the eve of 1871 the trades that one can call "traditional" were still very much in the lead: clothing, industrial arts, fancy goods, furniture...'[38] As for the provinces à la Comtesse de Ségur (also to be encountered in some of Zola's novels, such as *La Faute de l'abbé Mouret*), they were by and large untouched by technological or economic innovations, and often remained in the age of the stagecoach, the sailing ship and the oil lamp.[39] It was a world where rural folk, domestic servants, modest artisans and humble tradespeople greatly outnumbered workers employed in big industrial firms. Nevertheless, in *La Fortune de Gaspard*, this traditional microcosm suddenly finds its old-fashioned way of life upset when a new industrialist arrives to set up his wireworks. Similarly, the whole of traditional French society was affected by these irruptions, however limited, of modern capitalism in the shape of railways, large-scale industry and so on.

# 4

# Living standards, life styles and attitudes

## 1. Average living standards and disparities

### A better-fed and sturdier population

Although the size of the population remained virtually the same, its composition changed. First, it tended to age somewhat, owing to a low birth rate and a high infant mortality rate. Second, the growth of national income caused the 'average Frenchman', hitherto accustomed to restricting himself even on food, to devote his surplus wealth to food and drink (Table 13).

The last lines of this table are supported by ample evidence concerning the spread of drunkenness both in the countryside (at Mazières-en-Gâtine, 'the first effect of greater affluence was greater intemperance'[1]) and in the towns (such as Paris and Lille). Alcoholism, which could also be a means of escaping from poverty or of finding cheap calories, caused ever more extensive ravages.

Food consumption increased without changing its pattern. Before seeking to improve their diet, the French ate more of everything. Their individual ration rose from 2,480 to 2,875 calories, that is, the level recognized as being 'objectively necessary'. From this point of view, and according to today's criteria, France at the end of the Empire was on the point of ceasing to be an underdeveloped country. Hence the gradual disappearance of deficiency-induced diseases such as exophthalmic goitre, cretinism (which often accompanied it) and pellagra. Without actually receiving better medical care (the medical corps comprised more *officiers de santé* than true doctors), the French were becoming fitter. Their average height was increasing, thanks to a more plentiful diet.

From 1839 to the end of the Empire a partial and bloodless 'liquidation' of the 'undersized proletariat' took place, since among the annual intake of army recruits, the proportion of young men exempted because of insufficient height (below 1.56 m) fell from 16 per cent to 10 per cent. Less conclusively, the number of tall recruits (over 1.70 m), which had remained stable since 1820, gradually rose from 1863 onwards.

Table 13. *Annual consumption of foodstuffs, per capita and per diem (in grammes except where indicated)*

|  | 1845–54 | 1865–74 |
|---|---|---|
| Bread | 714 | 763 |
| Potatoes | 107 | 253 |
| Fruits and vegetables | 245 (?) | 265 |
| Sugar | 10 | 20 |
| Meat and fish | 78 | 100 |
| Milk and cheese | 168 | 208 |
| Oil, fats and butter | 17 | 21 |
| Wine (in litres) | 1.34 | 1.62 |
| Alcohol (in centilitres) | 0.47 | 0.75 |

*Source:* Toutain (**147**), p. 2015.

### The decline of illiteracy

The illiteracy rate, which mainly concerned young adults, minimizes the considerable weight of ignorance. But the number of Frenchmen who failed to receive a minimum degree of education decreased fairly rapidly. At the outset, the Empire benefited from the achievements of the July Monarchy (the Guizot law of 1833), but the schooling effort continued. While encouraging the rise of religious orders – to which, for a long time, it devolved the task of educating girls – the regime sponsored the founding of new schools by municipal councils, increased the number of schoolmasters (109,000 by 1863), upgraded their training in the *écoles normales* and granted a modest raise in their inadequate pay (increased from 600 to 700 francs in 1862 for teachers with five years' seniority; a further increase of 100 francs took place at the end of the Empire). Schoolmasters, now more competent, enjoyed higher social status and greater influence: henceforth they were often called *instituteurs*.

All the obstacles in the way of educational progress did not disappear overnight. In *La Fortune de Gaspard* (1865), a novel on 'the advantage of education for the people', the Comtesse de Ségur shows us the efforts of a schoolmaster to inculcate basic reading skills in his rowdy pupils with sharp blows of the rod; but pupils often missed school, for their parents – like Gaspard's father, despite his being a wealthy farmer – tended to regard education as a useless luxury and a convenient excuse for idlers to avoid farm work. This did not prevent the same parents from attending prize day in order to rebuke the poor schoolmaster sharply. Yet Gaspard's father eventually made honourable amends. Similarly, the peasants of Mazières discovered the benefits of schooling the moment they realized that it was responsible for the social promotion of the children of the town's artisans and tradespeople. All it took was the construction of a new school and the arrival of a 'good *instituteur*' who had graduated from the *école normale* for the number of pupils to rise rapidly from 48 (out of 174 children of school age) in 1856 to 140 in 1869 (of whom 23 paid no tuition). Even though schooling remained too brief and too intermittent to be anything more than superficial, the spread of education was bringing about far-reaching changes in the human environment.

Table 14. *Educational attainment*

|  | 1851 | 1856 | 1866 | 1872 | 1881 |
|---|---|---|---|---|---|
| Illiteracy rate (% unable to write) | | | | | |
| conscripts | 38.7 | 35.8 | 25.5 | 21.5 | 16.1 |
| husbands | | 31 | 26 | 23 | 15 |
| wives | | 47 | 39 | 35 | 23 |
| both spouses | | 39 | 32.5 | 29 | 19 |
| Schooling rate (% of children attending school in the 5–14 age group) | | | | | |
| boys | 55 | | 70 | | 78 |
| girls | 48 | | 66 | | 76 |
| combined | 51 | | 68 | | 77 |

*Source:* Toutain (**117**), pp. 216 and 227.

### Disparities

It is not enough to talk about the 'average Frenchman', his food intake or his educational level: considerable inequalities persisted despite the collective progress. The fate of the comfortably-off and the wealthy contrasted with that of all the *Misérables*. It was during the Second Empire that Victor Hugo wrote his novel – set in the previous period – and that he began to use the term to designate those he saw as poor unfortunate souls far more than dangerous criminals. Thabault has left us a portrait of one of these paupers, who lived in the Vendée:

> He was called 'Fourteen' because he was the fourteenth child of his family. In his childhood he had scrounged for bread. He himself had had six children. His wife and five of his children had died of tuberculosis and destitution. He was left with one child, a small hunchback...This small hunchback died too. The life of poor Fourteen was thus in all respects deplorable.[2]

The poor and the non-poor were two human breeds whose fates diverged. Their attitudes to the problems of living differed, and the former usually had more children than the latter. In Bordeaux, the number of children per 100 families dropped from 80 to 53 in bourgeois families and rose from

91 to 105 in those of the popular classes between 1853 and 1885.[3] The same pattern was repeated in Lille and also in Mazières, where only the bourgeoisie had small families, whereas poor households often had between three and five children.

Nor did the two groups offer the same resistance to death. While the children of the rich often suffered from the same mortality rate as the children of the poor, on account of their having been put out to nurses, the destitute, in their later years, succumbed more frequently to epidemics (cholera in Bordeaux in 1854), they were alone exposed to certain diseases (scrofula and putrid infections in Bordeaux) and they were the prime victims of the scourges of the period (consumption and lung congestion, enteritis and syphilitic rickets in Lille). Finally, the destitute were often afflicted with prolonged illnesses well before their death – when they were not actually disabled. The deformed gnomes depicted by Daumier in his popular scenes contrast strikingly with the florid bourgeois portrayed by Ingres.

Even the young men of the popular classes who were declared fit for duty by recruiting boards presented features somewhat different from those of the 'well-to-do youths', as the researches of Le Roy Ladurie and N. Bernageau have shown.[4] Using a sampling of the 300,000 personal files concerning conscripts of the class of 1868 (called up in 1869), they distinguish between 'replaced' and 'non-replaced' recruits. Since 1818, young men who drew an unlucky number could avoid the harsh obligations of a six- or seven-year-long military service by 'paying for a man' (between 1858 and 1863, this system was replaced by a basically not very different exemption arrangement). A stand-in cost on average 1,700 francs in 1868. Replacements constituted an additional inequality in life, a privilege of affluence; thus they represent, if not a means test, at least a rough but valid indication of non-poverty, enabling one to distinguish between the destitute – that is, the unreplaced (to whom one could add the proxies, who were poor wretches) – and all the others (those replaced). As the files were kept up to date for at least fifteen years after the recruiting board examination, several features of the conscripts' lives can be statistically compared (Table 15).

Those who were born into great poverty were thus far more exposed to the possibility of becoming delinquents, migrants, uprooted (and 'mobile parents engendered far more have-nots than stable parents'); of reaching only a puny height; lastly, of not even acquiring a 'knowledge of ABC'. The intersection of the variables 'replacement' and 'education' enables one to draw an even sharper distinction between two borderline groups, that of 'have-nots all down the line, both ignorant and ragged', and that of the financially and educationally advantaged. Blanqui had already said that 'the Empire put wealth and education on one side', poverty and ignorance on the other. In actual fact, the period had inherited the problem of poverty. In Paris in 1847, between 70 per cent and 80 per cent of the population were destitute individuals who left nothing or next to nothing when they died – not even enough to entitle them to a paid burial. But the *fête impériale* did not reduce the pervasiveness of poverty. In Paris in 1862, Haussmann calculated that the number of poor who would have to be fed at the slightest rise in food prices would be at least 1,200,000 (that is, over 70 per cent of the population);[5] in Bordeaux in 1873, 76 per cent of those who died left no inheritance and, in 1868, in

Table 15. *Characteristics of army recruits called up in 1869*

| | Conscripted directly | Conscripts replaced by substitutes |
|---|---|---|
| | (in percentages within each category) | |
| Height | | |
| 1.70 m and above | 18.9 | 26 |
| 1.65–1.69 m | 30.4 | 33.6 |
| 1.60–1.64 m | 33.3 | 28.8 |
| Under 1.60 m | 17.2 | 10.8 |
| Education | | |
| Illiterates | 32.6 | 15 |
| Geographical mobility* | | |
| In agricultural professions | 12.21 | 3.89 |
| In non-agricultural professions | 19.18 | 15.06 |
| Deliquency | | |
| Among conscripts from the popular classes alone | 3.19 | 0.54 |

* Calculated on the basis of the number of cases in which the young conscript's residence was different from that of his parents.

the whole of France, 78 per cent of all conscripts were not replaced, in most cases because their families did not have the means to purchase a substitute for them. Society continued to rest on a broad base of poverty and on a considerable income gap.

Nor was the general improvement accompanied by a greater uniformity in spatial terms. While often modifying earlier human and economic geographical patterns, progress did not entail the disappearance of regional and local inequalities. Indeed, to a great extent, it perpetuated the old frontier that – in a very rough sense – ran between two Frances along the Saint-Malo–Geneva line, as Baron Dupin and d'Angeville had noted in the

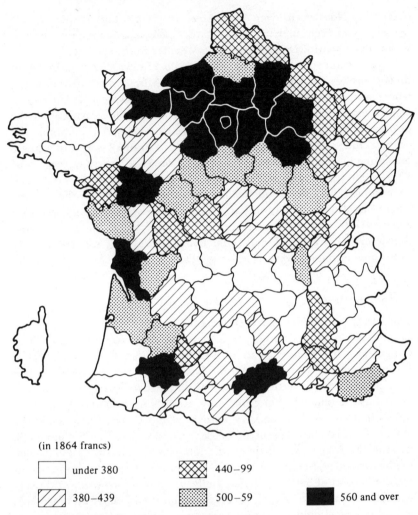

(in 1864 francs)

| | | | |
|---|---|---|---|
| ☐ under 380 | ⊠ 440–99 | |
| ▨ 380–439 | ▦ 500–59 | ■ 560 and over |

6 Disposable income per capita in 1864
(Based on N. Delefortrie and J. Morice (**146**), p. 67)

first half of the century. To the north, the inhabitants remained often taller (partly for ethnic reasons) than their undersized but sturdier southern kinsmen.

The separation between a less ignorant northern France and a benighted southern France was less sharp under the Empire, for much educational progress had been achieved in the south-east. Nevertheless, Maggiolo's survey shows that in 1871–5 the northern zone remained well in the lead in respect of the educational level, since in all the *départements* of the north, except the Nord itself, over 80 per cent of grooms and 70 per cent of brides signed their marriage certificates – percentages that the central, western and south-western *départements* were far from reaching.[6]

With certain exceptions, the Saint-Malo–Geneva line continued to divide the less developed regions of the south from those of the north, where prosperous forms of agriculture were more widespread and industrial centres more dynamic. This explains the considerable disparities in the disposable annual income per capita (national average: 477 francs): the south included 22 'poor' *départements* (below 380 francs) as against a single one in the north (the Vosges, 372 francs). Conversely, there were 4 'rich' *départements* (per capita income over 559 francs) in the southern zone (particularly in wine-producing regions) and 11 in the northern zone. There was also a considerable gap between the wealthiest *départements* (the Seine, 917 francs; the Eure-et-Loire, 677 francs) and the poorest (the Finistère, 282 francs). Finally, the lives of rural folk differed greatly from those of the inhabitants of large urban centres.

## 2. *The rural world*

The rural world remained preponderant in the France of the Second Empire. Admittedly, a rural exodus took place in areas such as the Haut-Languedoc (the *arrondissements* of Villefranche and Castelnaudary lost 16 per cent of their inhabitants), the Basses-Alpes and the Isère – in this last *département*, the movement became widespread, affecting the mountain as well as the plain. But in other rural areas, the population grew, as in the Côte-d'Or. Within the very borders of the Loir-et-Cher, while the *cantons* of the Perche and even of the Beauce lost some of their inhabitants, those of the Sologne saw their population increase. On the national level, the rural population remained remarkably stable (if one takes into account the annexation of Savoy). The only effect of migrations was to rid over-populated rural areas of their excess inhabitants and above all of workers in declining scattered industries. It was primarily rural artisans who left the villages of the Haute-Saône or of Picardy.[7]

Nevertheless, the rural population often retained its variety: in Mazières, a 'town' (*bourg*) of 250 inhabitants, one found notables (the doctor, the *officier de santé*, the veterinary surgeon, the notary), State employees (the tax collector, the schoolmaster, the gendarmes, 3 roadmen and, 'a total novelty', 2 rural postmen), artisans and tradesmen (2 clog-makers, 'a considerable novelty, 1 cobbler employing 1 workman', 1 baker, 3 grocers and 6 café-owners; 5 masons, 3 joiners, 1 cartwright, 1 rope-maker and 1 pit sawyer; but 'the weaver had disappeared'). All these individuals were indirectly connected with the land. And the land was the source of livelihood for farmers and their families, who still represented

Table 16. *The rural population: size and dependence on agriculture*

| | 1856 | | 1866 | |
|---|---|---|---|---|
| | 000s | % of total population | 000s | % of total population |
| Rural population* | 26,190 | 72.7 | 26,470 | 69.5 |
| Population dependent on agriculture | 19,140 | 53.1 | 19,600 | 51.5 |

\* Or population of communes comprising fewer than 2,000 inhabitants gathered round the urban nucleus.

one Frenchman in two nationwide. If agriculture continued to claim so large a share of the population, it was because no agrarian revolution had occurred.

### Agricultural progress and backwardness

The acreage of exploited land increased, thanks in particular to extensive reclamation in the Landes (where pines were planted under the supervision of the engineer Chambrelent), the Brenne, the Sologne and the Dombes, and to the construction of irrigation canals in Provence. The emperor set the example by having his estates at Mimizan (Landes) and La Motte-Beuvron (Sologne) drained, and by subsidizing the company assigned to continue the drainage of the Dombes. Prefects often took an interest in the 'improvement' of insalubrious *cantons*. But it was above all the farmers themselves, thirsting for new land, who forged ahead in their clearing operations, eating away at moors and forests just about everywhere. In the region of Les Andelys, for example, 3,700 hectares were cleared between 1840 and 1860. In the country as a whole, the area of land under cultivation increased by 1,500,000 hectares during the Empire, reaching a level unparalleled in all of French history (26,500,000 hectares).

At the same time, in various areas, farming methods improved, allowing for a better use of the soil. While there was often little change in age-old systems of crop rotation, new practices in Picardy and in the Beauce made it possible to substitute artificial grassland for fallow (which still occupied 5 million hectares in France). Furthermore, thanks to railways and by-roads, it became possible to lime or marl acid soils in cold areas and to sow them with wheat instead of lower-grade cereals. As soon as the railway reached Rennes (1857), Breton peasants began to enrich their soil with lime deposits from the Mayenne, and buckwheat and rye gradually gave way to wheat.

The railway also led certain farmers to abandon traditional mixed farming and to concentrate their efforts on crops for which they already knew that their lands were especially suited. Thus the peasants of the Léon and the Trégorrois became specialized in market garden produce and strawberries, which until then they had only been able to deliver to markets in Brest and Morlaix; now this produce reached Paris and, after 1860, even Britain. Also, for similar reasons, enclosed farmland regions (*bocages*) were increasingly given over to livestock breeding (Basse-Normandie) or more particularly to cattle-fattening (Charolais, Pays d'Auge). In the Bas-Languedoc, the 'vineyard revolution' broke out: the rhythm of plantings changed suddenly, and 220,000 hectares of the Hérault were under vines in 1864 as against 114,000 in 1850. The same trend towards single-crop farming developed in the better areas of the northern Beaujolais. In the Corbières, the 98 inhabitants of Périllos,[8] accustomed to living in autarky and to producing in very adverse conditions the cereals that they needed for their own nourishment, suddenly sacrificed to vineyards 40 of their 140 hectares of arable land, for they found it more advantageous to sell 300 hectolitres of wine a year (on average) in order to buy 150 quintals of wheat. But alongside these areas of progress, there were a great many regions where the peasants had so far been integrated in no more than a very marginal way in the market economy. Even in the still rich and prosperous 'lands of the Garonne'[9] the traditional farming system (wheat, maize, vineyards) described by Arthur Young at the end of the eighteenth century survived virtually intact.

The increase in the various forms of agricultural production was neither steady nor widespread. There were several epidemics of epizootic diseases; vineyards, first devastated by oidium towards 1854 (which led to their disappearance from the Oise and from Lorraine), suffered the first attacks of phylloxera at the end of the Empire; *pébrine*, a silkworm disease, practically wiped out the mulberry tree. Cereal harvests remained subjected to the hazards of the weather and were sometimes drastically reduced (in 1853, 1855, 1861 and 1867). Furthermore, this period marked the beginning of the decline of oleaginous and tinctorial plants and – despite a short-lived boom brought on by the American Civil War – of linen and hemp. In contrast, there was, by and large, a significant increase in the production of wheat (which gained ground at the expense of rye and buckwheat), potatoes, beets and, to an even greater extent, husbandry products. All in all, over twenty years, 'the final product of agriculture' rose by 69 per cent,[10] but if one takes price rises into account, the increase in the amounts produced did not exceed 25 per cent. This appreciable growth – which, however, was not more rapid than in the preceding period – tended to lose speed in the 1860s.

Considering the fact that more land was coming under cultivation and fallowing was being abandoned, there was still only a very gradual improvement in yields. While wheat yields per hectare reached 20 quintals in the Beauce, the national average stagnated at around 11 quintals (compared to 15 to 20 in the Netherlands and in the German States). Yet in several regions (Picardy, Lorraine, the plain of Caen) the practice spread of sowing in closer rows and of dressing the soil more often. But the improvement in yields was blocked by the lack of fertilizers. Only a few modern large-scale farms used nitrates, phosphates and even Peruvian guano. Sometimes one could resort to traditional local methods such as *écobuage* (burning the grass collected on moors) or the reclamation of marine fertilizers (such as sea-marl and *tangue\**). In most cases, even in the Beauce, as Zola showed in *La Terre*, farmers big and small were on the look-out for every possible means of obtaining fertilizers. But, apart from human manure, virtually the only substance available to them was farm compost, which the livestock population, despite its increase, was unable to produce in sufficient quantities.

Far slower still was the modernization of farming equipment, which remained very primitive even in the mid nineteenth century. While deep-furrowing swivel ploughs were to be found particularly in the north and the Paris basin, most ploughing was done with a wheelless implement that still resembled the age-old swing plough. As for harvesting, progress consisted far more of substituting scythes for sickles than of using harvesters, which were still a rarity (9,000 machines for 3,600,000 farmers in 1862). Although 10,000 sowing machines and 100,000 threshers were in use, it was still a common practice – even in the Beauce, as described in *La Terre* – to sow by hand and to thresh by flail.

Agronomists and officials ascribed the persistence of archaic methods to peasant routine, but there were in reality several causes. The government itself, even while proclaiming its determination to modernize the country-side and taking credit for the results obtained, did very little in the way of direct intervention, except to send its prefects to deliver speeches in praise of the regime at agricultural shows. Worse still, the government, to a great extent, undid the agronomic achievements of earlier regimes and, by drastic budget cuts, sabotaged the farming education system set up by the Second Republic. The Crédit Foncier, founded for the purpose of aiding agriculture, supplied it with barely 15 per cent of its credit, which the institution reserved for big landowners. And although there were agricultural societies that did their best to spread technological progress, sometimes successfully (witness Rieffel's Association Bretonne in Brittany), these notables' clubs usually had little influence on the peasantry. For example, when the Société d'Agriculture of Autun began in 1863 to encourage farmers to replace departing day labourers by machines, its advice was heeded almost exclusively by the big landowners who belonged

---

\* Slimy sea-sand thus employed on the Normandy coast. (Trans.)

to it.[11] Lastly, far from mechanizing their estates, landowners often invested all their landed income in transferable securities or spent it in town; this was tantamount to an agricultural disinvestment. For lack of means no less than of education, the forsaken smallholder was condemned to abide by his traditional routine.

### Was the peasantry 'deproletarianized'?

The fact was that in the peasant world, wealth remained an exception. Landed property was highly concentrated (even in 1884, estates assessed at over 100 hectares represented 25 per cent of total acreage, and all those of 20 hectares and over, which belonged to fewer than 3 per cent of landowners, covered 51 per cent of appropriated land).

Table 17. *Agrarian work force in 1862 (in thousands)*

| | |
|---|---|
| Yeomen farmers | |
| Cultivating their own land exclusively | 1,813 |
| Working in addition as | |
| tenant farmers | 649 |
| sharecroppers | 204 |
| day labourers | 1,134 |
| Propertyless peasants | |
| Tenant farmers | 387 |
| Sharecroppers | 202 |
| Wage-earners | |
| Mainly day labourers and servants; also stewards | 2,975 |
| Total | 7,364 |

*Source:* Dupeux (**32**), p. 122.

Furthermore, the great estates were often in the hands of nobles and bourgeois (under the Empire, they held respectively one-fifth and one-third of the land – in value – in the Loir-et-Cher). Thus hardly one peasant in four managed to make a living by cultivating his own property. In addition, in 1862, fully-fledged farmers (3.2 million) were outnumbered by wage-earning farm hands (4.2 million, of whom close to 3 million did not own a single parcel of land).

But a static view fails to describe the reality of a world that was in no way immobile. No doubt it is impossible to isolate statistically, at the national level, the evolution specific to the Second Empire; one can only observe that between 1862 and 1882 the more impoverished categories diminished considerably (there were fewer proletarians and peasants who worked a small plot, and especially fewer landowning day labourers, whose number had dropped to 727,000 by 1882). One also finds a notable rise in the number of farmers who worked their own land exclusively, and in the number of tenant farmers, so that there were now as many farmers who ran estates as there were wage-earning peasants. Yet various indicators – particularly the increase in the number of land assessments (not exclusively due to inheritance-sharing) – and several local studies show that the Second Empire marked the beginning of a rising trend of estate and farm division in many regions (especially in the southern half of the country). At the same time the structure and nature of the peasantry at large were changing.

The (very relative) increase in peasant wealth may have been helped by demographic phenomena, by a falling birth rate (which, particularly in the south-west, restricted the number of persons liable to receive land) and also by the rural exodus, in areas where it occurred. By draining away the poorer peasants – along with ruined artisans – towards the towns, the rural exodus brought about a drop in demographic pressure that worked in favour of those who stayed behind (particularly in the Haut-Languedoc). In the Loir-et-Cher, too, 'emigration purged [the rural masses], relieving them of the poorest and most dangerous blood – a blood-letting of day labourers and lumberjacks....'[12] Almost everywhere, as in the Gâtinais, clearing and drainage enabled proletarians to become smallholders.

But the peasantry profited above all from the relative rise in incomes. Admittedly, land rent – the traditional source of income for landowners not engaged in farming – remained a heavy financial burden, and it was still rising (by 41 per cent in the Loir-et-Cher), even though it performed less dynamically than budding industrial profits. In certain regions, this led big landowners to sell their estates, for 'it [was] very tempting during the industrial booms of the Second Empire to exchange sluggish land rents against...a stake, in whatever form, in the future of an expanding sector'. At all events, land rents rose more slowly than peasant incomes.

Farm wages, until then very low, increased by as much as 66 per cent in the Loir-et-Cher; in the Aisne, unfed day labourers earned 1.25 francs around 1850 and 2.25 francs towards the end of the Empire. This prompted complaints from many landowners and big farmers, who blamed the abandonment of the countryside for the fall in supply on the labour market. But if day labourers had to be paid better wages, it was also because of rising demand, for agricultural progress was often obtained by more frequent tilling. For wage-earners, the number of holidays a year tended, if anything, to decrease. In consequence, poverty ceased to be a widespread bane and a dangerous scourge in rural areas. Gone were the chronic complaints about the existence of bands of vagrants. Not only did the number of wage-earners decrease somewhat, but their condition –

generally speaking, and taking price rises into account – became slightly less wretched. Some of them, particularly those who already owned a small plot, gradually succeeded in joining the category of yeomen-farmers.

In actual fact, farmers, whether landowners or tenants, reaped the greatest profits from this period. In the Loir-et-Cher, their profits rose by between 82 and 125 per cent, thanks to the combined effects of increased output and, more importantly, of rising prices. With a few exceptions (in particular in 1863–5), this was an unusually favourable period for agriculture, as bumper crops coincided with high prices. This undeniable prosperity had a stronger impact on farmers who were already integrated into a market economy; it thus chiefly benefited the more affluent peasantry. In varying degrees, and at different rhythms, 'the archaic and destitute peasantry that worked small plots gave way to a peasantry of sellers that gradually took on the consistency of a "middle class"',[13] Consequently, the peasant world, which displayed scant interest in politics, tended to support any government that guaranteed respect for property, and it became a factor of stability.

### Attitudes and ways of life

Despite their infinite regional variety, these peasants – whether day labourers, cultivators of small plots (*parcellaires*) or farmers – shared a common feature: they were tormented by the irrepressible desire to acquire a little – or a little more – of the land that they saw as the key to financial ease, a respected status and social promotion. Even the men from the Limousin who came to Paris every year to work in the building industry (the *département* of the Creuse alone sent up an average of 30,000 of these temporary migrants every year) devoted most of the funds they sent back by money order to their families or brought back home with them to the purchase of a few plots. Everywhere, the slightest surplus of income was devoted to the task. In consequence, the pressure from buyers caused land prices to rise from an average of 1,100 francs to nearly 2,000 francs an hectare, often reaching a value totally disproportionate to the potential yield. This increase was far more rapid than that of the incomes of many peasants, who were often forced into debt in order to purchase a coveted plot.

This devouring passion for land utterly destroyed the feeling of patriotism in a number of peasants; it could even stifle all sense of family: in *La Terre*, the old Fouan, urged by his children to share his estate among them, at long last gives in to their demands, whereupon his children leave him penniless and eventually even assassinate him. No doubt this is an extreme case, but the theme of Zola's horror story is not purely fictional. In the course of the agricultural survey conducted in 1866–70, the minister and several witnesses criticized estate-sharing carried out by ascendants:

'The crimes committed in order to hasten death [are given] a sort of encouragement [by this practice]...The head of the family, once he has disposed of his property, becomes a creature despised and rejected by his children, sent from one to the other with a life annuity that he often does not receive.'[14]

Harsh on themselves, the peasants lived a life of toil, like the pain-ridden hoer (*Homme à la houe*) painted by Millet. Children, women and men slaved away until they died or until, like Fouan, they found themselves with their 'backs broken' by a lifetime's labour. In their concern to save enough to purchase the land they so desired, they preferred to carry out their routine tasks more often rather than upgrade their equipment or use new fertilizers.

Prosperity brought no great upheavals in living conditions. Admittedly, prefects and mayors – such as the mayor of Cormeray (Loir-et-Cher) in answer to a survey of 1862 – asserted that 'the local population now enjoys a certain affluence...Everyone is indulging in a previously unheard-of degree of comfort...The inhabitants eat far better than in the past.' In actual fact, progress was often imperceptible, for the peasants, again in order to save money, practised an extreme frugality. In particular their living quarters hardly changed, as Michel Chevalier observed during the Empire:

> At present most peasants are very poor. The houses they live in can be called – no less appropriately today than in La Bruyère's time – dens. None of life's amenities and comforts are to be found in them. These buildings lack the most indispensable features, even hygiene.

Such was the Fouans' three-hundred-year-old patrimonial home, patched up with boards, covered with rotting tiles and always damp – especially as it had sunk one metre into the ground. An official survey carried out in 1872 in 46 *départements* also concluded that

> a single room with a very low ceiling often serves as a dwelling for an entire family. Animals sleep intermingled with men, women and children. The inhabitants feed on rye, potatoes, maize and chestnuts. Some persons describe as a great event the fact of having eaten meat a few times in their lives.

Finally, in most rural areas, works and days seem to have followed one another as in the past. Mores remained brutal and attitudes primitive even among the peasants of the Beauce – so close to Paris – of whom Zola left a reasonably faithful portrait.[15] Religious beliefs, too, changed little. Often, as in the diocese of Orléans,[16] parishioners were baptized, took their first communion, had church weddings and religious burials, but the men rarely practised, and these gestures were simply customs followed out of awe for a religion intermingled with crude superstitions. Yet even as horizons broadened, the outlook and culture of rural folk were imperceptibly changing. In certain regions, this evolution was hastened by specific circumstances, such as temporary emigration in the Limousin. In areas where emigration took place, it led to a more widespread use of birth control, to dietary improvements (masons had grown accustomed to eating meat regularly) and better clothing and to the development of certain hygienic habits. But emigration also hastened the process of dechristianization already under way; it accelerated the spread of literacy and the use of French in the countryside, while songs in Limousin *patois* began to disappear.[17]

Similarly, in Provence, as a consequence of the advent of railways and the attraction of Marseilles, which intensified age-old migratory movements, 'a majority of the population experienced changes more rapid than those of any earlier period in its economic life, its social organization and even its language. [Hence], as a conscious reaction against this overly dynamic present, there arose a magnificently orchestrated form of traditionalism: the Félibrige.' Founded in 1854 with the aim of preventing the abandonment and death of the Provençal idiom by restoring it to the dignity of a living literary language (as illustrated in 1859 by Mistral's *Miréio*), this movement was deeply 'conservative; it corresponded to the landed and rural world of western Provence, where old-style mixed farming and traditional society lived on – to that part of the land that still turned its back on Marseilles...'[18]

Lastly, the reading habits of the French peasantry were gradually changing. For centuries the peasants had been accustomed to reading, at evening gatherings, chapbooks adapted to their tastes, with more or less modernized themes, particularly the Bibliothèque Bleue series already familiar to their ancestors at the time of Louis XIV. This literature was supplied to them across France chiefly by the inhabitants of the Pays de Comminges, who were peasants themselves. But the 'Gascons' were carrying only two million of these volumes in their bundles in 1869, as against nine million in 1847–8. The irremediable decline of the chapbook trade was partly due to the painstaking control exercised by a commission set up in 1852 for the purpose of restricting the circulation of pamphlets that might be used as a medium by the opposition; it was due even more to the spread of education, affluence and communications. Gradually peasants got into the habit of purchasing popular novels at licensed booksellers in rural towns or at railway station bookstalls. They also began to read serial magazines. By their reading habits, peasants were introduced to urban civilization, and were increasingly attentive to the city.[19]

Yet city-dwellers knew little about rural folk, since, as the *Revue des Deux Mondes* of 15 October 1879 observed,

> the circle of naturalistic observation stops at the ring of town walls; its
> novelists have barely looked at – and in most cases do not even seem to

suspect the existence of – the millions of beings who, on the other side, till, sow and reap, and who in actual fact constitute the true French people.

## 3. Workers and towns

In contrast, workers, not all of whom were townspeople, represented only a portion of the urban masses. Their number barely increased (the industrial population made up 28 per cent of the total population), and they were often a long way from forming a homogeneous class aware of its individuality. For there were great differences among workers, in the first place those related to the branch in which they were employed and to their occupation (skilled or unskilled). There were even workers who remained half-peasants, like the miners of Carmaux.

Above all, what an antithesis between the two stereotyped portraits one can draw of the worker in large-scale industry and of the craftsman in an urban workshop! The second figure, heir to a long tradition and often the only one to bear the name *ouvrier*, was generally a skilled labourer who had completed his apprenticeship. He was relatively well educated and had a taste for reading; his family life was beyond reproach and he rarely set foot in taverns. His wife stayed at home; the family had few children and attentively looked after their education. In short, he was a man who naturally belonged to the working-class élite. But we have very inadequate information about how he actually lived, and of the extent to which his living conditions worsened during the Second Empire.

The proletarian in a concentrated factory was often a country-dweller just recently uprooted from his environment. Totally unskilled, he performed a monotonous and harassing task in the service of the machine. His wife and his many children were also caught up in the modern factory. Their lot seems to have been particularly wretched and their sufferings acute. In order to round off the family income, the wife would prostitute herself (this was known as the 'fifth quarter' of her day), and often the entire family succumbed to alcoholism.

But between these two images, there were a great many overlapping cases and intermediate degrees. Furthermore, the living environment of workers also shaped their habits and outlook. This was demonstrated by G. Duveau,[20] who suggested a distinction between four types of workers:

(1) Workers (male or female) who lived scattered throughout the countryside and held a wide variety of jobs; for example, the weaver of the Picardy plains, who 'breathed the air of the great outdoors', remained thoroughly imbued with peasant traditions, and had few opportunities for personal contacts and so of being affected by ideological dissemination.

(2) Workers in medium-sized urban centres such as Orléans or Montereau, which had diversified their activities but lacked large factories. Workers in these towns kept their simple, patriarchal mores; they were often born in the towns and their sense of unity owed less to their professional life than to their common origin.

(3) Wage-earners in small provincial towns where a single firm exercised total domination. Such was the situation of the metal-worker at Le Creusot, who was 'the man from Schneider', or the watch-maker at Beaucourt, who was 'the man from Japy'. They lived under the sway of sprawling factories and all-powerful bosses.

(4) Finally, workers in large urban centres such as Paris and Lyons. Whether they worked in the 'penal colonies' run by Cail or Gouin – steam-engine manufacturers in Vaugirard and Batignolles who employed between 1,000 and 2,000 persons depending on the economic situation – or, as was more frequently the case, in small workshops, Parisian workers

> breathed a comparatively liberating intellectual atmosphere...A man imbued with the great city no longer reflected exclusively on his own fate; he was to a certain extent the heir to all the dreams accumulated by the city over the centuries...Paris rocked in the same lulling rhythm the wallet-maker in a small workshop of the Faubourg Saint-Antoine and the metal-worker at the Cail factory.

They thus shared an attachment to republican and socialist ideas, as well as a Béranger-style chauvinism. But it is very difficult to generalize even about the working-class environment of Paris alone, described by D. Poulot in *Le Sublime* (1863) and by Corbon in *Le Secret du peuple de Paris*. One would also have to take into account the impecunious workers who plied their trade at home, not to mention the temporary migrants who lived apart from the population in squalid furnished rooms (*garnis*).

### The working-class standard of living

As the sole resource of industrial proletarians was, by definition, their wages, changes in their living standards were contingent on the movements of these wages. Under the Empire, the average money wage paid to workers finally began to rise, after three decades of decline or, at best, stagnation. But as prices too began to rise during the same period, the nominal wage index must be divided by the cost of living index in order to evaluate the real wage – or the purchasing power – of the working man (Table 18).

These figures must be interpreted with caution, first, because there is no fully satisfactory index of the cost of living for the working classes, and second, because employment trends cannot be included in the calculations. It is likely that there was less unemployment in 1856 than in 1852; consequently, there must have been only a negligible decrease in aggregate

Table 18. *Nominal and real wages (index 1900 = 100)*

|  | 1852 | 1856 | 1869 |
|---|---|---|---|
| Nominal wage | 49 | 55 | 72 |
| Cost of living | 81 | 114 | 101 |
| Real wage | 60 | 48 | 72 |

*Source:* Lhomme (**154**).

remuneration between these two dates. One can only conclude, with J. Rougerie,[21] that the material condition of the Parisian (and no doubt of the French) worker did not worsen *on average*, contrary to the argument of 'absolute pauperization' long defended by 'classic' Marxists:

> Poverty was still a fact, but there is no doubt that workers of the 1850s and 1860s (decades when work was plentiful and wages rising, even if the cost of living was rising sharply too) were better off than their predecessors of the 1840s (a period of falling or stagnant wages, uncertain work prospects and endemic dearth).

But to discuss the reality of pauperization is to argue on the basis of misleading averages, forgetting the hard facts and the tragic fate of many categories of workers. Witness the female worker employed at home, described by J. Simon in *L'Ouvrière* (1861); earning at best

> a 2-franc wage, housed in a slum, dressed in rags, [she] has 59 centimes a day for food, provided she is lucky enough to stay healthy 365 days a year. The immense majority of female workers receive 50 and even 75 centimes less. How do they live?

Frightening too was the fate of workers – mostly Belgians from Flanders – employed by large-scale industry in Lille.[22] Their working day lasted from 13 to 15 hours, and the stiffness of competition even led industrialists to reduce the time allotted to meals – regarded as 'wasted time' – and to force their employees to eat as they worked. This was in exchange for a daily wage of some 2.50 francs, quite inadequate to feed a family, especially as fines and factory lighting costs were often deducted from it. Women too had to enter the factory, where they were all the more welcome as they were paid even less (1.50 francs at most). Even very young children were caught up in the factory – despite the law of 1841 and the efforts of work inspectors – and the working day inflicted on them was just as long. For them, there was no apprenticeship (which would have been too costly for their parents). At best, they attended school from noon to one in the afternoon, but as they were already exhausted by six or seven hours' labour amid the deafening noise of machines, what could they learn while eating their lunch in these 'midday classes'? Yet the self-interest of industrialists – who paid even less for child labour – coincided with the parents' need for the meagre supplementary income thus obtained.

All worked in very dangerous conditions. Cramped quarters, exposed gears that caught hold of hair or clothing, the habit of cleaning machines without turning them off so as not to lose a moment, fatigue brought on by uninterrupted toil – all these factors contributed to an increase in the number of accidents, which in most cases were blamed on the imprudence of the victim, who thus received no compensation. While a veritable dietary revolution was taking place in Paris, where less bread and more meat was being consumed, workers in Lille were reduced to 'stuffing themselves' with bread, starchy foods and potatoes. They dwelt in horrid slums, sometimes in one of the cellars denounced by Victor Hugo,[23] often in a room looking out on a sordid courtyard (*courée*). The slightest mishap spelled total indigence. If a worker was unable to pay his rent to the *cabaretier* landlord, his entire family had to pack up and 'move out by stealth'. At the sight of this debilitated population, J. Simon noted in 1859: 'Nothing is more appalling than this degeneration of the race...'

The chief escape from this life of misery lay in the tavern, 'the working man's church' (Leroy-Beaulieu): for him, 'it was a home away from home, more welcoming, more cheerful and more fraternal than the family slum'. It was also the cell of a clandestine form of socialism. At the same time, the working class consummated its break with religion: 'Indifference towards religious matters was primarily due to the fatigue engendered by a ninety-hour working week and to the spiritual vacuum inevitably created by such a rhythm.' As for the clergy, who visibly preferred to practise charity than to change the established social order, they were losing all influence over the masses, even as they strengthened their hold on the bourgeoisie by means of the secondary schools (*collèges*) that the Falloux law gave them the right to open.

### Social repression

While pauperization was not, on the whole, an absolute phenomenon, it was at least a relative and subjective one. Broadly speaking, the gap widened between all the popular elements on the one hand and the affluent social categories on the other. The income gap in particular was growing, since the profit boom often contrasted with the extremely moderate increase in wages. In the textile industry alone (artisan sector excluded), the average annual profit for entrepreneurs has been put at 31,900 francs, and the average wage at 565 francs.[24] Differences in wealth were accentuated even further, and greater national prosperity did not reduce inequalities. No doubt the rate at which the gap deepened between rich and poor varied according to the locality, but in Lille – an extreme example – the gap became an abyss. A study of the inheritances left behind by deceased Lillois reveals the existence of a highly inegalitarian society. A privileged albeit slightly expanding minority received nine-tenths of all the estates, while the ever more numerous members of the popular classes left an ever smaller share of worldly possessions (Table 19). The contrast was sharp indeed between an upper bourgeoisie on its way to exercising an overwhelming hegemony and the popular masses, 'who suffered the effects of a genuine "economic drift"'.[25]

Table 19. *The inequality of inheritances in Lille*

|  | 1821 | 1856–8 | 1873–5 |
|---|---|---|---|
| Deaths by social class (%) |  |  |  |
| Governing classes | 7.06 | 8.1 | 9.07 |
| Middle classes | 30.74 | 32.4 | 23.35 |
| Popular classes | 62.19 | 59.4 | 67.55 |
| Percentage share of total value of estates left by each category |  |  |  |
| Governing classes | 57.6 | 89.9 | 89.82 |
| Middle classes | 40.9 | 9.5 | 9.94 |
| Popular classes | 1.4 | 0.4 | 0.23 |

Furthermore, classes became more watertight and social structures more rigid. The common man had fewer chances of achieving social promotion. While a number of employers had risen from the ranks of the people, they now tended to form a caste from which workers were increasingly disbarred. The importance of acquired status was enhanced:

> After 1860, in the textile bourgeoisie of Rouen, the only survivors were the great industrialists, of whom there were few; they formed a closed circle in which social promotion was no longer but a memory. The same was true of Paris... Ever since the mid nineteenth century, a business aristocracy had been emerging – an aristocracy that, with a few exceptions, recruited its members on the basis of birth and was becoming increasingly exclusive.[26]

The worker thus acquired the conviction that his condition was immutable and that he would henceforth have great difficulty escaping from it. Often he also felt cut off from the rich at work (in localities where large-scale industry was developing), driven away from them towards the poor neighbourhoods of 'Haussmannized' cities.

In cases where the cleavage was particularly sharp, as in Lille, the local population experienced a true 'emotional partition. Neither of the two sections felt itself any longer in unison with the other.' This led to the disappearance of the festivals and processions that had once testified to social harmony in Lille.

Furthermore, the painful feeling of frustration among the poor turned into antagonism, as Michel Chevalier noted:

> There is a chasm between the bourgeois on the one side and...the worker on the other. The bourgeois feels nothing in common between himself and the proletarian, commonly regarded as a rented machine to be used and paid for only for the length of time that one needs it. Similarly, for a great number of proletarians, the bourgeois is an enemy whose superiority they accept for the sole reason that he is stronger... Today there are two warring natures: the bourgeois nature and the proletarian nature.[27]

The poor thus became new barbarians threatening society.

### The transformation of the big cities; Paris

The urban population rose considerably (9,130,000 persons in 1851 and 11,590,000 in 1866), and, what was even more unprecedented, the benefits of urbanization were chiefly felt by what were already sizeable cities: in 1851, 5.4 per cent of Frenchmen lived in towns of more than 50,000 inhabitants; in 1866, nearly 11 per cent. While the secondary urban centres experienced stagnation or only modest growth, the big towns (except Rouen, a victim of the crisis in the cotton industry) expanded rapidly, exerting an ever stronger and more wide-ranging influence. The development of Saint-Etienne and Lille, which grew respectively (between 1851 and 1866) from 56,000 to 97,000 inhabitants and from 76,000 to 155,000, was especially spectacular, even though it was partly due to the extension of the area of these towns. Similarly, the population of Lyons soared from 177,000 to 324,000. The growth of the great urban centres was not necessarily linked to industrialization, and trading towns expanded just as rapidly. The population of Bordeaux rose from 130,000 to 194,000; that of Marseilles from 195,000 to over 300,000 at a rate of 3 per cent a year, owing to an influx of men from Provence and even from Italy. In each of these towns, population growth was precisely due to an influx of immigrants, who often still came from the surrounding region, but did not integrate themselves overnight into the established population. They often appeared as nomads who had fairly considerable difficulty merging into the mainstream of urban life.

The greatest expansion took place in the capital, whose rate of growth was very rapid at first, and later slowed somewhat (Table 20).

In 1866 only one-third of the inhabitants of Paris were born in the city, and 61 per cent came from the provinces (6 per cent were foreigners). Although an increasing number of *départements* were beginning to feel the attractive force of Paris, most immigrants were still arriving from fairly nearby regions (of northern and eastern France). They were drawn to Paris by the nominally high wages (but the cost of living was higher in the capital than in the provinces), perhaps even more by employment opportunities and, for some, by the hope of achieving social promotion there.

The narrow confines of the now overpopulated capital were widened overnight. On 1 January 1860 its surface area doubled and its boundaries were moved out from the old wall of the farmers-general to the fortifications built in 1841–5. Thus Paris, annexing the eighteen suburban communes of the *petite banlieue* all around it, expanded to roughly its present size and was divided into 20 *arrondissements* (instead of 12). By driving farther afield the firms that sought to avoid the customs tax barrier (*octroi*), the annexation precipitated the industrialization of new suburbs. For example, the plain of Saint-Denis experienced a 'full-scale industrial explosion'; in Vanves, cultivated land gave way to built-up areas.

Table 20. *The population of Paris (within the city limits of 1860)*

|  | Absolute figure (in thousands) | Annual % growth rate |
| --- | --- | --- |
| 1846 | 1,234 | 3.99 |
| 1856 | 1,500 | 2.14 |
| 1861 | 1,668 | 1.54 |
| 1866 | 1,800 | 2.0 |
| 1870 | 1,980 (?) |  |

Furthermore, the physiognomy of Paris, which, with its labyrinth of narrow winding streets, had scarcely changed since 1789, was brutally transmogrified under the Second Empire. The close-knit fabric of the older neighbourhoods was pierced by wholesale demolitions that Saccard, in Zola's *La Curée*, discovered thus from the top of Montmartre:

> Down there, in the Halles quarter, they have cut Paris in four. Yes, the great crossroads of Paris, as they say. They're clearing the area around the Louvre and the Hôtel de Ville. When the first network is finished, then the great dance will begin. The second network will pierce the city everywhere and so connect the *faubourgs* to the first network. The city's truncated sections will suffer the pangs of death in plaster...One cut here, one cut there, cuts everywhere. Paris slashed by sabre-cuts, with its veins open...

The area surrounding Notre-Dame was also cleared and the dilapidated houses that covered the Ile de la Cité were razed. And how many new boulevards, broad, long and straight, lined with pavements, often intersecting at right angles or radiating out from vast squares! The Boulevard Sebastopol, inaugurated by the emperor in 1858, was the model artery. Extended shortly thereafter by the 40-metre-wide Boulevard de Strasbourg and, beyond the Seine, by the Boulevard Saint-Michel, it formed the north–south axis that cut across the east–west axis leading from the Etoile to the Place de la Bastille. To these must be added a host of other boulevards (Boulevard Malesherbes, the Grands Boulevards) and streets nearly as wide (Rue de Rennes).

The houses demolished were replaced by residential buildings over four storeys high (used for letting) or by private townhouses such as those adjoining the Parc Monceau. Other new constructions included a variety of public, functional or cultural buildings: the Halles market, near the intersection of the major arteries leading to the railway stations, 'landing stages' such as the Gare du Nord (1861–6), designed by Hittorf, town halls in the *arrondissements*, prisons (La Roquette), as well as schools and churches. A number of green spaces were added; the Parc Monceau and the Buttes-Chaumont were redone, and the Bois de Boulogne and Bois de Vincennes were laid out. At the same time, the supply of drinking water was improved by a series of public works, aimed in particular at harnessing the Dhuys and the Vanne. Underground, an extensive gas supply network and a modern sewage system were built.

Although this spectacular metamorphosis was accomplished essentially by private companies (even the building of the boulevards was contracted out to concessionary firms, the State's chief commitment being to carry out the necessary expropriations by decree), the impulse came from Napoleon III and Haussmann. In his enthusiasm for the project, the emperor pressed for fast results, and often paid attention – not without ostentation – to the smallest details. His intervention seems to have been decisive on a number of occasions. He is said to have thought up the general plan for the new boulevards, according to the account of Haussmann, to whom on 29 June 1853 he showed 'a map of Paris on which he had personally traced – in blue, red, yellow and green, in order of priority – the various new avenues that he wanted built', and that were often actually constructed. Indeed, there were maps of Paris in all his residences. It was also Napoleon III who, having found Baltard's first blueprints for the Halles sheds too massive, advised him (perhaps at Viollet-le-Duc's instigation) to use only iron and glass, and added, handing the architect a sketch: 'What I need is wide umbrellas, nothing more.'

Haussmann reigned at the Hôtel de Ville from 1853 to January 1870 almost as a minister of the capital. At first merely a high-ranking civil servant who knew how to surround himself with a team of competent technicians, he gradually acquired greater freedom of action. And even if his relationship with the emperor was not as consistently harmonious as has been assumed, his driving ambition overcame all opposition – that of the Parisians upset in their habits, that of certain ministers (he got on rather poorly with Rouher, Baroche and Billault) and above all that of the *budgétaires* (most notably certain deputies from the provinces) who concurred with the Cour des Comptes and the Conseil d'Etat in criticizing his dubious management practices. As the State bore only a small share of expenses – incurred especially as a result of costly expropriation settlements – Haussmann resorted to expedients such as issuing more or less illegal loans or drawing on the resources of the Crédit Foncier, his sole justification being the theory of productive expenses. The debts of the city of Paris eventually reached the colossal sum of 2,500 million francs! No wonder that Haussmann soon became the *bête noire* of all the opposition; in 1867, he was denounced in a pamphlet by Jules Ferry entitled (in keeping with the prevailing fashion for puns) *Les Comptes fantastiques d'Haussmann.* The documentation for this work has been provided by Léon Say, a representative of the world of finance who had very close connections with the Rothschilds and also with the Orleanist *Journal des Débats.*

The motives of Napoleon III and of his prefect of Paris (assuming they were identical) were very complex. Obsessed by recent memories, the two men may have been guided by a concern to maintain order when they destroyed alleys propitious to barricades and built impressive barracks from which there radiated outwards a series of rectilinear avenues apparently suitable for artillery fire or cavalry charges. One such avenue was the Boulevard du Prince-Eugène, now the Boulevard Voltaire, which kept under surveillance the restless inhabitants of the Faubourg Saint-Antoine.

The emperor also saw these gigantic projects as a means of avoiding unemployment for the workers. As Gobineau observed ironically,

> the city is being demolished from every angle in order to give masons, carpenters, blacksmiths, locksmiths, roofers, painters, joiners, tapestry-makers and cabinet-makers – in short, every profession imaginable – the satisfaction of rebuilding.

Yet Haussmannization also led to a greater concentration of the working-class population in the capital, and thus increased the social peril.

Furthermore, as a sovereign concerned with greatness and glory, Napoleon III embellished Paris in order to make it the equal of London and even the capital of capitals. For reasons of prestige, he freed the buildings of the past from their decrepit surroundings and ordered the construction of grandiose monuments aimed at impressing visitors drawn from the world over, as well as Parisian high society. Hence, for example, the pomp given to the 140-metre-wide Avenue de l'Impératrice, which led to the Bois de Boulogne.

Above all, Napoleon III and his prefect displayed a keen awareness of the most urgent priorities, chiefly those of a demographic and sanitary nature. Paris in the mid nineteenth century was a city without air or

light, unhealthy and underequipped, whose inhabitants were crammed
with great difficulty into buildings to which extra storeys had already been
added. How could it have coped with a heavy increase in its population
without dying of apoplexy or asphyxiation? 'Given its expanding population, it was impossible to preserve the old Paris as it was' (Rouher,
1867); a drastic remedy therefore had to be administered.

A new setting was also required for the capitalist city, with its department stores, big banks, and above all its railway stations, which inevitably
engendered a pressing need for wide thoroughfares:

> Industrial growth and the lively development of commerce were
> shackled by the yoke of the city's medieval core...Paris had to be
> redone in such a way that the city would become a 'productive environ-
> ment' capable of satisfying the needs of the new mode of production.[28]

These tasks were not carried out arbitrarily or artificially. The lengthy
statistical researches of Halbwachs[29] show that the piercing of new streets
was less the cause of subsequent movements of traffic and population than
a response to genuine needs: 'The city was transformed as and when the
patterns of population dictated...'

Indeed, a number of other towns were modernized during the same
period. While some of them slumbered, such as Aix, which remained in
1857 'a mausoleum of the seventeenth and eighteenth centuries', a considerable amount of renovation was carried out in Cherbourg, Le Havre,
Rouen, Blois (in order to unclog the centre and facilitate the crossing from
the bridge to the railway station) and Besançon (building of a dock on the
right bank of the Doubs, conveyance of drinking water). The major urban
centres were, on their own scale and with varying degrees of success,
'Haussmannized' after the Parisian model. In Lyons, the prefect Vaïsse
and his technicians vitalized the bustling quarters cramped between the
Saône and Rhône, turning them into a London-style City. Bordeaux,
expanded in 1865 and surrounded by a ring road, was equipped with
water, gas, main sewers, markets and public transport; while the administration, confronted with a bourgeoisie hostile to lavish expenditure, did
not disembowel the old quarters, it ridded them of their 'dens of rats and
cholera' and disengaged the cathedral. Marseilles underwent the greatest
transformations, with the construction of the prefecture, the Chamber of
Commerce palace (inaugurated by the imperial couple in 1860), the
cathedral and Notre-Dame de la Garde. A town particularly vulnerable
to cholera, it was at long last equipped with a sewage network. Beginning
at La Joliette (completed in 1853), a series of ports stretched northwards:
Arenc, followed by the Port Impérial. Lastly, as a link between La Joliette
and the lower end of the Canebière, between the new commercial centre
and the old, the Rue Impériale (now Rue de la République) was driven
through the old quarter. At Lille, however, Haussmannization failed,

perhaps because the municipality was completely taken up by the most urgent projects. Lille too was suffocating and totally lacked green spaces, but its enlargement led to new, sordid quarters being built alongside old, unrenovated quarters, separated only by a few unattractive bourgeois avenues. The city had been decentred.

The end result of this modernization is debatable and has been criticized, most notably as concerns the capital. Yet one can speak of the undoubted success of an approach to town planning – the word *urbanisme* did not exist at the time – based on spaciousness and renovation, and adapted to the needs of the great modern city. To be sure, Haussmann was wrong to give the impression that nothing had been accomplished before him. His work remained to a great extent unfinished: large sections of old Paris, as well as a number of slums, still remained, and the city continued to display signs of illness (cholera struck again in 1866 and 1867), but the urban fabric built during the Empire has, for the most part, weathered the test of time until the 1960s. It is as if Paris had gone from the eighteenth to the twentieth century overnight.

The aesthetic results have also provoked controversy. Haussmann has been called a ripper, a vandal guilty of numerous irreparable acts of destruction, carried out without discernment. One can share Baudelaire's melancholy:

> Le vieux Paris n'est plus, la forme d'une ville
> change plus vite, hélas! que le cœur d'un mortel
> (Old Paris is no more; a city's shape
> changes faster, alas, than a mortal's heart)

but one is obliged to observe that a number of renovation projects existed at the time that were even less respectful of the past. As for the new Paris, viewed in isolation, its elements no doubt lack artistic vitality. Nevertheless, after being so maligned, they are now recognized as possessing some qualities after all. When they disappeared, Baltard's pavilions became 'a higher expression of the capacities of the nineteenth century', remarkable 'for their use of materials, their broad treatment of space and a sort of neo-Gothic elegance in a regular and cubic structure'.[30] As for the Second Empire townhouses bordering the Parc Monceau, their originality was discovered when they became endangered. More generally, the geometrical lines of the new town planning, long accused of being a monotonous imitation of Anglo-Saxon or Germanic styles, constitute a striking setting that highlights the surviving older monuments, and

> the spirit of classical French beauty lives on in the aesthetics of the general composition. While lacking architectural genius, the project is informed by the principles of taste that had become national traditions. This urban aesthetic is an offspring of Versailles.[31]

Haussmann gave an air of grandeur to Paris.

But the modernization of the big cities was a political failure. The Parisians, the Lyonnais and shortly thereafter the Marseillais were the first to vote massively for the opposition, for the prefects' iron-handed approach to town planning had aroused numerous forms of discontent. Even more, it had – most notably in Paris, but also in Lille and Lyons – helped to trigger an acute housing crisis, which engendered deep popular discontent. Haussmann's street penetrations destroyed bourgeois town-houses as well as more modest housing. Admittedly, more buildings were put up than torn down, but the new rents were much higher. All of those expelled who did not have the means to be rehoused on the spot (workers, artisans, employees, low-ranking civil servants) tried to find lodgings near by, but they were driven back further and further. Louis Lazare, in *Les Quartiers pauvres de Paris* (1868), recounts the exemplary odyssey of a cabinet-maker and his family who lived comfortably in the Rue Tixanderie, near Les Halles, where they paid an annual rent of 110 francs. Driven out by renovation, they move to the Rue de Ménilmontant, with the intention of returning to their old quarter. But in their reconstructed building, the landlord wants to get rid of working-class tenants, and in any case the rent is prohibitive. In the Rue de Ménilmontant too the rent becomes too expensive (180 francs). The family therefore moves to Belleville, but the extension of the city's boundaries and the start of renovation work in Belleville drives the rent up to 250 francs. And so the family moves once again, this time to the Pavé de Charonne. The more fortunate among these expelled inhabitants eventually found accommodation in apartment buildings where they paid far higher rent for smaller lodgings. Others crowded into the slums that survived in the annexed faubourgs or into those that mushroomed in the new, undeveloped suburbs, which often lacked roads and water supply. And what a race to go every day to one's place of work, still located in old Paris!

Previously, rich and poor had lived in the same neighbourhoods, often in the same buildings, the former occupying only the lower storeys. This close proximity and the encounters in staircases and in the street made for a certain familiarity. Now two antithetical cities had been engendered by social segregation: on the one hand, the quarters inhabited primarily by the well-to-do (the centre) or the rich (the west); on the other, the popular *arrondissements* to the north (the population of Les Batignolles soared from 5,000 to 65,000), east and south, teeming with newly-arrived immigrants and the poor expelled from the centre. 'A red belt encloses and lays siege to the centre of town – a horseshoe that breaks off only between Les Ternes and Auteuil.'[32] Thus, wrote Lazare, 'two very different and hostile towns have been created in Paris: the city of luxury surrounded, blocked by the city of poverty. You have exposed every kind of seduction to every kind of envy.'[33] It was a dangerous situation, but for the time being the bourgeoisie was often quite content to live apart, to be rid of the irksome promiscuousness of the rabble and to occupy an ostentatious position in the city.

## 4. Bourgeoisie and civilization

### The varied world of the bourgeoisie

Whereas a part of the aristocracy, preserving its social prestige, stood aloof with its traditional decorum and good taste (wintering in the Faubourg Saint-Germain, summering on its rural estates), the social life of the Second Empire had a bad reputation. It was described, in *La Curée* for example, as the triumph of immorality, a union between gambling and debauchery – the money obtained by rapidly and dishonestly earned gains from stock market or real estate speculation and the money spent in no time by a frivolous society tormented by a huge appetite for all forms of sensual delight and seeking out every kind of easy or even corrupt pleasure. The capital became a 'new Babylon', an immense den of iniquity, famous for its demi-mondaines like 'la Païva' (the expression 'demi-monde' was introduced in a play by Alexandre Dumas the younger in 1855), for its 'lionesses' recruited among actresses, such as Blanche d'Antigny, and for its countless courtesans (*lorettes*). As the actors of *La Vie parisienne* (1866) sang – the words were by Meilhac and Halévy, the music by Offenbach:

> Du plaisir à perdre haleine,
> Oui, voilà la vie parisienne.
> (Pleasure until you're out of breath –
> Yes, that's life in Paris.)

While 'society' had indeed become cosmopolitan and multifarious, the 'horrors of the *fête impériale*' denounced by the entire opposition were attributable only to a tiny, visible minority. They did not faithfully reflect the life of the bourgeoisie of the Second Empire, not even that of the predominantly Parisian upper bourgeoisie. Alongside the profiteers of the regime and the *nouveaux riches*, who were often no more than passing comets, the old dynasties – who augmented their wealth considerably – joined the *fête* with restraint and often continued to lead a quiet life. Furthermore, the bourgeois class was less than ever a homogeneous group. The bulk of its members belonged to the 'good' bourgeoisie (wholesalers, industrialists, professionals and civil servants), to the world of shopkeepers or even to that needy *petite bourgeoisie* that one has trouble distinguishing from the populace (perhaps the lower limit of the bourgeois categories could be drawn at the families with an annual income of 5,000 francs in Paris and 4,000 in the provinces).

These bourgeois by and large preserved their traditional virtues of integrity and seriousness in business, of hard work (even in a wealthy family a young man was expected to work) and of barely diminished prudence. 'Bourgeois' life was, by definition, peaceful. Lisa, the pretty *charcutière* of Les Halles in *Le Ventre de Paris*, symbolizes this mentality. She 'does not think highly of Saccard', the feverish speculator, and she expresses her profession of faith in these words:

> I have nothing on my conscience...I am not involved in any shady deals...We who lead such a quiet life, who take fifteen years to feather our nest, we whose sole concern is to raise our daughter and lead our ship safely to port, we are decent folk.[34]

Money was indeed the predominant, almost exclusive concern of many of these bourgeois, for example those portrayed in Labiche's *La Cagnotte* (the nest egg). They were against everything that could threaten the power of money or the success of their business ventures: war, income taxes (which already existed in Britain), the slightest infringement of property rights and – above all – disorder, whose terrible consequences Lisa described to her husband: 'You don't want them to come and plunder your shop, empty your cellar and steal your money. Stay at home, then, you big fool, eat well, make money and keep your conscience clear.' While it is dangerous to generalize about so diversified a class, these bourgeois who increased their earnings and became more aware of what separated them from the people did their best to distinguish themselves from the latter, to stand apart.

Their first gesture was an ostentatious display of money. This was an instinctive *nouveau-riche* behaviour for some bourgeois, about whom Madame Dosne, Thiers's mother-in-law, observed: 'These latter-day gentlemen cannot be reproached with hiding their recently acquired fortune.' More generally, the bourgeoisie was determined to be classed by its style of living, which, while some sometimes restrained out of a sense of thrift and less 'showy' in the provinces, implied that every bourgeois, at his or her own level, was keen to display a certain degree of luxury.

The chief showcase of the bourgeoisie was housing. New urban development satisfied 'the good bourgeois, the *rentiers*, the captains of industry who had long suffered because of their inability to display their wealth'.[35] The most affluent established themselves in private townhouses with lavishly decorated façades, the others in the solid freestone buildings put up along Haussmann's street penetrations. All these buildings were alike, as if to provide a clear statement of class cohesion. The bourgeois flat always included a dining room and at least one living room; both usually overlooked the street and were the object of painstaking attention. In the living room, decorated with a varied array of opulent-looking furniture, one found a juxtaposition of Louis XVI-style pieces – back in fashion – and a piano (often), padded seats, a divan or a sofa and consoles laden with vases. In order to give it a 'rich look', the dining room, furnished in Henri II style, was adorned with silverware that was often only electroplated (*ruolz*) (the emperor gave the example by ordering 3,000 pieces of *ruolz*-ware). The table was always very copiously garnished, even for ordinary meals. Formal dinners, which in the provinces were often still held only once a year, were gargantuan. The fare would include four or five meat or fish courses, several vegetables and all manner of wines and desserts. The bourgeois was becoming 'the eater',[36] the fat man who in *Le Ventre de Paris* felt himself to be at war with 'the thin'. Furthermore, in order to practise such a style of living, the family could not dispense with servants, at the very least a general help, at best a cook, a valet (often in livery), chambermaids and nannies.

Clothing and finery were another way of showing off one's wealth. While men wore heavy watch chains and charms on their chests, women flaunted their jewellery and strove, according to their means, to keep up with fashions. The wealthier women patronized the great designers, such as Worth, who made the empress's clothes. For indoor wear, shawls – if possible, of cashmere – were the fashion. For 'going out', an expensive silk crinoline, decorated with ribbons, lace, flounces or flowers, was a must almost until the end of the Empire. Finally, recreations provided something of an opportunity for parading: in the provinces, families made Sunday strolls the rule. In Paris, the bourgeoisie attended boulevard cafés with brightly lit terraces, racecourses, theatres such as the Théâtre de Vaudeville or the Théâtre des Variétés, and the Bois de Boulogne and Bois de Vincennes. On every fine day in the spring, the wealthier bourgeois submitted to the ritual promenade in the Bois de Boulogne, an opportunity to display – as described in the opening of *La Curée* – the luxuriousness of feminine outfits and the splendour of equipages. Travel was a way of getting together with members of the same social set in spa towns (Vichy, Plombières) or on the beach at Deauville (launched by Morny).

Sensing that if he was to win over these bourgeois, he had to play on their craving to be noticed, the emperor went about satisfying it. In the provinces, sumptuous receptions held at prefectures put notables in the limelight, and the court, which Napoleon III – despite his great personal simplicity – intended as a dazzling showcase, afforded the *grande bourgeoisie* a chance to take part in the magnificent celebrations at the Tuileries and invited them to receptions at Compiègne, where guests came to stay in successive series according to a carefully organized hierarchy.

The élite also distinguished itself from the people by its educational level. Bourgeois families, aware of the importance of education for their children, put their sons through a secondary schooling too expensive to be accessible to others. Lycées and collèges numbered only 101,000 pupils in 1850 (of whom 53,000 in private schools) and 150,000 (80,000 in private schools) at the end of the Empire. This represented less than 5 per cent of all boys old enough to attend, and hardly more than 6,000 baccalaureate diplomas were issued every year. Secondary education provided the sons of the bourgeoisie with 'a professional culture for notables' that prepared them to be the nation's future leaders. It thus enabled their class to maintain its social ascendancy. Secondary education also ensured their moral training, and, through the study of Latin – the language to which the bourgeoisie turned to obtain 'its passwords' – it was designed to make them acquire elevation of thought and nobility of style, and ultimately to instil into them the dominant social ideology.

Lastly, the bourgeois tried to make their fortune, or their relative affluence, respectable by following a line of conduct acceptable from all points of view and by obeying a set of passively accepted rules, such as the obligation for men not to go out without gloves and, even less, without a top hat. If a number of petty bourgeois remained staunchly anti-clerical – hence Voltaire's return to favour under the Empire – many of them, outwardly at least, had gone back to religion since 1848 in a mechanical reaction of social defence. In the provinces, the men regularly attended Sunday services, while their wives devoted themselves to charity. It was this society – in which clericalism was far more prevalent than genuine belief – that Sainte-Beuve denounced in 1869 at the rostrum of the Senate. In their conviction – shared by the Emperor – that morals and religion were a good thing, the bourgeois were careful to lead an 'honest' or at least outwardly irreproachable life. Furthermore, they made themselves into champions of rigid principles that they carried to an excessive degree of prudery. While heartily applauding Labiche's vaudevilles, the irony of which they did not regard as very subversive, they also showed a predilection for works that extolled finer feelings, such as Octave Feuillet's *Roman d'un jeune homme pauvre*; they held in abhorrence whatever diverged in too provocative a manner from their time-honoured usages and their assumptions. Beaming and satisfied, these dogmatic bourgeois, whose 'idiocy' was cruelly denounced by Flaubert and Labiche, no doubt often displayed narrow-mindedness and conformism. What scandals were provoked in their ranks by works accused of outraging public morality and religion, such as *Madame Bovary* (the object of a pontificating indictment by the prosecutor Pinard, who later became Minister of the Interior in 1867), *Les Fleurs du Mal*, *Thérèse Raquin* and several novels by the Goncourt brothers! All of these works were subjected to prosecution. The sight of Manet's *Olympia* made the bourgeoisie choke with indignation.

### Artists and writers
The Second Empire has also suffered from a poor reputation in intellectual and artistic fields. French thought did undergo a relative

decline, and lost its formerly privileged position. Whereas most discoveries were the work of foreigners (Darwin, for example), French scientists were less productive, with the notable exception of Claude Bernard (author of the *Introduction à l'étude de la médecine expérimentale*, 1865) and Pasteur, whose work was only just beginning. Philosophical creativity seemed to be on the wane. Instead of building new theories, philosophers revived eclecticism or, with Littré, the positivism of Auguste Comte. There was little progress in the currents of political thought: between *L'Ancien Régime et la Révolution*, Tocqueville's last great work (1856), and Prévost-Paradol's *La France nouvelle* (1868), liberalism was dealt with in works of only honourable quality. The French socialist ideology, which had expressed itself essentially before 1850, gained little depth even as Marxism was being edified. The surveys of Le Play – an advocate of a social Christianity heavily tinged with paternalism – and the studies of Michel Chevalier did not revolutionize economic thought. This lack of vitality was perhaps partly due to the heavy constraints imposed by the regime in its early days on all means of expression, to the inadequate funds allocated for research and to the general climate of a society that exhibited scant concern for intellectual innovation.

More generally, writers and artists found themselves in an ambiguous situation. They were living in a world incapable of satisfying them. They felt no sympathy for a regime born of violence and run by a sovereign not very interested in literature, whose wife admitted her almost total ignorance of the arts; they were disappointed, too, by the attitude of the very masses on whom some had pinned all their hopes. In consequence, many of these writers and artists locked themselves up, like Leconte de Lisle, in their 'ivory tower' and became resolutely apolitical. Many of them, too, like Théophile Gautier and, later on, the Parnassians, sought a form of expression that would be 'a luxury for the very few' and were determined to engage in art for art's sake. The younger writers and artists in particular, who felt at odds with the materialist and conformist society around them and were disgusted with their native class, took refuge in the ever more closed world of Bohemia; they lived apart in Montmartre or Montparnasse, accepting poverty the better to scoff at the bourgeois whom they scorned and provoked by their outrageousness.

But while some persisted in refusing to become integrated into a world whose judgements and constraints they feared, and preferred to remain pariahs, for many the *Scènes de la vie de bohème* described by Henry Murger were only a passing episode. Most notably for artists, success depended on the emperor – who was intent on becoming their protector and patron – and on all the officials who controlled prizes and State commissions and regulated access to theatres, concert halls and painting salons (held every other year until 1861, and yearly thereafter), outside of which it was difficult indeed for painters to make a name for themselves, for lack of private galleries. Furthermore, vast and lucrative outlets were offered to artists, provided they were willing to please a bourgeoisie eager to flaunt its opulence by purchasing works of art – clients such as the *manieur d'affaires* (big businessman) who, in Dumas the younger's *La Question d'argent*, declared with disarming ingenuousness: 'You will see my mansion and I will show you my paintings and statues, because I have been told that a man in my position must have a taste for the arts. I am utterly ignorant in the matter, I have paid a lot for all of this, but I'm afraid it may not be worth very much.' Ultimately, success seems to have been worth a few concessions. Hence the complex relationships that were established between authors and a society that perhaps they secretly loathed – relationships sometimes laden with silences, implications and repressed feelings. A characteristic case was that of Flaubert, the *Idiot de la famille*,[37] a victim of official moralism who was none the less extremely happy to lead a *dolce vita* at court and in the salon of Princesse Mathilde, and who shared with the bourgeois readers he detested certain unbearable secrets, born perhaps of the revelation – repressed since 1848 – of the existence of the proletariat.

### Literary and artistic renewal

It is tempting to divide the works produced during these years into two groups. The first would include commercial productions, which were successful and at times brilliant, but also superficial, conventional and conformist. In music, Gounod and Bizet triumphed while Berlioz, more a man of the past, remained misunderstood, and Wagner's *Tannhäuser* was hooted down by the Parisians. Architects complied with electicism and the taste for pastiche, successively building churches in Romanesque (Saint-Augustin), Gothic (Sainte-Clotilde) and Renaissance (La Trinité) styles. Charles Garnier mingled all genres for the Opéra, which remained unfinished and is in a sense the symbol of the Second Empire style characterized by Zola as an 'opulent bastard of all styles'. This was the heyday of the *peintres pompiers*, of the sort of painting that 'instead of serving Art, as it believes it is doing, is at the service of the Bouvards and Pécuchets, its consumers',[38] who demanded heroic, noble, edifying, virtuous or sometimes naughty paintings. Among these painters, who were proud of their subjects and their craft, one can mention Winterhalter, the official portrait painter of the court, Meissonnier, who specialized in battle scenes from which not a single gaiter button was missing, and Cabanel, whose *Vénus* dazzled the chroniclers of the 1863 Salon. The second group of creative artists would include the reprobates, those who remained outcasts or were the focus of scandal – but who were often recognized as geniuses by posterity. However, one should not carry this antithesis to excess. Not all the *pompiers* were mediocre imitators of conventional models. While contemporaries may have laughed at them, the works of Labiche or Offenbach are not without savour. Lastly, in the field of sculpture, Carpeaux – who was awarded several major commissions by the regime (although his *La Danse* was accused of being an affront to decency) – combined technical perfection with an inspiration that enabled him to rediscover the graces of the best classical style while hinting at a strangely modern realism.

The currents of the past did not disappear overnight. Classicism lived on with Ingres; romanticism cast its dying – and sometimes most glowing – lights in the paintings of Delacroix and Fromentin, and in the great works of Hugo, who wrote *Les Châtiments*, *La Légende des Siècles* and *Les Misérables* in exile.

But a reaction did take place. In deliberate opposition to romanticism, the new generation attached greater importance to elegance of form. It had greater faith in intelligence than in imagination, and was intent on grasping reality. These concerns were evidenced in poetry, with Leconte de Lisle, Heredia, F. Coppée and Sully Prudhomme. Realism made even greater inroads among novelists, who described without complacency and often even in a caricatural manner the foibles of the rich and the pretensions of the middle classes while denouncing the plight of the poor. Flaubert wrote *Madame Bovary*, a portrayal of provincial mores, and *L'Education sentimentale*; the Goncourt brothers composed their novels with a twofold concern for the most painstaking exactitude and for artistic writing; finally, Zola's early works foreshadowed naturalism, the extreme form of realism. The same determination to describe mores prevailed in theatre (Dumas the younger, E. Augier); the same desire to represent scenes from daily life was shared by painters like Courbet, Millet and Daumier.

Going beyond this reaction, one can discern the outlines of revolutionary currents in music (with the young Fauré, who composed his first vocal works) and, above all, in poetry and painting. Symbolism was heralded by Baudelaire (who died in 1867), ever in search of new sensations and a secret vision of the world, and by the early work of Verlaine and Mallarmé. In painting, 1863 marks a decisive break: in that year, the artists turned down at the Salon were allowed by Napoleon III to exhibit their works in the 'Salon of the reprobates' (Salon des Réprouvés). Among them were Manet and Pissarro; soon joined by Sisley, Claude Monet, Renoir and others, they formed the current later called Impressionism. As Pierre Francastel has shown,[39] their movement challenged the concept of pictorial space that had been forged in the age of the Renaissance and had subsequently served as the basis for all painting; what was about to blossom was an interpretation of reality. According to Malraux, Manet's *Olympia* marked the appearance of 'painting whose subject was irrelevant': it signalled 'the birth of modern art'.[40] These were revolutionary changes, which some interpreted as the first signs of a crisis of civilization.

# 5

# The good years, 1852–61

The first years of the Empire were presented in the official propaganda as a period of triumph. At the very least, during the first legislature, there prevailed a calm that contrasted with the previous storms.

## 1. The first legislature (1852–7)

### The seizure of the country

The government had little to fear from the assemblies, least of all from a Legislative Body that comprised but a single declared opponent, Montalembert. While the debates adroitly presided over by Morny were nevertheless rather animated at times – so much so that the government had to withdraw several bills dealing with financial or customs matters – they had no impact on the country at large, which was where the decisive battle was being waged. The regime, which rested on universal suffrage, could not last unless it continued to enjoy the massive support of the French people. Having been established by surprise, it was in danger of being worn away by the exercise of power and having to contend with renascent forms of opposition. It was for the administration to ensure the 'conquest' of the country (in the sense in which Zola spoke of *La Conquête de Plassans*) and, while maintaining order, to prevent any turnaround in the opinions of as yet very inexperienced voters.

The terror that followed the *coup d'état* gradually relented, but in January 1853 there remained, in prison or exile, 6,153 victims of repression who had not yet been amnestied. The prefects and their civil servants, the police, the magistrates and the army (the National Guard, for its part, was reduced to a purely ceremonial role on public occasions) all co-operated in a strict enforcement of legislation curtailing freedoms, a task carried out with an often distrustful and sometimes quite excessive zeal. Two events that occurred in the north are a telling indication of the climate that was settling over the country.[1] In 1853, in the Cambrésis, the *commissaire de police cantonal* (a post created by the Empire) discovered that an industrialist in Masnières had had the doors of his factory painted red; the official immediately interpreted this as 'a blatant manifestation of this manufacturer's advanced ideas and something of an act of bravado directed at the government'. It took a lot of persuading to make the *commissaire* admit that the industrialist had merely wanted to use an inexpensive paint made of crushed brick. In 1855, a domestic quarrel followed by a denunciation led the police to discover the existence of a worker society that professed republican and vaguely socialist ideas, *La Cocotte* (the casserole). Its members were recruited from among the miners and workers of Anzin, and it maintained connections with militants in Paris, refugees in Brussels and London and the convicts on Belle-Ile. Although this association apparently did not intend to resort to violent action, the ten members apprehended by the police were tried and subjected to heavy sentences (ranging from two to four years' imprisonment for four of them).

Everywhere, taverns could be closed down arbitrarily. Newspapers were kept under a harassing surveillance in which ample use was made of unofficial notifications and official warnings. Hence a debased press that no longer dared to speak its mind. Chapbook catalogues were severely purged. Teachers were the victims of the brutal methods of the imperious Fortoul, who abolished the safe tenure of university professors.

In conjunction with this repression – which, on the whole, had very little occasion to exercise itself – an active propaganda campaign was led in favour of a regime that was not content with muzzling the opposition. In order to direct public opinion and secure a broad consensus, the government used all the means at its disposal, most notably its prefects, who addressed themselves directly to the local inhabitants when touring their *départements* to organize recruiting boards. They spread the good word at agricultural shows and made contact with the appropriate notables at receptions held at their prefectures. If necessary, they founded imperialist newspapers in their *départements*, but often the weapons they wielded (the granting or withdrawal of official notices, the secret funds that enabled them to win over certain editors) were adequate to ensure the servility of the existing local press. In 1860, the pro-government press exercised a monopoly in half the *départements*.[2] Propaganda also took on forms better suited to a popular audience: it worked its way into chapbooks, inspiring imagery or news-sheets (*canards*) in praise of the sovereign. The emperor had his own publicists and propaganda agents; to reach out to the working class, he called on Armand Lévy and Hugelmann, two revolutionaries of 1848, as well as Darimon, a friend of Emile Ollivier.

The themes exploited were always more or less the same: criticism of sterile political games and of the former parties that succeeded only in dividing the French; praise for the emperor who had saved the country from anarchy and had, in addition, brought prosperity and a glorious peace. Not without skill, propaganda language was adapted to the audience to which it was directed. To notables, one spoke about order and the 'red spectre' threatening property, while the following assertion was made to the workers in 1855:

> Ever since his accession, H.M. Napoleon III has sought every occasion to come to the rescue of the labouring classes. How many workers' housing estates, model public baths and washing houses, free or moderately priced, how many children's homes and mutual aid societies have been established both in Paris and in the *départements*![3]

Even the emperor's marriage, which had a 'deplorable effect' (Rémusat) in the salons, seemed an opportunity to woo popular opinion. On 17 January 1853, Morny told Persigny the theme to exploit:

> You can be sure that among the people they say: 'Ah! Ah! There's a man who doesn't stick to the rules. He doesn't try to satisfy his vanity by running after the princesses who bring misfortune on France. Instead, he's married a beautiful lady whom he loves!' And the emperor will have the women, but also the workers and peasants, on his side...[4]

These efforts seem to have borne fruit. No doubt the attitude of the working and urban masses remained ambiguous and somewhat inscrutable. Aversion to the regime often coexisted – particularly when troops left for the Crimea or Italy – with displays of attachment to the emperor, whom many regarded as 'poorly advised'. Napoleon III was acclaimed by the artisans of the Faubourg Saint-Antoine and the silk workers at Lyons. But when the imperial couple visited Lille in 1853, despite the presence of a crowd of spectators at his entrance into the city, curiosity may have prevailed over enthusiasm. All in all, with the exception of the slate-quarry workers of Trélazé, who revolted in 1855, secret societies such as *La Marianne* initially encountered little active support in a working-class world that, despite its reservations about the regime, remained calm and even apathetic.

The rural masses, who had opted for the future emperor by 1848, benefited more obviously from the economic evolution, and took a respectful view of an administration that had greater sway over them. Thus rural society granted the regime a nearly unanimous vote of confidence. Béranger sensed the vital importance of this:

> The peasants! That's where every government must get its greatest support! The peasants will defend Napoleon less out of sympathy than out of self-interest. They form a mass of 20 or 22 million individuals. That's a formidable army, and it would be a fine thing to command it.

As for the aristocracy and especially the bourgeoisie, often already attached to ideologies other than Bonapartism, they were divided, sometimes within the same family. If one simplifies the picture, one can distinguish, on the one hand, the 'obstinate individuals' whose reaction was conditioned by political tradition, indomitable pride and intellectual or moral habits; they persisted in fighting the regime, or at least in refusing to co-operate with it. 'Thus it cannot be said that the whole bourgeoisie supported the Empire.'[5] On the other hand, we find the '*résignés*', whose conduct was dictated more by class interests. Without being converts, they rallied to the saviour of society and supplied him with the political personnel he needed. More than one *petit bourgeois* must have thought like Lisa, Zola's *charcutière*: 'I'm grateful to the government when my business is doing well, when I can eat my soup quietly and sleep without being awakened by gunshots.'

Official propaganda, which relentlessly vaunted the beneficent action of the regime, was especially successful in that it appeared to be corroborated by the economic situation (rising profits and employment) and was directed at a generally contented population: 'On the mind of the citizen, prosperity acted like an anaesthetic.'[6]

### The alliance of throne and altar

Lastly, the Empire enjoyed the backing of the Church, with whom it reached something of a self-interested entente, based on an exchange of friendly services. A large majority of Catholics and clergy welcomed the restoration of an empire that stood for the principles of social conservatism. Louis Napoleon appeared to them as the man who had saved the Church from annihilation. Louis Veuillot, a cooper's son whose paper, *L'Univers*, wielded considerable influence over the priesthood at large, rallied enthusiastically to a regime which, so he expected, would ensure the triumph of faith. The bishops, except for a few legitimists, delivered extravagant encomiums for the sovereign, 'the man of God's right', the man chosen by providence to shower favours on the Church.

Admittedly, Napoleon III displayed little interest in religious questions, and several of his ministers remained wary of the clergy's aspirations. But the government wanted to promote the social and moral influence of religion, which it saw as a dependable weapon in its struggle against revolutionary propaganda and in favour of order; furthermore, the government was determined to win over a clergy that, with the introduction of universal suffrage, became a powerful electoral force, often the only one capable of inducing legitimist voters to rally to the regime. Accordingly, while a climate of moral order was taking hold, the government protected and honoured the clergy, included it in all public solemnities and lavished numerous material advantages on it (such as an increase in the funds allocated to religious affairs, which made it possible in particular to increase the stipends of the upper clergy; grants to communes for repairing and rebuilding presbyteries and churches; gifts). In addition, the government refrained from implementing the provisions of the 'Organic Articles' that hindered the Church of France's relations with the

Holy See. On the whole, the Empire granted the Church exceptional privileges: 'In an oppressed society, [the Church] preserved the most extensive freedoms that it had enjoyed since the Concordat'; it was given every opportunity to open educational establishments and to further the development of teaching orders, which were entrusted with a considerable number of primary schools.

All of this gave the Church a great expansionary impetus. The number of ordinations rose appreciably, the clergy exercised an ever greater influence over the moneyed classes and Sunday services seem to have been better attended. Some bishops tried to take advantage of these favourable circumstances in order to rechristianize their dioceses (for example, Monseigneur Dupanloup in the diocese of Orléans), but the successes obtained were generally short-lived. Furthermore, the privileged position of the Church remained precarious. The government refused to commit itself to abrogating the Organic Articles and making church marriages compulsory (this prevented Pius IX from coming to anoint the emperor): it established unilaterally the budget for religious affairs each year; it could always go back on simple administrative practices or, by reviving unenforced legislation, abolish illegal privileges that guaranteed a certain independence to the Church – an independence that an authoritarian government could not tolerate for very long. The regime also became concerned about the spread of an ultramontanist movement that its own attitude had encouraged. Fortoul, who had already attempted to restore the State's authority in the educational sphere, was succeeded in 1856 by the Gallican Rouland – a move that seemed to portend a hardening of religious policy.

Within the Church itself, various tensions emerged. Intransigent Catholics like Veuillot, hostile to the principles of 1789, were challenged by the small group of liberals around Lacordaire, Monseigneur Dupanloup and Montalembert. In 1856, this group found in *Le Correspondant* a platform from which to launch an attack on *L'Univers*. A few bishops, such as those of Luçon and Poitiers, still faithful to legitimism, constituted an irksome opposition to the regime. But virtually all the clergy rallied to the Empire. Even when they remained in sympathy with the legitimate monarchy, they did not hesitate to provide assistance to the civilian authorities and extol the government, so helping to win over many legitimists.

The government's relations with Protestant ministers and rabbis, most of whom were on the State payroll, posed very few problems. But the *réformés* often manifested a barely concealed attitude of reserve, possibly because the Protestant spirit implied 'a certain concept of political society involving respect for liberty, democracy and popular sovereignty'[7] – a position scarcely compatible with acceptance of an authoritarian regime.

The attitude of the Jews varied considerably: in Alsace-Lorraine, they rallied; in the Vaucluse and the Hérault, they were already in opposition.

### Weaknesses of the oppositions

During the first years of the Empire, opposition groups survived often as scattered remnants. The ranks of the representatives of the 'old parties', both royalist and liberal, were thinning out, their members having rallied to the regime or retired out of disgust with politics. Those who remained determined opponents acted out of dynastic loyalty, out of the horror that filled scrupulous men at the sight of an illegal regime engendered in violence and practising immoral methods or out of an attachment to liberal and parliamentary forms of government. The opposition was handicapped by the constraining persistence of old cleavages, for the attempts to achieve a merger at the top between the Comte de Chambord and the d'Orléans family failed, owing to the Comte's intransigence over the principle of the symbolically significant white flag. Not without hesitation, certain realignments were carried out.

On the far Right, if one can use the term, the pure legitimists obeyed the Comte de Chambord's directives to abstain from political activity. They were seemingly tempted by the ideal of a return to absolutism, by 'white Bonapartism'. Intransigent in politics as in religion, they isolated themselves in a sulking 'domestic emigration'.

Other legitimists, such as Berryer and Falloux, refused such abstention and sought to participate in political life at least at the local level. They were members of parliament and 'liberals in order to be conservatives without risk',[8] espousing the views of the most conservative of the Orleanists, who, with Guizot, regretted that the July Monarchy had already moved too far towards democracy. Whether at the grass roots level, in the salons or in the various academies that made up the Institut, these three currents coalesced. 'The Académie Française then became, under Guizot's aegis, a true "pro-merger" political academy, ranging from Montalembert to Berryer.'[9]

Somewhat apart stood a certain number of Orleanists who rejected the idea of a merger and claimed allegiance to the Duc d'Aumale, who had always defended the tricolour flag. They accepted the revolution of 1830 in all its aspects; they were liberal in politics and also in religious matters, as they were often spiritualists or rationalists themselves – when they did not, like the young Prévost-Paradol, feel an intense hatred for Catholicism. What separated these men, such as Thiers and Rémusat, from the more moderate republicans was not so much a disagreement as to the form of the regime (Rémusat stated his 'indifference to a choice between a monarchy and a republic')[10] as their stubborn rejection of universal suffrage.

The hostility of all these liberals expressed itself mainly in the guise of witticisms in salon conversation, carefully calculated allusions or quotations from Tacitus cleverly worked into speeches in the Law Courts or at the Académie, as well as historical or philosophical studies. Another outlet was the election to the Académie Française of candidates hostile to the master, such as Dupanloup, Berryer, the Duc de Broglie and Falloux. None of this could make much impact in the country at large. Accordingly, pessimism spread to the leaders of this troopless opposition. One of them, d'Haussonville, admitted: 'During the first years of the Empire, the latent but obstinate opposition that existed among many faithful supporters of earlier regimes was at a loss for a foothold. The country was visibly satisfied.'[11]

The republicans too, albeit to a lesser extent, were weakened by the loss of those who defected or rallied to the Empire. Above all, they had suffered far more from the repression that followed the *coup d'état*, and they were still being hounded by the police. Many leaders remained in gaol or in exile, for a general amnesty was not decreed until 1859. The existence of these martyrs – whose sufferings were recounted with emotion – instilled into the militants both a fierce hatred of a regime whose crimes they could not forget and a fervent worship of the Republic.

The 'republican party constituted a sort of cluster whose contours are hard to discern'. Socially speaking, it was extremely varied and deeply divided. Exiles composed a distinct group, living off their wits throughout the world but especially in Britain, Belgium, Switzerland and Savoy. Within the country, while the republican idea seemed to survive only in isolated rural *cantons*, it enjoyed a fairly broad popular following in the towns, particularly among artisans and workers. Students were still often republican, most notably in Paris. And republicans were to be found in all the strata of the bourgeoisie, among small shopkeepers, professionals, intellectuals, lawyers (Emile Ollivier), newspaper editors (at *Le Siècle*, for instance) and even prominent industrialists (Dorian in Saint-Etienne, Magnin in Dijon). In the Isère, 'no less than its rivals, the republican party was run by bourgeois..., by socially prominent men, usually lawyers, whose profession guaranteed them total independence'.[12] In Paris, these notables met in the salons, such as that of Madame Hérold and especially that of Madame d'Agoult, who hosted Jules Grévy, Carnot, Littré and the economist Dupont-White as well as keeping in contact with exiles like Louis Blanc.

The old divisions dating from the Second Republic persisted, leading to quarrels and even duels among exiles. Disagreements broke out over the conduct to adopt. Dyed-in-the-wool republicans, particularly those in exile, were all the more intransigent as they believed the Empire would not last: they resolutely opposed all participation in elections, and *a fortiori* the oath required of members of the Legislative Body. In France itself, while there were regions such as the Isère in which the generational conflict was hardly visible, in others, most notably in Paris, the older republicans – the idealists, willing to abide by what the exiles prescribed – clashed with younger, more realistic colleagues. This dispute came into the open during the elections of 1857, but as early as 11 May 1855, Emile Ollivier, although himself the son of an exile, observed in his diary:

> The republican party, such as it has constantly manifested itself to this day, has displayed two very serious faults. The first is that it has always confined itself to the realm of the absolute...; the second, that it has always appeared unaware...of the existence of an art of life, which consists in knowing the ways of dealing with men.[13]

During these silent years, the republicans acted very unobtrusively, confining their actions to demonstrations organized at burials of members of their camp, plots discovered by informers or assassination attempts against the emperor often inspired from abroad. But an underground activity was deployed with the aim of introducing into France clandestine literature (such as Victor Hugo's *Les Châtiments*) that customs officers tried to stop at the borders. An invisible and unrelenting effort was made, especially in Lille, to peddle these seditious writings and recruit new sympathizers in taverns and elsewhere. In the end, the republican ideology was making renewed progress.

### The regime's policy course and the Crimean War

Governing a country in which the opposition counted for so little and political life appeared to be at a standstill seemingly posed few problems. This somewhat misleading impression was due to the surveillance that was exercised over the means of expression and that virtually forbade the press from discussing politics. In reality, by means of a number of polemics ostensibly concerning history, religion or events abroad, a continuing discussion was being pursued on the proper course to be followed by the regime.

Bonapartism brought together elements of widely differing origins – democrats, Orleanists and so on. Furthermore, for having crushed the 'reds', it drew the encumbering support of certain 'whites' – outspoken opponents of the Revolution's achievements, staunch followers of the reactionary philosophy expressed by Joseph de Maistre, intransigent Catholics. Among these was Veuillot, who thundered against all aspects of modern society, the 'abominations of industry' and science, political and religious liberalism, the bourgeois spirit and so on. Taking advantage of their opponents' crushing defeat and of the opportunity left open to them to speak up, these extremists urged the emperor to follow their advice. But the pro-government camp and its fringe primarily comprised good bourgeois, faithful to the revolutionary tradition, often Gallican, sometimes anti-clerical; they were convinced that Bonapartism contained a strong reformist element that was worth preserving. The emperor himself was attached to the principles of 1789; he had already refused to give in to the pretensions of the clergy on certain essential points (education, the Organic Articles); he also felt that if he countenanced a reinforcement of the 'reactionary tilt' involuntarily displayed by the regime in the course of the repression that followed the *coup d'état*, he would be in danger of 'being cut off from the masses', at least from the petty bourgeois who declared, along with Monsieur Homais: 'I am for the profession of faith of the Savoyard vicar and for the immortal principles of 1789'. In Paris itself, the most widely read daily was *Le Siècle*, a republican newspaper that had more or less rallied to the regime; its views were Voltairean and above all anti-clerical, its speciality being 'priest-gobbling' (*bouffer du curé*). Accordingly, the emperor made a series of imperceptible adjustments in order to preserve a balance among his supporters and keep to a middle course. He consistently refused to ban *Le Siècle* and often allowed the anti-clerical or liberal press to engage in low-keyed or violent polemics with its opponents, most notably *L'Univers*.

The figure of Béranger, one of the glories of his day, was the object of one such skirmish. Béranger's songs had exalted the Napoleonic legend. In his old age, he abstained from voicing any political opinion and denied being an imperialist. He typified the resigned republican, satisfied on the whole with the advent of the Empire, to the point of declaring around 1853: 'Don't you see that we have been delivered from the white flag forever? Don't you see this is the triumph of the revolution?' But Veuillot concentrated his attacks on the author of 'Le Dieu des bonnes gens', on the anti-clerical bourgeois who stood for everything he detested. In November 1853 *L'Univers* launched into a first polemic with *Le Siècle*, which defended the 'national poet' against 'these vile sermons'. In April 1855, *L'Univers* repeated its scathing attacks, to which *Le Siècle* reacted forcefully. This time, the government, which was trying to substantiate the notion that the old poet was favourable to the regime, intervened. Summoned by the director of the Sûreté, Veuillot was advised to cease his attacks against 'this worthy old man'. There was no aftermath to the incident, but Veuillot vented his rancour in a letter in which he complained of the existence in the administration of 'a number of low-class rascals recruited from the republican party'; his relations with the government – which was determined not to swing towards reaction – became chilly.[14]

Foreign policy was to provide the opportunity for the regime to confirm its course and for polemics to be revived. As early as 24 May 1853, Napoleon III invited Britain to conclude an entente aimed at supporting the Ottoman Empire against Russia; with the outbreak of hostilities between Russians and Turks, France and Britain declared war on the tsar on 27 March 1854. What were the emperor's aims in committing his country – then in deep financial trouble – to such an adventure? He does not seem to have acted in order to satisfy Catholic circles (the question of the Holy Places had been settled in the meantime), and even less out of economic motives. Pursuing a more distant aim – the revision of the treaties of 1815 – the emperor, by intervening against the pillar of reaction, sought to secure the support of liberal Britain for the future and to break up the entente among the conservative powers (Russia, Prussia and Austria) – in short, to clear the ground so as to have a free hand for his later moves.

After the failure of the expeditionary force sent to the Dobruja, operations were shifted to the Crimea. French troops, commanded first by Saint-Arnaud (soon a victim of cholera), then by Canrobert and finally by Pélissier, had to endure harsh sufferings during the interminable siege of Sebastopol, especially as the supply corps proved to be very inadequate. The emperor, who transmitted his orders by electric telegraph, contemplated going to the spot to take command of the troops, and abandoned the idea only at his ministers' entreaties. On 10 September 1855, the allies finally entered Sebastopol, but were incapable of striking a decisive blow against Russia. Austria's mediation and the accession of a new tsar led to the conclusion of the war on 18 January 1856; all the belligerents met at the Congress of Paris, held from 26 February to 30 March of that year.

Although French opinion had not called for a war in the east, the conflict was fairly popular at first not only among Catholics, who saw it as a crusade against Russia, but among a number of liberals and even republicans with Béranger-style patriotic feelings. But controversies soon developed: businessmen and peasants thought it was time to stop, whereas Catholics, who also favoured a compromise peace, called for a rapprochement with Austria (which had just signed a concordat with the Pope). This, it was thought, would ensure the emergence of a conservative bastion in Europe, the 'Holy League' denounced by *Le Siècle* – which advocated instead a revolutionary war to be waged in Poland, Italy and elsewhere. Napoleon III appeared to be on the verge of opting for the second solution, since in May 1855 he dismissed his Minister of Foreign Affairs, Drouyn de Lhuys, an advocate of the conservative solution, and brought Cavour's Piedmont, an irreconcilable foe of Austria, into the anti-Russian alliance. Later, when it was learned that in the course of the 'revolutionary' session of 8 April 1856 Cavour succeeded – with British and French support – in bringing the Italian question before the Congress, the controversies became 'sharp and protracted'. Throughout this affair,

Napoleon III's policy remained ambiguous. Out of fidelity to the principles of 1789 – by which he meant the fall of the *ancien régime* in all of Europe – he was led to align himself with Britain and Piedmont rather than draw closer to Austria. In so doing, he took a distinctly 'leftward' turn in 1855, thus forfeiting the support of *L'Univers* and, more generally, that of his most determined followers at the time of the *coup d'état*. Nevertheless, he did not intend to satisfy all the revolutionary demands voiced in *Le Siècle*. Between the 'whites' and the 'reds', Napoleon sought to be 'blue'. The middle course he tried to follow tended instead to draw him closer to the liberal-leaning *Journal des Débats* and *Revue des Deux Mondes*; paradoxically, however, this condemned him to give his support abroad to the very liberals whom he was fighting in France itself.

All the same, the emperor's achievement was overwhelming: by convening the Congress of Paris, he had taken a spectacular revenge on those European nations that had recognized the Empire with bad grace and subjected him personally to a humiliating 'matrimonial blockade'. His good relations with Britain had enabled him to split the front of the conservative monarchies, and he now proceeded to draw closer to Russia. Yet he failed to obtain any tangible benefits, and the treaties of 1815 were left untouched. Some time later, according to Emile Ollivier, he confided to his ministers:

> The Empire is still a recent creation; it is subject to the tribulations of childhood; the Empire is visibly strong and flourishing, but people are waiting for it to undergo the test of its primal, hereditary and fatal disease, which I shall call the reaction to the 1815 treaties. So long as the European crisis predicted for the past forty years has not arrived, no one will enjoy the present or believe in the future. The eastern war could have been the expected revolution, and it was with that hope in mind that I waged it. Great territorial changes could have taken place as a result, had not Austria's indecision and the slow pace of military operations reduced to mere jousting the seeds of a great political revolution.[15]

On the domestic front, the situation was brilliant. At the time of the World Fair of 1855, the Congress of Paris and the birth of the imperial prince (March 1856), the regime seemed to have reached its apogee, and the *fête impériale* an acme of splendour. Order reigned everywhere. Disproving the pronouncements of Guizot, exiled republicans and Marx, who had predicted its swift and catastrophic downfall, the Empire succeeded in surviving and acquired the temporal dimension that made it a regime, not a mere episode. The government issued an increasing number of decrees concerning economic matters; the emperor's concern with social issues took the form of measures in favour of mutual aid societies, poor houses, working-class housing and so on; an attempt was made to enact a reform of secondary education devised by Fortoul, which called at the end of the *quatrième* for 'students to branch off into a literary section or a scientific section' (*bifurcation*). Yet, particularly if one compares this period to the years that preceded or were to follow it, one observes that this strong regime did little in the way of innovation, as if its only aim were to maintain order. There were no spectacular decisions taken to implement a 'Napoleonic idea', as if Napoleon III were being restrained by his conservative backers, whom he felt strong enough to resist but not yet to provoke.

## 2. The phase of initiative

### The elections of 1857

Napoleon III decided to call an election in June 1857, thus shortening the life of the Legislative Body by nearly a year. The climate seemed favourable to him: had he not brought the French a glory that satisfied their pride, and a prosperity barely tarnished by the world monetary crisis? Perhaps he was impatient to sound out public opinion, with which he was determined to remain in harmony. The atmosphere was quite different from that of the 1852 elections, held in a terrorized country in the wake of a plebiscite. But – and the government was aware of this – the stakes this time were high. For the Minister of the Interior, Billault, 'it is essential that people should not say, in France and Europe, that the imperial government has lost ground among the masses'. The official candidates – chiefly incumbent deputies – were the beneficiaries of all forms of pressure, as described by the poet Ponsard, an opposition candidate in Vienne:

> Mayors, police commissioners and rural policemen made the rustic herd vote as they wished. Those who carried my ballots were arrested and my posters torn up; my ballots were seized in voters' hands and even in peasants' houses, after their occupants were subjected to threats of all kinds; mayors were promised fairs, churches, roads and relief for the victims of last year's floods.[16]

In the ranks of the opposition, a few legitimists tried their luck. The Orleanists, however, generally proclaimed their indifference to these 'administrative elections'. As for the republicans, while standing in some one hundred constituencies, they often deliberately let the official candidate stand against men who did not belong to their party, such as Ponsard, who was shocked above all by the climate of moral order – as he explained in his manifesto:

> Wherever one goes, the only talk nowadays is of authority, religion, morals and family, which means that people want to hold on to their property and to the consideration that goes with it...The bourgeois bore me with their brutal egoism and I much prefer to try out the unknown than return to healthy traditions.[17]

In Paris, the republicans decided to stand; after laborious negotiations, the manager of *Le Siècle*, Havin, succeeded in imposing the presence in their ranks – alongside the veterans of 1848 – of a few young candidates determined to take the oath, if elected, in order to have the right to sit in parliament. Among them were Emile Ollivier and Darimon.

The final result of the elections was cause for satisfaction for the government, its candidates having polled nearly 5.5 million votes, or 90 per cent of the total. Rural areas in particular 'voted well'. Nevertheless, the abstention rate remained high (35.5 per cent of registered voters). More worryingly, the republican opposition made inroads in several major towns, narrowly losing in Lille and winning a seat in Lyons. Above all, the republicans won 5 of the 10 Parisian constituencies (in the central and eastern parts of the capital). The 1858 by-elections gave the republicans two of the three Paris seats that had become vacant in the interval. Thus five republicans sat in the new Legislative Body: Emile Ollivier, Darimon, J. Favre, E. Picard and Hénon. By demonstrating the surprising persistence of the republican movement in the larger towns, these elections aroused the emperor's discontent and anger. Some ministers suggested, if not the abolition of universal suffrage (as Fould contemplated), at least a return to a repressive policy designed 'to nip agitation in the bud'.

### Orsini's assassination attempt and the law of general security

On the evening of 14 January 1858, on their way to the Opera (then located in Rue Le Peletier), the imperial couple escaped a lethal assassination attempt fomented by Felice Orsini, a native of Romagna. Orsini had hoped, by eliminating the emperor, to provoke a revolution in France that would have spread to Italy. Panic-stricken officials, realizing the extent to which the survival of the regime depended on that of the emperor, reacted with great violence. While relations with Britain – where the attempt had been prepared – chilled, the emperor was urged from all quarters to 'depart from his mercy'. The ministers called for an authoritarian reaction, and in several regions, particularly in working-class centres, the police and public prosecutors imposed a climate of intimidation and terror, and carried out several arrests.[18] Many saw this as a favourable opportunity to exploit the emotional reaction in the country with the aim of eradicating the virus that had wrongly been regarded as extinct and, since the elections, was once again provoking fear.

Napoleon III himself eventually lost his calm. At the same time as he set up a Privy Council to ensure the transfer of power in the event of his death, he allowed the enactment of a series of repressive measures, despite the failure of the investigation conducted on national territory to uncover any accomplices of Orsini. Several newspapers were banned and

*Le Siècle* was spared only as the result of Havin's personal appeal to the sovereign. Above all, as *Le Moniteur* put it, it was the army's duty to play 'a political role in times of crisis'. Accordingly, five marshals were appointed to supervise the prefects, while General Espinasse, a tough-minded officer who believed it was 'time for the good to find reassurance and for the wicked to tremble',* was appointed on 7 February Minister of the Interior and General Security. In a circular sent to each prefect, the minister ordered them to arrest a specified number of suspects in their *départements*. In order to systematize and legalize this repression, a law of general security was finally voted and promulgated on 27 February despite certain misgivings voiced in the Conseil d'Etat and the speeches of Ollivier and several conservative deputies in the Legislative Body. The law, soon called 'law of suspects', was aimed chiefly at the republicans; it stipulated that any individual having planned to act against the government was liable to a fine or imprisonment, and that anyone who had already been sentenced for political motives since 1848 could be arrested, deported and exiled without trial. From March onwards, however, the law – which was not abrogated until 1870 – seems to have been enforced only in a few exceptional instances (as in the Nièvre in 1858–9), and in June Napoleon III replaced Espinasse at the ministry. All in all, this brutal repression claimed some 430 victims, most of them sentenced to deportation to Algeria.

### Intervention in Italy to 1860: the break

Exploited in France against the republicans, the Orsini plot was used at the same time by the emperor as a starting-point for a curious campaign aimed at preparing chancelleries and French opinion for his intervention in the Italian peninsula. This process was plagued by hesitations and marked by a series of highly surprising developments. First, during Orsini's trial, his lawyer, the republican deputy Jules Favre, read to everyone's amazement a letter from the accused to the emperor begging him not to intervene against a possible rising of Italian patriots, as he had in 1849. The terms of the letter had no doubt been suggested to Orsini by the prefect of police Pietri (a Left Bonapartist); they were made public by J. Favre only with the emperor's permission, and were reproduced verbatim by *Le Moniteur*. As the sovereign could not go against his ministers and spare Orsini, the latter, before his execution, sent Napoleon III a second letter, which was passed on to Cavour and published in Turin. In addition, *Le Siècle* was soon allowed to reappear and engage in polemics on the subject of the miracles at Lourdes (which occurred in

---

* As the prince-president had put it in the wake of the events of 13 June 1849 (see Maurice Agulhon, *The Republican Experiment, 1848–1852*, trans. by Janet Lloyd (Cambridge, 1983), p. 100). (Trans.)

February 1858) and the temporal power of the Pope – also the favourite target of E. About's column in *Le Moniteur*.

In May 1858 the emperor conveyed to Cavour an invitation to meet him at Plombières, where he would be taking the waters. On 21 July, the meeting took place there in total secrecy, unbeknownst even to the ministers. Napoleon III made the unwritten promise to help liberate Italy from the Alps to the Adriatic with the aim of reconstructing it along federal lines; in exchange, he asked for Savoy and possibly Nice. The marriage of Prince Napoleon with the daughter of the king of Piedmont was to symbolize the planned alliance. Despite the chill response from Britain, the distrust of all the conservatives – whether Bonapartist or 'liberal' – and the reluctance of his ministers, Napoleon III concluded a defensive treaty with Piedmont on 10 December. An incident with the Austrian ambassador on 1 January 1859 at the reception of the diplomatic corps was followed by the publication of an unofficial pamphlet by La Guéronnière, *L'Empereur Napoléon III et l'Italie*, promising that France would keep revolution out of Italy while satisfying the Italians' national aspirations. After these portents of war, it was finally Austria that opened hostilities by attacking Piedmont (29 April).

Throughout this period, *Le Siècle* and *La Presse* were the only major newspapers to campaign in favour of French intervention in Italy. The liberal press and, even more so, the conservative papers were hesitant or hostile. As for the government-leaning press, it seemed to be acutely embarrassed. The 'enlightened classes' wanted peace, particularly businessmen, who became worried (the stock market fell), and Catholics (intransigents and liberals alike), who feared for the Pope's temporal power. Why then did the emperor enter into this conflict? To be sure, he had always felt a deep sympathy for the Italian cause, but he also saw this as an opportunity to consummate his break with the clericalists and conservatives and win over the urban masses, who were strongly attached to the nationhood principle. In January 1859 he endeavoured in the following terms to convince his ministers of the domestic and foreign benefits of the operation:

> If France, while driving the Austrians from Italy, protects the power of the Pope, if it opposes extreme policies [the 'middle course' once more] and declares that with the exception of Savoy and Nice it is not out for any conquest, then it will have the support of Europe...Public opinion in Europe will regard the French government not only as the anarchists' ogre, but as the regime determined to display its strength at home so as to be able to break its own bonds, to deliver and civilize nations...On the domestic front, the war will at first awaken great fears; traders and speculators of every stripe will shriek, but national sentiment will put paid to this domestic fright; the nation will be put to the test once more in a struggle that will stir many a heart, recall the memory of heroic

times and bring together under the mantle of glory parties that are steadily drifting away from one another day after day.[19]

On 10 May, the emperor, wishing to take personal command of his troops, left the Tuileries for the Gare de Lyon in combat dress. All along his route, he was cheered by the populace, who sang the 'Marseillaise'. Popular enthusiasm was undeniably sincere, even if the demonstration was prepared in advance.

The campaign was extremely short: after their victory at Magenta (4 June), the French troops, under the emperor's command, defeated the Austrians at Solferino in a bloody, confused and inconclusive battle. Then, suddenly, on 12 July, Napoleon III concluded a preliminary peace agreement at Villafranca, although it fell far short of fulfilling France's war aims or those of Piedmont, which annexed only Lombardy. The French sovereign had several motives for calling an abrupt halt to the operations. First, with the Prussian threat to mobilize along the Rhine, 'the war was about to assume proportions incommensurate with France's interest', as he put it. Second, while Napoleon III personally demonstrated greater strategic ability than has been stated, the French army's weaknesses were cruelly revealed: 'part of the cavalry became panic-stricken (on 25 June). This incident certainly upset Napoleon III. The victorious army could not inspire much confidence so far as further hostilities were concerned. As for the sanitary condition of the men and horses, it was deplorable.'[20] In France itself, whereas *Le Siècle* was urging the pursuit of a revolutionary war, the ministers wanted to limit its scope. Certain opponents, like Thiers, tried to exploit the anxiety of Catholics and the concern of 'all those who are no fonder of revolution in Europe than of revolution in France'. 'Villafranca marked the reconciliation of the emperor with the conservative party', Darimon noted.[21] Lastly, the emperor feared that the revolutionary process he had triggered in Italy by his intervention might lead him too far. On their return from Italy, the troops paraded to popular applause on 15 August, Saint Napoleon's day.

In central Italy, however, even in Romagna (which was part of the Papal States), constituent assemblies proclaimed the inhabitants' desire to be annexed to Piedmont. Napoleon III took the initiative once more by arranging for the publication on 22 December 1859 of a new unofficial brochure by La Guéronnière, *Le Pape et le Congrès*, in which he advised Pius IX to help solve the national problem by agreeing to the dismemberment of his States. But the Pope condemned the brochure, and in March Napoleon III allowed Piedmont to annex the insurgent territories (Romagna included), in exchange for handing over Nice and Savoy to France. This transfer was conditional on the consent of the local population, which voted overwhelmingly in favour in April. The emperor thus regained a measure of popularity, except among Catholics.

### The *customs* coup d'état

Despite his long-standing support for free-trade ideas, and the Pereires' efforts to make him put those ideas into practice, Napoleon III had so far hesitated to do so, knowing how strongly French industrialists – with a very few exceptions – espoused protectionism. In October 1859, Michel Chevalier, seemingly on his own initiative, held a series of decisive talks in Britain, returning to France with Cobden, the apostle of free trade. The two men were received by Napoleon III, who welcomed their proposals. The timing seemed right to him: it was in his interest to improve his relations with Britain while he was still involved in the Italian imbroglio; he also wanted to slow the rise in prices that drew complaints from consumers, and to help industrialists and railway companies to purchase equipment at low cost – in short, to restimulate an economic expansion that was apparently running out of steam. A round of negotiations briskly conducted by Rouher and Chevalier led to a draft treaty that was examined in a cabinet meeting and, despite opposition from Magne and Walewski, adopted by the emperor. At the same time as a vast programme of public works was announced, *Le Moniteur* of 15 January 1860 published a letter from the emperor dated 5 January informing the country of the treaty, to be signed on the 23rd. Some have spoken of this episode as a 'customs *coup d'état*', for this very well-kept secret came as a total surprise. The Legislative Body was not consulted, but the emperor, since 1852, was perfectly entitled to conclude a commercial treaty single-handedly.

The treaty, signed for a ten-year period, involved concessions by both countries: France abolished all import bans, exonerated most raw materials and foodstuffs from customs rates, and fixed *ad valorem* duties on manufactured goods and coal that were not to exceed 30 per cent (25 per cent from 1864); the United Kingdom agreed to let in a great number of finished products duty-free and drastically reduced its wine tax. No doubt this was not a true free-trade agreement, but in a country as strongly protectionist as France had been until then, it provoked a customs revolution. The treaty was followed by a series of commercial agreements with most European nations (with Prussia in 1862) and by a number of decrees that freed exchanges for the older colonies.

### Foreign ventures

Colonial expansion was actively pursued during the Second Empire, although the emperor did not follow a coherent plan. In Senegal, Faidherbe, appointed governor in 1854 at the request of oil producers in Bordeaux, enlarged the colony and developed peanut production there; in the Levant, Napoleon III intervened to protect the Catholic Maronites (this expedition also fulfilled the expectations of the silk makers in Lyons, who hoped to find a supply of raw silk in the area); in the Far East, in order to protect endangered Catholic missionaries, French sailors occupied Saigon (1859) and later Cochin-China, moving on both towards Cambodia (which placed itself under France's protection in 1863) and in the direction of the gigantic Chinese market (exploration of Laos by Doudart de Lagrée, 1866–8). The surface area of French colonial possessions eventually tripled.

Governing and administering these colonies raised complex problems, particularly in the case of Algeria, now fully conquered after the submission of Kabylia in 1857.[22] Efforts were undertaken to equip the country (for instance by building railways), and plans were made to carry out irrigation work and introduce new crops. At certain points the French sponsored the establishment of major concessionary companies, which were supposed to assume responsibility for public works but often failed in their mission. Without going into the details of Algeria's political evolution, one can say that the emperor at first displayed little concern for the country, allowing the military to conduct an authoritarian policy. He then unsuccessfully experimented with a Ministry for Algeria and the Colonies, entrusted in 1858 to Prince Napoleon, who resigned nine months later. But, from 1860 on, Napoleon III gradually came to envisage new types of relations between the Algerians and France. This 'Napoleonic idea' came into sharper focus after the emperor's visit to Algeria in September 1860; inspiration was also provided by certain Saint-Simonians. Napoleon III's innate generosity seemed to prompt his interest in the fate of the Moslems. At Algiers, he declared:

> Our first duty is to look after the well-being of three million Arabs whom the fate of arms has placed under our domination...To raise the Arabs to the dignity of free men, bestow education upon them while respecting their religion, improve their existence by extracting from this land all the treasures that Providence has buried in it - such is our mission.

This speech was shortly followed by the senatus consultum of 22 April, which made the tribes 'the inalienable proprietors of their lands'; a further senatus consultum of 14 July 1865 left 'the Algerians free to choose French citizenship while granting them unconditional enjoyment of French civil rights: [it] represents perhaps the most liberal measure of our colonial legislation'.[23] Finally, the emperor contemplated transforming Algeria into a protectorate whose government would be entrusted to the great Moslem chiefs – an 'Arab kingdom'. This policy – an extremely liberal one for its time – was astonishingly bold. But it was barely implemented, and one can regard it as a failure. The emperor had to contend with hostility from established authorities, rivalry between civilians and soldiers and, above all, the settlers' resolve to drive out the natives and appropriate their lands.

'The kingdom's grand design' may have concerned Mexico. By 1858, according to Schefer,[24] Napoleon III was directly preoccupied by his Mexican plan, and the expedition itself lasted from 1861 to 1867. The facts are familiar: Mexico, torn by a civil war between Catholics and anti-clerical liberals, ceased to pay its debts; accordingly, France, Britain and Spain embarked on a joint military expedition aimed at protecting their nationals' interests, but the British and Spanish withdrew almost immediately. French troops under Bazaine advanced with difficulty to Mexico City, where they stayed on to protect the new emperor of Mexico, Archduke Maximilian. But in 1866–7, under pressure from the United States, Napoleon III ordered their evacuation, soon followed by Maximilian's execution. Why this involvement in a costly and distant expedition, in a country where French interests were seemingly so minor? It is doubtful whether the intervention of Morny, who had a stake in the debts to be collected by the Swiss banker Jecker, carried very much weight in the emperor's decision. Nor is Napoleon III's desire to please his Catholic subjects a sufficient explanation. Economic aims were not absent: well before his accession, Napoleon III had dreamed of an inter-oceanic canal (a cherished scheme of the Saint-Simonians) across Mexico, a country whose wealth he exaggerated; and would it not be an ideal market for France? No doubt he also felt a desire to increase prosperity not only in France, but also throughout the world, most notably in countries with a Latin civilization. Summing up recent interpretations of this not yet fully elucidated problem, one historian recently concluded:

> Latinity [was] the conquering Napoleonic ideology...Napoleon III wanted to establish French greatness in the world by forcing countries, if need be, to accept the well-being and progress that emanated from France, heart of universality; this domination was not self-interested, but altruistic, in the best Saint-Simonian spirit. While Mexico had rejected it, Africa, instead, had recognized it...[25]

### Towards a more liberal regime

On the domestic front, the emperor made a few moves towards liberalization in small successive doses. In an attempt to ingratiate himself with the republicans, he issued a decree on 15 August 1859 granting 'full and total amnesty to all persons condemned for political crimes and offences or subjected to general security measures'. The exiles came home, except for a few die-hards like Quinet and Hugo.

Next, the decree of 24 November 1860 came as a surprise first of all to the ministers (who learned about it only on the 22nd) and to public opinion, for it brought about the first change in the Constitution: henceforth, in response to the emperor's speech at the opening session, the Legislative Body and also the Senate were to discuss each year the terms of an address; furthermore, the emperor would designate ministers without portfolio to defend and explain government policy before the two assemblies. Thus the deputies would once again be put in the presence of ministers – admittedly of men specialized in this task. *Le Moniteur* and all the newspapers were allowed to publish full stenographic transcripts of debates in the two assemblies: the country was no longer kept in the dark about these proceedings.

Lastly, readers of *Le Moniteur* of 15 November 1861 had the surprise of finding both a long letter sent to the emperor from Tarbes by Fould, in which he sharply criticized over-expenditure, and a reply from Napoleon III, who approved the terms of Fould's indictment, appointed him Minister of Finance and entrusted him with the task of reform. This led to the senatus consultum of 31 December 1861, whereby the government renounced the practice of raising supplementary and special funds by decree without a vote by the Legislative Body, and the deputies were to vote the budget no longer by ministry but by section – a move that increased their control.

The impact of these reforms must not be exaggerated: this was still a far cry from a parliamentarian or liberal regime, and Fould was the first to concoct misleading budgets, in this case to conceal the heavy costs of the Mexican expedition. However, it is interesting to observe that the emperor was not obliged to make these concessions by public opinion; he acted entirely on his own initiative. Why then did he alter the Constitution, even as little as he did? Was it in order to move in very gradual steps towards the crowning of the edifice? Or rather to take into account a situation that was changing because of his other initiatives? He perceived the criticisms being voiced, and foresaw that they would gain in intensity. By granting minor satisfactions to the republicans, the conservatives – who might be tempted by Orleanism – and the *budgétaires*, he hoped to forestall the dangers already visible on the horizon.

# 6

# Decline and fall

## 1. Deterioration (1858–63)

### Causes

Although in the early 1860s the regime was still basking in glory and power, it later experienced increasing difficulties. Admittedly, its decline was not continuous, and the *fête impériale* often shone with all its usual splendour, for example at the World Fair of 1867. However, as Napoleon III put it that very same year, 'problems have appeared on the horizon and are beclouding it', and the government seemed to have ever greater difficulty controlling the general situation.

First, the emperor, on whom everything rested, was governing with a weaker hand. He was subject to increasingly frequent attacks of the stone (lithiasis) – from which he had long been suffering – and appeared to his entourage to be 'prematurely aged'. As he had also begun, in 1860, to write a *Life of Caesar*, a very time-consuming project despite the assistance of Victor Duruy, his presence became more and more 'intermittent', and he left greater initiative to his ministers. But the cabinet, now composed of ageing men, would have liked to preserve the status quo, and had difficulty adapting to new circumstances.

Furthermore, passing time sapped the original foundations of the regime: the Empire had derived its initial strength from the failure of the Second Republic and from the fear of 'anarchy'. These memories and arguments were losing their hold over men who were beginning to forget the past; they had no effect on the new generation, which, being far more concerned with the constraints of the present, aspired both to a freedom whose risks it had not experienced and to greater social equality. Thus the young bourgeois turned away from the Empire, as the Bonapartist Granier de Cassagnac observed: 'Just try to find the ambitious young men who are embarking on a conservative career, and give us their names! You won't find any. The opposition is taking in, gathering, assembling everyone.' Moreover, the regime had devoted scant attention to the task of training its future personnel among the younger generation.

152

The new currents of thought developed on the sidelines of the regime, often simultaneously in opposition to it and to the Church, which the Empire was accused of having excessively favoured. The rising generation, resolutely positivistic, not only spoke out against a Church whose head condemned the modern world with intransigence but also refused to support the Empire. This was even true of Renan, who had rallied in 1860, and been rewarded for it by the Legion of Honour and a chair at the Collège de France. For having in his inaugural lecture referred to Jesus as an 'incomparable man' – which caused an immense scandal among the conservatives – Renan was barred from giving his course, and later removed. He refused all new appointments and all compensation from the government. 'Pecunia tua tecum sit', he replied – keep your money. And he sent his colleagues a letter of explanation that contains the most clear-cut definition of what the human sciences ought to be: 'If there is', he proclaimed, 'a history forbidden to criticism and set aside as divine, then historical science ceases to exist.'[1] Taine, for his part, came across as a liberal, hostile to the Second Empire: he abhorred plebiscitary democracy, was favourable to decentralization and admired British institutions. Many other celebrated anti-clericals like Littré had espoused the republican cause.

The ideas of the free-thinkers were spread by organizations such as freemasonry, which, after a period of decline prior to 1861, augmented its influence considerably and took in a growing number of republicans recruited among lower-ranking local notables. In the Isère, the administration regarded most masonic dignitaries as 'belonging to the advanced party'.[2] While the lodges often abstained from open political intervention, they enabled the regime's opponents to band together.

At the same time, the international situation and the economic climate worsened, and the Empire seemed indeed to have lost the lucky star that had so favoured it at the outset. In the foreign sphere, the army was unable to impose victory in Mexico, and its failures, gradually denounced by the opposition, eventually made public opinion – which had never been in favour of the expedition – aware of the Empire's decline. The American Civil War and the succession of crises in Europe (the Italian conflicts, the rising of the Poles, whom Napoleon III had eagerly wanted to assist by an intervention, the Schleswig–Holstein affair, the Austro–Prussian war of 1866) perpetuated an unhealthy climate. Admittedly, France eventually did not take part in any major European war, but public opinion lived in a state of uncertainty, indeed anxiety, fearing an unforeseen initiative by this surprise-prone sovereign. Furthermore, economic prosperity, hitherto one of the regime's great propaganda themes, was suffering a number of setbacks. The cotton shortage brought many firms to a standstill, especially in Normandy, and the bankruptcy of Mirès, followed by the difficulties of the Pereires, rebounded on the regime. At the same time, as we shall see, the working class was stirring once again: the Empire was no longer even maintaining social order.

Lastly, what worked against the emperor was the fact that, by a deluge of personal initiatives, most notably his intervention in Italy and in customs policy, he had breached the tacit contract that tied him to his conservative supporters. The latter had accepted, not without distrust, a constable-emperor, provided he did not go against their convictions or interests. At the very least, they were determined not to allow him to commit new violations.

### Facing the rising tide of opposition

The anxiety displayed by many Catholics at the first announcement of the emperor's intervention in Italy turned to wrath when the integrity of the Papal States was breached. Their emotion reached a peak when Piedmontese troops – with no reaction from the imperial government – invaded the Marche and Umbria, scattering at Castelfidardo the Papal zouaves commanded by Lamoricière (many of these volunteers were young French legitimists). The Pope's only remaining possession was the region of Rome, where French troops were protecting him – but for how much longer? Accordingly, the Catholics organized the first open campaign of criticism directed against the emperor's policy. This agitation took the form of pastorals issued by certain bishops, the organization of petitions sent to the Senate and the publication of pamphlets; *L'Univers* did its best to ignite the lower clergy in the more Catholic regions. In the Legislative Body itself, some Catholic deputies, despite their having been elected as official candidates, took advantage of the slightest opportunity to conduct full-scale interpellations* on the subject of the government's Italian policy. The discussion on the opening address in January 1861 enabled them to state their case; one of them, Keller, enjoined the government to abandon its equivocal policy once and for all: 'Are you revolutionaries? Are you conservatives?' In the course of the debate, a vote on the Roman question produced but a narrow majority for the government in the Legislative Body (161 for, 91 against), and an even more slender one in the Senate (79 to 61).

Taken aback by this unrest, the government reacted. Rouland conducted a narrowly Gallican policy, hampering the development of religious orders by a strict enforcement of the laws concerning them. The exceptional advantages hitherto enjoyed by the clergy were abolished for good. The government now issued warnings to the Catholic press, and by

* Interpellation: formal demand by member(s) of French parliament in public session for explanation of government policy or ministerial conduct. (Trans.)

January 1860 it had banned *L'Univers*. Finally, Persigny, back in the Ministry of the Interior, launched a brutal attack on the Society of Saint-Vincent-de-Paul: this lay association devoted to charity – which, however, included a number of legitimists and clericalists – was ordered to expel its most hostile members and to accept, just as the freemasonry had, a government-appointed president. As it refused to comply, several hundred of its chapters, scattered throughout the country, were suppressed.

Yet the government did not want to drive to the wall a clergy whose support it still needed. Conversely, clerical agitation was often aimed less at overthrowing the regime than at putting pressure on its policy. In the ranks of the episcopate, violent outbursts such as those of Monseigneur Pie remained the exception. Many moderate bishops, little inclined to break with the authorities, behaved like the bishop of Bayonne, who first contented himself with private entreaties before publicly voicing his emotion on Christmas Day of 1859 – although he refrained from openly attacking the government. Even the lower clergy, despite its growing ultramontanist feelings and – in this same *département* – its espousal of legitimism, often conducted only a very peaceful form of opposition, for 'despite everything, it was even more fearful of the republican alternative'.[3] And on the whole, the violent opposition of certain clericalists met with only limited response in the country at large, for the popularity of the Pope's cause was still confined to a minority of Catholics.

The irritation of protectionist groups also helped to splinter the government majority in the Legislative Body. The discussion of bills designed to complete the treaty of 1860 thus enabled a minority of deputies, in particular the Norman industrialist Pouyer-Quertier, to air their grievances on the subject. To be sure, opposition from employers was not unanimous. The industrialists of the Dauphiné, for instance, were rather happy about free-trade agreements that might favour the glove, silk and paper industries. And while furious protectionists blamed the treaty for the slightest economic difficulty leading to unemployment, the masses were still fairly impervious to such propaganda. Although less visible than clerical opposition, the hostility of these protectionists – who were doubtless more anxious to prevent the emperor from harming their interests than desirous of replacing him – was a force to be reckoned with. It is likely that the protectionists often supplied the revived opposition with the funds it needed for its campaigns.

Within the ranks of the 'government' majority itself, 'the Italian affair and the commercial treaty loosened tongues', Emile Ollivier observed. The emperor was thus deprived of the apparently unconditional support of those conservatives who had backed the regime from its inception. Whether they were intransigent protectionists or staunch clericalists – and fairly often they were one and the same – they began to think that had they allowed him less room for manoeuvring, they could have prevented the moves they were now criticizing. In their newly-found distrust, they sought to curtail the emperor's personal powers; they therefore had to obtain parliamentary guarantees, and consequently the word 'freedom' regained all its attractiveness in their eyes.

But at this point the liberal opponents, who were previously isolated and had merely represented a distinguished coterie, discerned an unhoped-for opportunity to win back a larger audience among the 'better-off classes'. Recovering their courage, they did their best to take advantage of the situation. The better to lure disgruntled conservatives, they ably displayed their protectionist beliefs or soft-pedalled their free-trade sympathies. Even more astonishing appeared to be their support for the temporal power of the Pope, suddenly expressed by Protestants like Guizot or spiritualists like Victor Cousin, Villemain and Thiers – who was obviously preparing his political comeback. It is also curious to find Prévost-Paradol among the defenders of the Society of Saint-Vincent-de-Paul. Sensing that these liberal opponents could cleverly win over many restless conservatives, and that they therefore constituted a potentially dangerous threat, the government sought to put an end to the pamphlet campaign organized by the Orleanists and to censor their articles in the press. At the same time, Persigny attempted to woo these selfsame Orleanists by asking his prefects to 'show the notabilities of earlier governments the consideration they deserve' – but his policy was a total failure.

### The elections of 1863

The legislative elections were to serve as a means of measuring the extent of the political thaw. By early 1863, even before the opening of the election campaign (10–31 May), the situation seemed very complex. There were three hundred opposition candidates, representing a broad spectrum of opinions. Although they often combined their efforts, they pursued widely divergent goals. Some were irreconcilable adversaries of the Empire and determined to overthrow it. This was the case of the legitimists who, contravening the orders of the Comte de Chambord, stood for election; of prominent Orleanists who, like Rémusat or, in the Isère, Auguste Casimir-Perier (son of the ex-premier), now openly plunged into the struggle. Both camps were joined by the more intransigent clericalists. The republicans especially stood in great numbers, despite the senatus consultum of 1858, which, by requiring all candidates (and not just those elected) to take the oath, posed an awkward problem of conscience for many: Proudhon came out in favour of a blank vote, while, from London, Ledru-Rollin preached abstention. In the provinces, the designation of republican candidates caused no serious difficulties, but in Paris protracted manoeuvring pitted the veterans of 1848, the few supporters of working-class candidacies, incumbent deputies and newspaper managers against one another. Eventually, a list of nine names was drawn up that included in particular the incumbents (Ollivier, Darimon, J. Favre and E. Picard), Havin, manager of *Le Siècle*, J. Simon (despite his earlier fierce hostility to taking the oath) and also Thiers, chosen not without hesitation because of his attitude under the Second Republic. Lastly, other candidates, also standing as opponents, were above all champions of freedom and, not being overly concerned with the form of the regime, remained on the whole rather inclined to accept the Empire providing it underwent major changes. This was the attitude of the 'independent' candidates, chiefly Catholics or protectionists. They shared with many Orleanists a desire to see the establishment of a vast 'liberal union' extending from the more moderate republicans to parliamentarian legitimists. But for the time being the creation of this alliance was still blocked by dissensions focusing most notably on the Roman question.

As for the choice of official candidates, it turned out to be a complex matter. Persigny would have liked to sponsor only unswerving loyalists, but he was finally obliged to accept, alongside the unconditional supporters of the imperial dictatorship who were now being called 'the Mamelukes', a number of less compliant men, more open to liberal ideas. He sought at least to obtain by every possible means the election of his candidates: he clamped down on the opposition press with renewed rigour, and sent out pressing circulars to his prefects enjoining them to bring into play all the mechanisms of the official candidacy. The pamphlet entitled *Les Elections de 1863*, by Jules Ferry, then a young lawyer, describes all the administrative pressures exerted in rural areas. Nevertheless, in a fairly frequent number of instances, prefects and, even more so, mayors, civil servants and priests displayed less zeal than previously for government candidates, and the latter made a point of proclaiming their independence. All in all, this election was less firmly managed than the earlier ones, especially in the towns.

The outcome unquestionably constituted a partial defeat for the government (Table 21).

Despite the increase in the number of voters and, especially, the sizeable drop in the abstention rate (27 per cent instead of 35.5 per cent in 1857), government candidates polled slightly fewer votes, while opposition candidates scored a combined total of three times as many votes. But their gains can be partly explained by the participation of voters who had abstained in 1857 for lack of an anti-government candidate in their constituency. In the event, there was no opposition landslide, at least in rural France, which by and large remained loyal to the Empire despite some inroads of republican ideology in the east and south-east and clerical influence in the west. However, the opposition carried nearly all the major towns, including Marseilles, Lyons, Lille, Bordeaux and Toulouse. And the nine seats in Paris were won by the republican 'list', which obtained 63 per cent of the votes. While Orleanist leaders were roundly defeated in many constituencies (these 'distinguished men' remained rather unpopular), the republicans, who emerged as the true winners, captured 17 seats, to which should be added the 15 'independent' deputies elected. Thanks to the mechanism of elections on a majority basis, the Legislative Body remained composed primarily of official candidates. But many of these owed their election to Catholic or conservative votes, and the government could no longer count on their compliance as easily as in the past.

Table 21. *Results of the legislative elections*

|                        | 1852       | 1857       | 1863       | 1869        |
|------------------------|------------|------------|------------|-------------|
| Registered voters      | 9,836,000  | 9,490,000  | 9,938,000  | 10,417,000  |
| For the government     | 5,248,000  | 5,471,000  | 5,308,000  | 4,438,000   |
| Against the government | 810,000    | 665,000    | 1,954,000  | 3,335,000   |
| Abstentions            | 3,613,000  | 3,372,000  | 2,713,000  | 2,291,000   |

*Source:* Dansette (**1**), p. 441.

## 2. The regime's failures

### An uncertain policy

While the republicans and liberals hoped that the progress of primary education and the propaganda of emergent social groups (doctors, apothecaries, notaries and so on) would eventually enable them to win over the rural population, the regime's supporters were in total disagreement over the proper way to stem the rise of the opposition. Some advocated a return to a more authoritarian policy, while others favoured further concessions to satisfy the moderate opposition. In June 1863, the emperor dismissed Persigny and carried out a sweeping cabinet reshuffle. At the same time, he replaced the ministers without portfolio with a single Minister of State to act as his spokesman before the assemblies. This move was intended to establish a dialogue between the government, represented by the Minister of State, and the deputies. But the emperor was reluctant to go any further.

Morny, however, persisted in his efforts to transform the regime. He was convinced, as he wrote to his half-brother after the elections, that only 'two forces remain: the emperor and democracy. Democracy will steadily gain strength; it is urgent to satisfy it if we do not want to be swept away by it.'[4] Therefore it was necessary to implement genuinely liberal reforms, and to grant deputies the right of interpellation and amendment. For Morny, institutional change would be carried out by a great coalition government (*ministère de fusion*), in which he dreamed of bringing in representatives of every political current. Hence his show of politeness towards 'illustrious former parliamentarians', whom he looked forward to finding in the new Legislative Body; hence, too, his much earlier attempts to woo the republican 'five'. Morny had paved the way for Emile Ollivier's switch to the government camp. The process had begun in 1861 when Ollivier, frightened by the speech of the clericalist Keller, was moved to offer the emperor his conditional support. In 1862, Morny informed Ollivier of his plans and invited him to be the spokesman of his future cabinet. Finally, in 1864, Morny secured Ollivier's appointment as rapporteur for the law authorizing trade unions (*droit de coalition*), thus making him break publicly with his republican friends. But Morny died in March 1865, and this put an end to liberalization. Henceforth, and until 1869, the most influential man was Rouher, the minister without portfolio. Enjoying both the support of a clientele of intimates – whom he succeeded in appointing everywhere – and the favour of Napoleon III, 'his position depended solely on the emperor's will, which he himself all too often controlled' (Maupas). While Rouher probably had no deep-seated political beliefs, his authoritarian temperament made him both little inclined towards liberal reforms and jealous of a now isolated Emile Ollivier. By refusing new concessions, he displeased all the opposition groups, whose 'common programme' comprised the five 'necessary freedoms' demanded by Thiers in a major speech of January 1864: personal liberties, freedom of the press, free elections, right of interpellation and ministerial responsibility. Nevertheless, in the ranks of pro-government deputies, a new current was emerging, soon to be known as the third party: it brought together a number of official candidates who were genuine Bonapartists and strongly conservative, but liberal and parliamentarian by temperament. They too wished to check the emperor's initiatives in order to avoid any unpleasant surprises in foreign, religious or economic policy. Disappointed by the absence of new reforms, they tabled an amendment to the address in January 1866 which obtained 45 votes; in it they called for 'our institutions to advance wisely' towards a greater liberalism.

### The failure of social policy

Both generosity and calculation no doubt prompted Napoleon III in the early 1860s to embark on a new and relatively bold social policy. He had always felt a sincere desire to alleviate the poverty of the working masses, but until then he had done almost nothing for them. Was it not time now to seek their support, even as the 'upper classes' were increasingly distrustful of the Empire?

During the years of dictatorship, the labour movement survived. Mutual aid societies were founded, which, despite the precautions taken, frequently served as fronts for resistance societies, for working-class action continued to take the form of fairly frequent strikes (109 of them were followed by legal prosecution in 1853, 73 in 1856). At the same time, despite the regime's claims to have eliminated socialism, working-class ideology was advancing and evolving: the great surges of generosity of 1848 had lost their appeal as workers became concerned more with their professional fate than with the task of building a new society. They were also influenced by the ideas forcefully advocated by Proudhon, who advised the workers to concentrate on solving their own problems by themselves without bringing in the government or the opposition. Proudhon's anarchist and mutual-aid programme called for self-management of the masses and a pluralist and decentralized collectivism that he called 'industrial-agricultural democracy'.

The attempt to woo the working classes was made by the agency of the so-called Palais Royal group, in which Prince Napoleon figured prominently; its membership included both former Saint-Simonians (M. Chevalier) and publicists. The group published articles in newspapers such as *L'Opinion Nationale* and put out inexpensive, orange-coloured pamphlets. The first of these, *L'Empereur, le Peuple et les Anciens Partis*, presented Napoleon III as a popular prince with an inclination towards social reforms. Later, the group launched the idea of sending a delegation of workers to the London Exhibition of 1862; with the help of Tolain, a bronze-worker and great reader of Proudhon, it organized the election of delegates and contributed to their travel expenses. On their return, the delegates published their reports under the emperor's patronage, and availed themselves of the opportunity to demand the right of coalition and association already enjoyed by their British comrades.

In the 1863 elections and especially the by-elections of 1864, labour militants decided to field their own candidates, and, in order to refute the accusations of the republicans, sixty workers of the Seine issued a manifesto on 17 February 1864. This 'manifesto of the Sixty', 'the first class-based charter of a French labour movement on its way to adulthood',[5] proclaimed that the workers formed 'a special class of citizens requiring direct representation', but it did not discuss the question of political regime. Although a few of the Sixty, such as Tolain, were accused of being the creatures of the Palais Royal group, they were determined to keep at a distance from the regime.

Taking advantage of greater tolerance, militants organized producer and consumer co-operatives, set up numerous trade-unionist resistance societies and launched frequent strikes. Napoleon III pardoned the heavily sentenced leaders of a bitter strike by typographers (1862), and, in response to an appeal by Darimon, initiated a bill that eventually became the law of 25 May 1864, which made it legal for workers to form 'coalitions' provided the freedom to work was not infringed. But the successive waves of strikes that broke out in 1864, 1865 and 1867 soon posed the problem of the right of association and assembly, and called for new concessions. A circular from the Minister of the Interior of February 1866 advised prefects to display greater tolerance for strikers' meetings. Later, a letter from the Minister of Commerce of 21 March 1866, published in *Le Moniteur*, promised the same liberal attitude towards associations of a trade-unionist character. A law of the same year abrogated the article of the Code Civil that established the inequality of master and worker in the eyes of the law. In a related development, the International Working Men's Association, founded in 1864 as a result of contacts made at the London Exhibition of 1862, began to expand in France. According to Leroy-Beaulieu, who, it is true, was writing in 1871, 'in its early years [the International] was looked upon favourably in official circles; it was regarded as an ally. It was shown an ill-concealed tolerance. Thus it took root in the shadow of the regime.' It should be added that the emperor tried, without great success, to encourage the establishment of worker co-operatives, and sponsored a fund for popular associations intended as a source of loans to these co-operatives.

While workers made extensive use of their new rights, the working-class élite did not rally to the Empire – far from it. The failure of this very open-minded social policy was due to its overly paternalistic aspect, the people's harsh living conditions (particularly following the poor harvest of 1867) and the persistence of revolutionary memories and traditions, most notably in Paris. The first militants were often Proudhonians wary of joining in political struggles, but they were wrongly accused of sympathy for the regime. Furthermore, many workers were soon to be won over to the ideas of Blanqui, whose prestige was enhanced among these followers by his hatred of the Empire and by his revolutionary zeal. For having taken part in a republican demonstration over the tomb of the Italian Manin (late 1867), the Paris chapter of the International was disbanded and its leaders replaced by a more resolute team, from which moderate Proudhonians were excluded. The newcomers included Varlin, for whom 'political revolution and social revolution are intertwined and cannot do without each other'. Everywhere, members of the International and of labour societies rallied to the radical republican opposition.

*The failure of reform (1867–8)*

Disappointed by the failure of his attempt to woo the working classes, the emperor was obliged to mollify the ever more uneasy 'upper classes' – particularly business circles – who were increasingly worried by foreign developments and by the emperor's silence. The announcement of an alliance between Prussia and Italy – concluded, it was sensed, with the emperor's help – created apprehensions about a possible French intervention in a major European war. The subsequent triumph of the Prussians over the Austrians at Sadowa (3 July 1866), which came too suddenly for the emperor to impose his armed mediation, was regarded as a diplomatic defeat for France and a source of serious complications, since it raised the thorny question of the compensations France requested of the victor. Lastly, the Catholics feared that the evacuation of Rome by French troops in 1866 (in accordance with the convention of 15 September 1864) would expose the city to Italian attack. As it turned out, these troops had to be sent back to protect the Papal States against Garibaldi's volunteers (Mentana, 4 November 1867), but this raised fears of a war with Italy. Thus France appeared to be isolated, with two new and hostile powers at its borders. In this uneasy climate, there were times when Rouher was unable to control the majority of the Legislative Body, which went so far as to acclaim Thiers. There was a great danger that an anti-dynastic 'liberal union' would eventually bring together the Orleanists, who sometimes considered the possibility of a republican regime in the future, and the republicans, who were winning an ever greater following in the towns. Heeding the advice of Walewski and Persigny, the emperor contemplated sponsoring the formation of a 'dynastic union' which the third party and the liberals might agree to remain in or to join. But this required new concessions, which Napoleon III explicitly promised in a letter dated 19 January 1867 and published in *Le Moniteur*. First, the right of debating the emperor's annual address was replaced by the right of interpellation. The ministers concerned would come with the Minister of State to defend their policies before the Legislative Body. Second, a senatus consultum empowered the Senate to send bills back to the deputies for re-examination. This was a further step towards a bicameral representative system. But, after many hesitations and even retreats (Rouher, for example, saw to it that the right of interpellation was very sparingly enforced), it was only in 1868 that the other promises contained in the letter of 1867 were kept. In May, a press law abolished preliminary authorizations and the practice of warnings, but press offences remained within the competence of courts of summary jurisdiction (and not of juries). In June, another law abolished preliminary authorizations for non-political and non-religious meetings, and granted freedom for adoption meetings. All these reforms were not enough to inspire genuine confidence among the liberals. To begin with, the parliamentary system they advocated was still a long way off (ministers were not responsible to the Legislative Body); in addition, instead of liberalizing the regime all at once, the emperor gave the impression of having conceded each measure one by one under duress. Finally, he kept on the same men to carry out a new policy – Rouher in particular, despite his having become the symbol of authoritarian methods. However, the emperor found it increasingly difficult to impose his will. In the country at large, government services seemed struck by anaemia. In parliament, government-sponsored bills had difficulty getting passed.

Thus Victor Duruy, Minister of Education since 1863, had many obstacles to overcome in his attempt to develop the education system. A left-wing Bonapartist (who basically had little interest in constitutional arrangements), he deeply upset the Catholics by his neutralist ideas about the role of religion in public education. Poorly regarded by most members of the majority, he had the greatest difficulty getting them to vote funds for his ministry.

His ambitious scheme of a primary school system designed as a major public service, to be free and eventually compulsory, dates from 1865. Only two years later was a law passed with the more modest aim of facilitating the spread of free tuition and upgrading the status of male and female schoolteachers. Duruy also established adult education programmes, and, in secondary education (where he abolished Fortoul's *bifurcation*), he introduced courses for girls – to the Catholics' great outrage. Finally, he breathed new life into a lack-lustre higher education system and founded the Ecole Pratique des Hautes Etudes.

The failure of the army reform scheme came as a vivid demonstration of the regime's enfeeblement and of the institutional stalemate. As early as the Italian campaign, Napoleon III had become clearly aware of the weakness of the military system established in 1818 and 1832: as a result of a seven-year military service, to which only a portion of the conscripts were obliged to submit, France now possessed what amounted to a mercenary army of barely 400,000 men, but no educated reserves. After long studies, and at a time when the Prussian threat made a reform more urgent, the emperor instructed Marshal Niel, Minister of War since 1867, to submit a complicated bill that provided for the call-up of all conscripts and the organization of a mobile National Guard to defend fortified towns and France's borders as well as maintain order. This scheme was unanimously rejected by the press and criticized in a spate of pamphlets; in the Legislative Body, it was denounced by the opposition (Thiers, J. Simon), greeted coldly by the deputies of the majority – whose eyes were already fixed on the next election – and limply defended by Rouher. Eventually, after countless concessions, a watered-down version was voted into law on 14 January 1868; practically the only innovation it introduced was the principle of a mobile National Guard, which, for lack of funds, was never set up. Instead, the discussion on the army law succeeded in arousing discontent among the bourgeoisie and anxiety among a peasantry strongly hostile to conscription.

### The elections of 1869

The elections of May–June 1869 took place in conditions very different from those prevailing in earlier elections. Not only was the emperor's prestige tarnished by his foreign policy setbacks, but the political climate, in the towns at least, had been transformed by the liberal laws of 1868. The republican opposition, most notably its angry young men, used the imperial concessions to lash out against the Empire. Meeting after meeting was held, frequently leading to violence – a situation reminiscent of the heyday of the 'clubs' during the Second Republic. Above all, there was an extraordinary proliferation of the press: in a single year, 140 newspapers were launched and, by the end of the Empire, the total print run for dailies had almost reached the million mark, five times more than in 1860. Of these newspapers, none scored a greater success than *La Lanterne*, in which Rochefort vented his biting irony; a best-seller among the workers, *La Lanterne* was soon printing 120,000 copies. In discussions and in books such as those by E. Ténot (a journalist of *Le Siècle*), particularly *Paris en décembre 1851*, the *coup d'état*, until then presented as an act of salvation, now became a crime and its victims, martyrs. The republican newspapers started a fund to put up a fitting monument to the deputy Baudin, who had died on a barricade on 3 December 1851. The government prosecuted them and, at the trial that ensued, their lawyer, Léon Gambetta, openly denounced the *coup d'état* and the men of 2 December. Thus, in Paris, the opposition was now impassioned and thoroughly revolutionary.

Rouher, for his part, held on to the system of official candidacies for this election, but here too the machine was beginning to jam: prefects and mayors often displayed less zeal, and in some cases candidates actually preferred not to make an open show of the government backing they enjoyed!

The results of the election[6] showed a sizeable decline in the number of votes polled by pro-government candidates (who lost nearly one million votes) and heavy gains by the opposition (who won 1,300,000 votes). The gap between the two camps narrowed even further. According to official figures, the 292 candidates returned included 216 government supporters (118 'official' candidates and 98 'pro-government liberals') and 74 opponents (25 republicans and 49 liberals).

The republicans carried all the larger cities, but at the same time they split into radical democrats (the irreconcilable opponents of the regime) and moderates; the former did not hesitate to stand, often successfully, in Paris, Lyons and Marseilles, against prominent republicans (Gambetta, for example, defeated Carnot in Belleville). In many other provincial towns, more moderate candidates were returned. Furthermore, the republicans made very few inroads as yet in rural areas, mostly in *cantons* in the south and the east already held by the 'démoc. soc.' under the Second Republic.*

Rural voters instead re-elected a great number of official candidates, as well as strongly anti-revolutionary clericalist or protectionist liberals, many of them former Orleanists.

All in all, in the new Legislative Body, realignments seemed inevitable. On the far Left sat the 25 irreconcilable republicans; at the opposite end, at most 80 pure Bonapartists, the 'mamelukes'; between them, a centre composed of both dynastic liberals and opposition liberals, hostile to the authoritarian regime but ready to rally to it one day if the Empire moved closer towards parliamentarianism.

### 3. The 'liberal Empire'

What could one do when faced with such an assembly? The emperor still seemed to hesitate, and the decisive move was to come from the liberal 'marsh': at the opening of the session, on 6 July 1869, 116 deputies 'asked to interpellate the government on the need to give satisfaction to the feeling that prevailed in the country, by involving the country more effectively in the management of its affairs' and by proceeding to 'form a cabinet responsible to the emperor and the Chamber'. Napoleon III grasped the need to avoid this interpellation and make concessions. On 12 July, Rouher came to announce the resignation of his cabinet, and read a message in which the emperor promised to yield on all the demands, even on the issue of tariffs. A transitional government was appointed to carry out the reform by senatus consultum. After being discussed during the summer (while the Legislative Body was prorogued), the senatus consultum was passed on 8 September 1869. Its chief provisions concerned the prerogatives of a Legislative Body totally freed from imperial tutelage. The assembly would henceforth share with the emperor the power of initiating legislation, vote the budget by section and approve customs rates. Lastly, it was stipulated (in Article 2) that the ministers, who could be chosen from among the deputies, were 'dependent solely on the emperor'; they were 'responsible', without it being specified to whom, but in fact everyone understood: to the Chambers. At the same

* See Maurice Agulhon, *The Republican Experiment, 1848–1852*, trans. by Janet Lloyd (Cambridge, 1983), pp. 75–6. (Trans.)

time, the emperor made contact with Emile Ollivier, whom he chose officially to be the head of the future government, in a letter of 27 December 1869 couched in terms characteristic of parliamentary practice: 'I ask you to indicate to me the persons who can form a united cabinet faithfully representative of the majority in the Legislative Body.' On 2 January 1870, Emile Ollivier succeeded, not without difficulty, in forming a cabinet composed of the emperor's creatures and members of the centre Right (liberal Bonapartists) and centre Left (liberals who accepted the Empire). Finally, the senatus consultum of 20 April 1870 completed the construction of a parliamentary system: besides reaffirming the principles of 1789, it transformed the Senate, which it deprived of its prerogatives in constitutional matters, into a second legislative chamber – an upper house – and confirmed the ministers' dual accountability to the deputies and the sovereign. But at the same time the regime continued to rest on plebiscite, for Article 13 specified that 'the emperor is responsible to the French people, to whom he retains his right to appeal'.

Despite very strong reactions from certain liberals and the Left, Napoleon III decided to call a plebiscite on 8 May 1870 on the following question: 'The people approve the liberal reforms carried out in the Constitution since 1860 by the emperor with the assistance of the senior institutions of State, and ratify the senatus consultum of 20 April 1870.' This clever question divided the opposition and put it in a quandary, for how could one accept the liberal reforms without simultaneously endorsing the sovereign, presented here as the man chiefly responsible for those reforms? While the more extremist republicans advocated abstention, the others, joined by Thiers, were inclined to vote against. The result was nevertheless an overwhelming 'yes' that prompted the emperor to remark gleefully: 'I'm back to my old score.' Indeed, 7,350,000 'ayes' were cast – almost as many as in 1851 and 1852 – as against 1,538,000 'noes'; even in the *département* of the Seine, where the 'noes' had it, the number of 'ayes' was double that of the number of votes polled a year earlier by pro-government candidates (Fig. 7). The Empire had apparently been reinforced.

However, the Ollivier government was preparing major reforms (a return to protectionism; decentralization; freedom of education at the secondary level), all designed to give satisfaction to businessmen, conservatives and clericalists. The fact was that the government regarded itself as liberal and parliamentarian, but not in the least democratic. It did not aim at winning over the urban masses; on the contrary, it was determined to take a firm stand against an increasingly extremist labour movement, which manifested itself by a new wave of strikes in 1869 and 1870. Ollivier sent troops to Le Creusot to back Schneider. His government also had to contend in Paris with opposition from radicals and

fewer than 25% of registered voters    35–59%

25–34%    over 50%

7 'Noes' cast in the plebiscite of 8 May 1870

revolutionary socialists, who increasingly took to the streets. When, on 12 January 1870, some 100,000 persons (according to certain estimates) attended the funeral of the republican journalist Victor Noir, shot in the course of a quarrel with Prince Pierre Bonaparte (a relative whom the imperial family kept somewhat at arm's length), Ollivier mobilized a considerable number of troops, and did not hesitate to gaol the popular Rochefort. In June 1870, he ordered the arrest of the principal leaders of the International, which he again disbanded. This agitation, which had been simmering continuously since 1867, did not necessarily imply that the revolution was imminent. Only in Paris were revolutionary elements present in any great numbers, and even many moderate republicans were frightened by the unrest in the capital. By its vote in the plebiscite, the country had also come down against revolution and in favour of order.

### 4. Collapse

Less than five months after this reassuring plebiscite, despite the fact that even in Paris the Left was, if anything, calming down and that the Empire – now accepted everywhere, except in some of the larger cities – seemed yet to have a good chance of surviving through change, the regime collapsed in the wake of a military defeat. The war of 1870 was the outcome of a complex dispute that dated from Sadowa and from the emperor's demands for 'gratuities' (*pourboires*); after continually lowering his claims, he was even refused Luxemburg. The critical point was reached when a prince of the Hohenzollern family stood as a candidate for the Spanish throne. The French government demanded and obtained the withdrawal of his candidacy (12 July), but Napoleon III wanted to obtain in addition a promise from Prussia that such an attempt would not be repeated. Kaiser Wilhelm merely eluded this excessive request, submitted by Benedetti; by means of the Ems telegram, however, Bismarck announced to the press that his sovereign had refused in an offensive manner to receive the French ambassador. Paris was swept by a wave of patriotism; the Legislative Body, despite Thiers, voted funds for a war that Ollivier, speaking for the government on 19 July, accepted 'with a light heart', because 'this war, which we are waging, has been inflicted upon us'.

Whereas for Bismarck this conflict was undoubtedly a desired means of achieving and consolidating German unity by a common struggle against 'the hereditary enemy', the aims of France's leaders are harder to discern. Many historians argue that while Ollivier was eager to keep the peace, the 'mamelukes', grouped together behind the empress, regarded a foreign diversion as an opportunity for bringing back the authoritarian Empire in the afterglow of success. The emperor, who, for that matter, took little heed of his ministers since the plebiscite, was – so the argument runs – easily convinced. This interpretation is questionable, for it is hard to see why Napoleon, whose regime appeared to have been strengthened by the recent plebiscite, would have put everything at risk in an adventure that he knew to be dangerous, since, two years earlier, he had himself denounced his army's weaknesses. No doubt his only intention was to score a diplomatic success by forcing the king of Prussia to back down.

The war began in disastrous conditions for France. Not only was the country isolated diplomatically, but it had an army of only 370,000 men at its disposal (of whom 60,000 were in Algeria and 6,000 in Civitavecchia) – a troop strength inferior to that of the enemy: by August 1870, Germany was able to 'rush over 500,000 men up to the front line, supported by 160,000 reserves in depots; at the same time, 190,000 men of the *Landwehr* made up a second-line army unmatched by France'.[7] To this one should add the mediocrity of many French field officers – whom the regime had often promoted because of their personal fortune rather than their ability – and a disastrously organized concentration of troops on the borders. In early August, all Napoleon III could count on was a very motley array of 235,000 men.

Consequently, defeat followed defeat: after Wissemburg (4 August) and Froeschwiller (6 August), Alsace had to be evacuated by MacMahon. In Lorraine, Bazaine allowed himself to be trapped at Metz. In an attempt to relieve him, what was left of the French troops – followed rather than commanded by a sick emperor – blundered into the Sedan basin, where they were encircled. By 1 September, the only possibility left was to capitulate. Napoleon III was taken prisoner.

When the news of this disaster reached Paris – where, after the first defeats, the Ollivier government had been replaced by a hard-line cabinet – the regime collapsed. On the night of the 3rd, the premier, the Comte de Palikao, summoned the Legislative Body at midnight. On the next day, while the deputies were still deliberating, groups of workers invaded the Assembly to demand that the emperor be deposed. Then, in keeping with an already established ritual, the republican deputies, in this case Gambetta and J. Favre, harangued the crowd in the Assembly before leading it to the Hôtel de Ville, where, while the empress fled to Britain, they secured the proclamation of the Republic and won applause for the formation of a 'government of national defence'. This ministry, from which the 'government republicans' had carefully excluded all the *clubistes* save Rochefort, was placed under the premiership of General Trochu, a popular and indispensable choice, given the military situation.

The new governing team undoubtedly lacked cohesion. While some of its members would have liked to call elections at once, the others succeeded in having them postponed in light of the inappropriate circumstances. Also, this government 'felt uncomfortable in its illegality'. Its task was to organize national defence, but Gambetta, who left an already besieged Paris in a balloon in order to organize new armies from Tours, was virtually alone in attempting the impossible. While Thiers's diplomatic missions in European capitals failed, the armies hastily raised in the provinces proved incapable of delivering Paris, where the government capitulated on 28 January 1871. As Bismarck had demanded that the peace be signed by a legal authority, elections were held on 8 February for a National Assembly. Predictably, the rural population, which constituted a great majority of the electorate, voted in favour of the defenders of order and the advocates of peace, who, in the event, were often monarchists. Having won a vote of confidence in 26 *départements*, Thiers was appointed 'head of the executive of the French Republic' and, in that capacity, assigned to negotiate the terms of the disastrous treaty of Frankfurt (10 May 1871), which called on France to hand over Alsace and Lorraine and to pay an indemnity of 5,000 million francs. In the meantime, however, the Commune revolt had broken out.

### 5. The Commune[8]

'The direct antithesis of the Empire was the Commune', said Marx. It is true that the Commune was indissolubly linked to earlier phenomena, such as the relative – and more intensely felt – pauperization of the working class, the consequences of the Haussmannization of the capital (where the poor sought to reconquer the urban centre from which they had been expelled) and the revolutionary fever that gripped the Parisians. In the provinces, by contrast, even town-dwellers generally displayed a degree of moderation. For several years past, the capital was no longer informed by the same aspirations as the provinces; it was virtually in a state of secession. The ordeal of the siege widened the gap. While the people of Paris were in arms – the government had to raise 250 battalions of the National Guard – the revolutionary forces of the capital organized themselves. In every *arrondissement*, vigilance committees were set up under the supervision of revolutionary elements (Internationalists, radicals and Jacobins). The 'Central Committee of the Twenty *Arrondissements*' appointed by these committees advocated all-out war and a democratic and 'social' government. Above all, it called for the election of a Paris municipal council, of a 'commune' derived directly from the people. The term 'commune', no doubt used first by the Central Committee, soon became popular, and came to embody 'all the social aspirations of the underprivileged'.[9] The uprising of 31 October 1870, triggered by the news of Bazaine's surrender at Metz and the announcement of a French defeat at the hands of the Prussians at Le Bourget, was aimed at toppling the provisional government, accused of being defeatist. But the Parisians did not yet follow the inhabitants of Belleville, who had taken to the streets. Admittedly, 'the word "commune" was born and had made steady progress during the siege, but it was not the siege that gave birth to the Commune'.

The insurrection was born of the defeat and the dangers that soon openly threatened the Republic – of the dual shock of the capitulation of 28 January and the election of a monarchist assembly. It was not led by the revolutionary organizations that had been active during the siege, but by a federation of National Guard battalions that emerged spontaneously from the people at the time of the February 1871 elections, and later appointed its own Central Committee. The Central Committee of the Twenty *Arrondissements* and the International eventually rallied to the Central Committee of the National Guard. By moving to Versailles, the National Assembly seemed to want to 'decapitalize' Paris and provoke the Parisians.

The decisive incident occurred on 18 March, when, in an ill-planned move, Thiers failed in his attempt to reclaim the National Guard's cannon on the Butte Montmartre; this led to the summary execution of the two generals in charge of the operation. The government hastily took refuge at Versailles. In the vacuum of power thus created, the Central Committee of the National Guard was led to take control of the situation. No doubt there was no plot involved, on either side: while the Blanquists were initially the only ones to take advantage of a situation that they had not created, Thiers acted far more out of panic than out of a desire to provoke. While negotiations with Versailles dragged on, elections were finally held in Paris on 26 March 1871. Out of 470,000 registered voters, only 230,000 took part, partly because many rich inhabitants had already left the capital. 'The Commune represented only about a half of the Parisian population.' In Haussmann's city, it was basically the popular strongholds in the east, the north (Belleville) and, to a lesser extent, the south that voted overwhelmingly in favour of the Commune.

Of the 85 deputies elected, 19 moderates refused to take up their seats. The others formed a Communal Assembly, but no one could tell whether it would be a simple municipal council or a counter-government. These *communeux* delegates, most of whom were manual workers or intellectuals (often journalists), covered a wide spectrum of opinions that are difficult to classify. But in early May an ideological split led to the emergence in their ranks of two camps that joined battle in a series of painful confrontations.

The majority was composed of pure revolutionaries, who made the political struggle their priority. The largest group consisted of Jacobins like Delescluze, who, without forming a true party, remained sentimentally attached to the Robespierrist tradition. Close to them stood the Blanquists, who worshipped the memory of Hébert. Despite the absence of their leader, arrested yet again on the eve of the insurrection, they formed a homogeneous group of men of action determined to battle against the bourgeoisie and the Church. Others too, including even some Internationalists, belonged to the majority.

The minority was composed of federalists and autonomists who were wary of the authoritarianism of the *majoritaires*, as well as socialists far more preoccupied with social issues. Many of them were workers. They included not only a good number of Internationalists, but also the Proud-honians and Bakuninists. Two forceful figures stood out in the minority: Vallès, a former school monitor turned journalist, and the bookbinder Varlin. Both, however, strove to preserve the Commune's endangered unity.

In actual fact, it would be an exaggeration to believe that the two currents were continually at war over the scheme to rebuild France. Witness the Declaration to the French People, which was voted by the Commune on 19 April unanimously with only one vote against, and which stands in a way as its testament:

> All were agreed at the time as to the need for autonomy and for Parisian freedoms, and as to the advantage of extending these freedoms to all French communes. All were agreed as to the need to destroy excessive centralization, which had become unbearable under the Second Empire; and at the same time as to the need to preserve the national unity achieved in 1790 in the course of the festival of the 'Federation', and the indispensable primacy of Paris, which, as usual, acted and suffered for all of France. This was indeed a programme, reasonably constructed and at least consistent, even if it did not solve every question; in it one could sense that the true revolution would be the antithesis of the State.[10]

Despite its divisions, this assembly, which sat for only fifty-four days running, implemented or at least outlined a considerable number of measures. First, a series of practical decisions: a moratorium on overdue bills for small traders, the cancellation of rents still owed by tenants, the requisition of vacant lodgings and the free restitution of goods pledged by the needier at the State-run pawnshop (*Mont-de-piété*). In addition, a series of measures on principle were voted: the abolition of conscription and of standing armies, to be replaced by people's militias, an attempt (inspired by Courbet) to liberalize art and, most notably, a radical educational reform, which called for free, compulsory, secular and even anti-religious education, more girls' schools and vocational institutions as well as a thorough change in teaching methods. Lastly, although its social policy remained rather vague, the Commune, at the instigation of its Labour and Exchange Commission (a sort of ministry run by members of the International), abolished fines and stoppages of pay, as well as night work for bakery workers. As part of its effort to co-operate with trade unions, the Commune reopened municipal enterprises and decided to hand over the workshops abandoned by owners who had left Paris to self-managing workers organized into co-operatives. In addition, in every *arrondissement*, it replaced employment agencies (*bureaux de placement*) by a labour exchange. Thus the Commune had distinctly socialist leanings – if one accepts the term 'socialist' in the very imprecise sense in which it was still often being used – but it lacked the time to pursue its schemes any further.

However, in a Paris once again besieged, public opinion expressed itself freely, indeed released its pent-up feelings. Revolutionary newspapers(such as *Le Père Duchéne* and Vallès's *Le Cri du Peuple*) were read avidly; new songs were sung all over town (Pottier was to write The Internationale during the 'week of bloodshed' [*Semaine sanglante*]); street corners were the scene of free and open discussions. The walls of the capital were covered with posters, notices and all manner of inscriptions. In the evening, Parisians would go to hold forth or listen to speeches at the revolutionary 'clubs' that had set themselves up in most churches in popular neighbourhoods. The inhabitants of the festive city were invited to join in by attending spectacular ceremonies, such as the one held on 28 March at the Hôtel de Ville for the proclamation of the Commune. Popular enthusiasm was roused by the free concerts at the Tuileries or by grandiose exorcistic ceremonies such as the destruction of the Vendôme column, a monument denounced as 'a symbol of brute force and false glory, an affirmation of militarism'.

But Paris remained isolated. While the peasants detested the new distributionists, the provincial towns, although sometimes won over to federalist ideas, did not follow suit. The 'commune' risings that did occur (Lyons, Marseilles) were but ephemeral episodes. Thiers, with Bismarck's connivance, consequently succeeded in raising a sizeable armed force. The 'free town', for its part, could count only on a National Guard that even Rossel, a young officer who had chosen the *communard* camp out of patriotism, was unable to discipline. Eventually, on 21 May, the Versaillais entered the city with no difficulty whatever. In their desperate attempt to stop them, the *communards* put up barricade after barricade and set fire to the Tuileries, the Hôtel de Ville and the Cour des Comptes. While the troops summarily shot everyone they arrested, the *communards* replied by executing hostages, including Monseigneur Darboy, Archbishop of Paris. The city, at long last brought to heel, suffered a frightening repression that claimed a total of one quarter of its working-class population.

Paradoxically – in appearance – the crushing of the *communards*, impassioned supporters of an ideal Republic, was ultimately to facilitate the advent of the Third Republic. The moderate republicans had by now severed all their connections with revolutionary elements, while the liberals realized that a non-monarchist government, based on universal suffrage, proved quite capable of restoring order. This liberal union, so frail when it first emerged in 1863, was to give birth to the new regime.

Later, all the self-designated heirs to 1871, and Lenin himself, drew exemplary lessons from the history of the Paris Commune. The socialists were to view it as the first of their revolutions. But, restored to its historical context, was it not in the first place a revolt by radical republicans, whose aim was often simply to fight 'for the Republic'? What was the deeper significance of this abortive revolution? Was it 'a Dawn or a Twilight?'

asks Rougerie, who replies: 'mostly a Twilight, possibly a Dawn'. I am inclined to agree with him that the *communards*, who were not yet modern proletarians in the true sense, and who religiously revived the words and rites of 1793, belong 'almost entirely to a prehistoric phase of the labour movement and of socialism'. This would make the insurrection, which 'carries the entire, decisive weight of all those that preceded it', the last revolution of the nineteenth century, the last deed of the revolutionary saga begun by the *sans-culottes*. But one can understand the strong reactions and the protests that such an interpretation provokes among all those who, with Charles Rihs, believe that 'the Commune, in the minds of the *communards*, was a Dawn. It is common knowledge that, in several respects, the Commune was a pioneer, an innovator, a forerunner.'[11] The debate remains open.

'Dawn or Twilight', modernity or tradition – these questions recur unceasingly for anyone who seeks to understand not only the Commune, but France throughout the Second Empire, its political significance, its economy and society, its people and their civilization. The truth is that, during this period, archaism and innovation were closely intermingled everywhere. One is astonished by the dualism of an age in which an eighteenth century that lived on and on and a twentieth century pregnant with all the problems of the contemporary period seemed to coexist and clash with each other. But the present-day observer is struck above all by the inroads of modernism that make the Second Empire such an immediate period for him: the gradual acceptance of universal suffrage, eventually linked with parliamentarianism, the birth of modern art, the rise of limited companies, the early developments of large-scale industry and the plight of its workers.

# Notes

Numbers in bold type refer to the bibliography on pp. 181–190.

**Foreword**

1 See (**16**).

### 1. The regime of Napoleon III

1 See (**59**), vol. V, p. 21.
2 See (**101**), p. 1.
3 In *Le Figaro littéraire* of 8–14 June 1970, Armand Lanoux portrayed him as 'a mafioso and a stand-in', while Jean Dutourd took his defence: 'He wasn't that little...'.
4 See (**1**), p. 51.
5 See Bibliothèque Nationale (Paris), Département des Manuscrits, no. 10292, fo. 195.
6 See M. Vaussard, *Histoire de l'Italie moderne* (Paris, 1950), pp. 187–8.
7 See (**59**), vol. IV, p. 359.
8 *Ibid.*, pp. 359–60.
9 Girard (**3**), p. 39.
10 *Ibid.*, p. 62.
11 Wright (**100**), p. 111.
12 To measure the concrete significance of these figures, and of those given in the rest of this book, one should ideally convert them into current francs. But prices have changed in such varying ways and consumption patterns have been so radically transformed that any conversion table would have only a very relative value. To give a very rough order of magnitude, it can be said that the franc of the Second Empire was worth about thirteen times the present-day franc.
13 Wright (**100**), pp. 109–10.
14 Rémond (**38**), p. 148.

### 2. The political personnel and political life of the Second Empire

1 Girard (**3**), p. 104.
2 Lhomme (**103**), pp. 156–7.
3 Maurain (**104**).
4 *Ibid.*, p. 230.
5 Wright (**100**), pp. 32–3.

175

6 Wright (**100**).
7 As late as 1869, as a statistical analysis of 269 of the 292 new deputies has shown, 35 per cent were landowners, 11 per cent former high-ranking civil servants, 16 per cent lawyers and 25 per cent representatives of the business world. The 'new strata' still made up an insignificant proportion. Furthermore, 52 per cent of these deputies enjoyed substantial incomes (at least 30,000 francs a year). See Girard, Prost and Gossez (**114**), p. 87.
8 See the previous volume in this series, Maurice Agulhon, *The Republican Experiment, 1848–1852*, trans. by Janet Lloyd (Cambridge: Cambridge University Press, 1983), pp. 177–8.
9 Payne (**164**), ch. 7.
10 For these examples and the preceding quotations, see Le Clère and Wright (**6**), pp. 82–3.
11 A. Gough, in *Conflicts in French Society* (**17**), p. 110.
12 As Fould put it in 1853. Le Clère and Wright (**6**), p. 39.
13 Daudet's description in *Le Nabab* (published 1877) of the prefects waiting patiently for an audience with Morny is hardly more flattering.
14 See (**6**).
15 *Ibid.*, pp. 204–5.
16 See (**10**), p. 32.
17 See (**14**), p. 239.
18 For a discussion of this, see Girard, Prost and Gossez (**114**).
19 *Ibid.*, p. 170.
20 Sabatier (**63**), p. 86.
21 Rémusat, quoted in Girard (**3**), pp. 24–5.
22 Dansette (**1**), p. 429.
23 E. Borne, 'Contradictions du bonapartisme', *France-Forum*, Paris, February 1970.
24 Balzac, *Le Médecin de campagne*, ch. 3, 'Le Napoléon du peuple'.
25 See (**65**), p. 397.
26 Quoted in Girard (**3**), p. 132.
27 Mérentie (**16**).
28 Guiral (**20**), p. 80.
29 Dansette (**1**), p. 27.
30 Girard (**3**), esp. p. 112.
31 Le Clère and Wright (**6**), p. 13.

## 3. Economic progress and change

1 Reinhard, Armengaud and Dupâquier, *Histoire de la population mondiale de 1700 à 1948* (Paris: Montchrestien, 1968), pp. 213–14.
2 The increase in this figure may be due to improved data-gathering.
3 R. Cameron, 'L'Economie française: passé, présent, avenir', *Annales: Economies, Sociétés, Civilisations* (*ESC*), September 1970.
4 Bouvier (**120**), p. 166.
5 Girard (**4**), p. 55.
6 Durieux (**108**), pp. 346–7.
7 On this still relatively unexplored question, see J. Bouvier, 'Sur les dimensions du fait financier, XIXe–XXe siècle', *Revue d'Histoire Economique et Sociale*, 1968, no. 2.
8 Bouvier (**120**), p. 166.

9 See (**135**).
10 Lévy-Leboyer, 'L'Héritage de Simiand: prix, profit et termes de l'échange au XIXe siècle', *Revue Historique*, January–March 1970.
11 See (**122**).
12 See (**134**).
13 Grothe (**109**), pp. 130–1.
14 Lévy-Leboyer in *Revue d'Histoire Economique et Sociale*, 1971.
15 See J. Chesneaux, *Une lecture politique de Jules Verne* (Paris: Maspero, 1971), ch. 10, 'L'Or et l'argent'.
16 Zola, *L'Argent*, in *Les Rougon-Macquart* (**48**), pp. 224–5.
17 Fohlen, *Une affaire de famille au XIXe siècle: Méquillet-Noblot* (Paris: A. Colin, 1955).
18 B. Gille (**129**), p. 570.
19 B. Gille, 'La Fondation du Crédit mobilier et les idées financières des frères Pereire', *Bulletin du Centre de Recherches sur l'Histoire des Entreprises*, 1954, no. 3.
20 D. S. Landes (**136**).
21 Bouvier, 'Systèmes bancaires et entreprises industrielles dans la croissance européenne au XIXe siècle', *Annales (ESC)*, January–February 1972.
22 Lhomme, *Economie et histoire* (Geneva: Droz, 1967), p. 184.
23 *Textes choisis*, Soboul, Angrand and Dautry, eds. (Paris: Editions Sociales, 1955), p. 147.
24 In *L'Empire industriel: histoire critique des concessions financières et industrielles du second Empire* (Paris, 1869) and *L'Economie politique de l'Empire* (Paris, 1870).
25 Maurain (**104**), pp. 138–9.
26 *Ibid.*, p. 261.
27 Bellanger, Godechot, Guiral and Terrou (**44**), p. 256.
28 Especially 'L'Exportation des capitaux français, 1850–1880', *Revue d'Histoire Economique et Sociale*, 1955; see also (**123**).
29 Girard, 'Le Chemin de fer Sète–Marseille', *Revue d'Histoire Moderne et Contemporaine*, April–June 1955.
30 Thépot, 'Un tournant dans l'histoire de l'industrie chimique française: la fusion Saint-Gobain–Perret–Ollivier (1866–1871)', *Bulletin de la Société d'Histoire Moderne*, 1967, no. 3.
31 Vial (**145**).
32 Bouvier (**119**), p. 29.
33 Fohlen (**128**).
34 Markovitch (**138**), vol. IV, p. 123.
35 Toutain (**117**), table 75.
36 For Lévy-Leboyer's index, see above, p. 69; for Markovitch's index, see the previous volume in this series, p. 83; for Crouzet's index, see (**126**); the index given by J. C. Toutain, *Le Produit intérieur brut de la France de 1789 à 1975* (still unpublished) points to an even slower rate of growth.
37 Lévy-Leboyer, 'Le Processus d'industrialisation: le cas de l'Angleterre et de la France', *Revue Historique*, April–June 1968.
38 Rougerie (**208**), p. 12.
39 Bleton (**46**).

## 4. Living standards, life styles and attitudes

1 Thabault (**75**).
2 *Ibid.*, p. 115.

3 Guillaume (**80**), p. 303.

4 'Le Conscrit et l'ordinateur: perspectives de recherche sur les archives militaires du XIXe siècle français', *Studi Storici*, April–June 1969, and 'Etude sur un contingent (1868)', *Annales de Démographie Historique*, 1972.

5 In a document quoted in *Rive Gauche*, 20 August 1865.

6 Fleury and Valmary, 'Les Progrès de l'instruction élémentaire de Louis XIV à Napoléon III d'après l'enquête de Louis Maggiolo', *Population*, 1966.

7 This 'active depopulation' characterized the period 1836–72, according to Pinchemel, *Structures sociales et dépopulation rurale dans les campagnes picardes de 1836 à 1936* (Paris: A. Colin, 1957).

8 Maureille, 'Périllos', *Revue de Géographie des Pyrénées*, 1947–8.

9 Chombart de Lauwe, *Bretagne et Pays de la Garonne* (Paris: Presses Universitaires de France (PUF), 1946).

10 Toutain (**151**).

11 Vigreux, 'La Société agricole d'Autun au XIXe siècle', typewritten Thèse de 3e Cycle, Dijon, 1970.

12 Labrousse, introduction to Dupeux (**71**).

13 *Ibid.*

14 Robert, '*La Terre*' *d'Emile Zola: étude historique et critique* (Paris: Les Belles Lettres, 1952).

15 Marcilhacy, 'Emile Zola, "historien" des paysans beaucerons', *Annales (ESC)*, 1957.

16 Marcilhacy (**74**).

17 Corbin, 'Migrations temporaires et société rurale au XIXe siecle: le cas du Limousin', *Revue Historique*, October–December 1971.

18 Agulhon, in *Histoire de la Provence* (Toulouse: Privat, 1969), pp. 484–5.

19 Darmon (**149**).

20 See (**153**).

21 See (**155**), p. 14.

22 Pierrard (**156**).

23 *Les Châtiments*, 'Joyeuse vie'.

24 Markovitch (**139**), p. 98.

25 Codaccioni (**78**).

26 Daumard, 'Evolution des structures sociales en France à l'époque de l'industrialisation, 1815–1914', *Revue Historique*, April–June 1972.

27 Quoted after *Rive gauche*, 25 July 1865.

28 Cornu (**88**), pp. 39–40.

29 Halbwachs, *La Population et les tracés des voies à Paris depuis un siècle* (Paris: PUF, 1928).

30 *Le Monde*, 14 July 1971.

31 Cornu (**88**), p. 34.

32 Rougerie (**208**), p. 19.

33 L. Lazare, *Les Quartiers de l'est de Paris et les communes suburbaines* (Paris, 1870).

34 See (**48**), vol. I.

35 According to a contemporary quoted in Pierrard (**156**), p. 101.

36 J. P. Aron, *Le Mangeur du XIXe siècle* (Paris: Laffont, 1973).

37 J.-P. Sartre, *L'Idiot de la famille* (Paris: Gallimard, 1972), esp. vol. III. For an introduction to a reading of this work, see Roche, 'L'Opposition au second Empire dans quelques-unes de ses expressions et représentations littéraires', in 'Colloque sur l'historiographie' (**16**).

38 Mathey, preface to '*Equivoques*': *peintures françaises du XIXe siècle* (Paris: Musée des Arts Décoratifs, 1973).
39 P. Francastel, *Peinture et société: naissance et destruction d'un espace plastique* (Lyons: Audin, 1951).
40 'La Vénus des Folies-Bergère et celle du Titien', *Le Figaro Littéraire*, 28 April and 5 May 1973.

## 5. The good years: 1852–61

1 Machu, 'Deux aspects de la répression policière dans le Nord à l'époque du second Empire', *Revue du Nord*, 1964.
2 Payne (**164**), p. 181.
3 Kulstein, *Napoleon III and the Working Class: A Study of Government Propaganda under the Second Empire* (Los Angeles: The Ward Richie Press, 1969).
4 Letter of 1853, quoted in Touchard (**23**), p. 307.
5 Barral (**66**), p. 166.
6 Dupeux (**71**), p. 618.
7 André Siegfried, quoted in Sabatier (**63**), p. 131.
8 Girard (**3**), p. 135.
9 *Ibid.*
10 See (**59**), vol. V, p. 80.
11 D'Haussonville, 'Souvenirs', *Revue des Deux Mondes*, 1 October 1923, p. 493.
12 Barral (**66**), pp. 167–8.
13 See (**57**), vol. I, p. 214.
14 Touchard (**23**), pp. 308–19.
15 See (**58**), vol. III, pp. 537–8.
16 Vier, *La Comtesse d'Agoult et François Ponsard d'après une correspondance inédite, 1843–1867* (Paris: A. Colin, 1960), vol. I.
17 Barral (**66**), p. 168.
18 Gaillard, 'Pourquoi la loi de sûreté générale', *Information Historique*, 1955, pp. 58–9.
19 Ollivier (**58**), pp. 538–42 (continuation of the text quoted above, p. 142).
20 Emerit, 'Une source pour l'histoire du second Empire: les souvenirs du général Desvaux', 'Colloque sur l'historiographie' (**16**).
21 Girard (**4**), p. 31.
22 The moves in Algeria, Syria, Egypt and Italy were part of a single Mediterranean policy of Napoleon III, which was a source of concern for Britain in the early 1860s.
23 Ageron (**185**); see also Y. Lacoste, A. Nouschi and A. Prenant, *L'Algérie, passé et présent* (Paris: Editions Sociales, 1960).
24 See (**180**).
25 Martinière, 'L'Expédition mexicaine de Napoléon III dans l'historiographie française', 'Colloque sur l'historiographie' (**16**).

## 6. Decline and fall

1 See Guéhenno, *Le Monde*, 26 September 1970.
2 Barral, *Le Département de l'Isère sous la IIIe République (1870–1940)* (Paris: A. Colin, 1962), p. 279.
3 Wright (**77**).
4 Quoted in Girard (**4**), p. 78.

5 Rougerie (**5**), p. 92.
6 See the results of the first round, p. 158 above.
7 Chanal (**198**).
8 It is impossible to recount here the various aspects of this episode, which, although brief, is so rich and so difficult to interpret. In order to gain a deeper insight into its complexity, the reader is advised to consult the works listed in the bibliography.
9 Rougerie (**5**), pp. 108ff.
10 Rougerie (**208**), p. 157.
11 See (**206**), p. 16.

# Bibliography

Interest in the period has spawned an abundant and very varied literature, of which the following items (as well as those cited in the notes) represent a carefully chosen selection. (Place of publication Paris unless otherwise stated. Trans.)

## Studies of general interest

*1. Recent works of synthesis*

1. A. Dansette, *Du 2 décembre au 4 septembre*, Hachette, 1972
2. J. Desmarest, *La France de 1870*, Hachette, 1970
3. L. Girard, *Problèmes politiques et constitutionnels du second Empire*, Centre de Documentation Universitaire (CDU), 1964 (stops *c*. 1857)
4. L. Girard, *Questions politiques et constitutionnelles du second Empire*, CDU, 1965 (covers the years 1857–70)
5. J. Rougerie, 'Le second Empire', in G. Duby, ed., *Histoire de la France*, vol. III, Larousse, 1972
6. B. Le Clère and V. Wright, *Les Préfets du second Empire*, A. Colin, 1973

And, more concise, but useful:

7. P. Aumoine and C. Dangeau, *La France a cent ans*, Fayard, 1965
8. P. Labracherie, *Le Second Empire*, Juillard, 1962
9. J. P. Miquel, *Le Second Empire*, A. Barret, 1979

*2. Older surveys*

10. M. Blanchard, *Le Second Empire*, A. Colin, 1950; new edn, 1966
11. P. de la Gorce, *Histoire du second Empire*, Plon, 1894–1904, 7 vols.
12. E. A. Jeloubovskaia, *La Chute du second Empire et la naissance de la IIIe République en France*, Moscow, Editions en Langues Etrangères, 1959 (orthodox Marxist interpretation)
13. C. H. Pouthas, *Histoire politique du second Empire*, CDU, 1954
14. C. Seignobos, in E. Lavisse, *Histoire de France contemporaine*, Hachette, 1921:

   Vol. VI. *La Révolution de 1848 – Le Second Empire*
   Vol. VII. *Le Déclin de l'Empire et l'établissement de la IIIe République*

15. A. Thomas, *Le Second Empire*, vol. X of J. Jaurès, ed., *Histoire socialiste*, Rouff, n.d. (*c*. 1900)

*3. More specialized studies*

16. 'Colloque sur l'historiographie', Aix-en-Provence and Marseilles, September 1972, summary by Mérentie, *Anthinéa*, no. 1; papers on 'L'Historiographie du second Empire' published in *Revue d'Histoire Moderne et Contemporaine*, January–March 1974

17. T. Zeldin, ed., *Conflicts in French Society: Anticlericalism, Education and Morals in the Nineteenth Century*, London, G. Allen & Unwin, 1970

18. M. Allem, *La Vie quotidienne sous le second Empire*, Hachette, 1948

19. P. Guiral, *La Vie quotidienne en France à l'âge d'or du capitalisme*, Hachette, 1976

20. P. Guiral, *Prévost-Paradol, 1829–1870: pensée et action d'un libéral sous le second Empire*, Presses Universitaires de France (PUF), 1955

21. P. Renouvin, *La Politique extérieure du second Empire*, CDU, 1947

22. M. Rubel, *Karl Marx devant le bonapartisme*, Paris and The Hague, Mouton, 1960

23. J. Touchard, *La Gloire de Béranger*, vol. II, A. Colin, 1968

24. J. Vier, *La Comtesse d'Agoult et son temps*, vols. III–V, A. Colin, 1961–2

*4. Research tools and reference works*

25. The *Annuaires statistiques de la France* (retrospective sections), Imprimerie Nationale

26. R. Rémond et al., *Atlas historique de la France contemporaine 1800–1965*, A. Colin, 1966

27. Bourloton, Robert and Cougny, *Dictionnaire des parlementaires*, Bourloton, 1891

28. J. Bouvier, *Initiation au vocabulaire et aux mécanismes économiques contemporains (XIXe–XXe siècle)*, Société d'Edition d'Enseignement Supérieur (SEDES), reissued 1972

29. A. Dansette, *Histoire religieuse de la France contemporaine*, vol. I, Flammarion, 1948

30. E. Dolléans, *Histoire du mouvement ouvrier*, vol. I, A. Colin, 1967

31. J. Droz, ed., *Histoire générale du socialisme*, vol. I, PUF, 1972

32. G. Dupeux, *La Société française, 1789–1970*, A. Colin, 1973

33. G. Duveau, *Histoire du peuple français*, vol. IV, Nouvelle Librairie de France, 1953

34. M. Beloff, P. Renouvin, F. Schnabel and F. Valsecchi, eds., *L'Europe du XIXe et du XXe siècle*, vol. I, Milan, Marzorati, 1959

35. R. Girardet, *La Société militaire dans la France contemporaine*, Plon, 1953

36. J. Maitron et al., *Dictionnaire biographique du mouvement ouvrier français*, Editions Ouvrières, 1964–6

37. F. Ponteil, *Les Institutions de la France de 1814 à 1870*, PUF, 1966

38. R. Rémond, *La Vie politique en France depuis 1789*, vol. II, A. Colin, 1969

39. A. Latreille, J. R. Palanque, E. Delaruelle and R. Rémond, *Histoire du catholicisme français*, vol. III, Spes, 1962

40. P. Renouvin, *Histoire des relations internationales*, vol. V, pt 1, Hachette, 1964,

41. Pierre Sorlin, *La Société française*, vol. I, Arthaud, 1969

42. L. G. Vapereau, *Dictionnaire universel des contemporains*, Hachette (several editions as early as the Second Empire itself)

*5. Sources and analyses of sources*

43. A. Gérard, *Le Second Empire: innovation et réaction*, PUF, 1972

These sources can be classified into three groups:

(1) Newspapers and magazines. See in particular:

44. C. Bellanger, J. Godechot, P. Guiral and F. Terrou, *Histoire générale de la presse française*, vol. II, PUF, 1969
45. R. Bellet, *Presse et journalisme sous le second Empire*, A. Colin, 1967

(2) Literary works. Novels are an even more valuable source than Victor Hugo's *engagé* poems and the plays of the period.

46. P. Bleton, *La Vie sociale sous le second Empire: un étonnant témoignage de la comtesse de Ségur*, Editions Ouvrières, 1963
47. M. Soriano, introduction to the Comtesse de Ségur, *La Fortune de Gaspard*, J. J. Pauvert, 1972
48. E. Zola, *Les Rougon-Macquart: histoire naturelle et sociale d'une famille sous le second Empire*, annotated by H. Mitterand, Gallimard ('La Pléiade'), 1960–7, 5 vols.
49. 'Colloque Zola', proceedings in *Europe*, April–May 1968

(3) Correspondence, memoirs and historical works of the period. Among the countless first-hand accounts referred to in recent surveys, the following should be mentioned:

50. The memoirs of the republican A. Darimon published between 1883 and 1887 under various titles, in particular *Histoire d'un parti: le Tiers Parti sous l'Empire (1863–1866)*, Le Dentu, 1887
51. T. Delord, *Histoire du second Empire*, Baillière, 1958–76, 6 vols.
52. M. Du Camp, *Souvenirs d'un demi-siècle*, Hachette, 1949
53. J. Ferry, *Discours et opinions*, vol. I, introduction by Robiquet, A. Colin, 1893
54. E. and J. de Goncourt, *Journal: mémoires de la vie littéraire*, vols. I–VIII, Editions de l'Imprimerie Nationale de Monaco, 1956–7
55. P. Guiral and R. Brunon, *Aspects de la vie politique et militaire en France à travers la correspondance reçue par le maréchal Pélissier (1828–1864)*, Bibliothèque Nationale, 1968
56. G. Lefrançais, *Souvenirs d'un révolutionnaire*, reprinted La Tête des Feuilles, 1972
57. E. Ollivier, *Journal (1844–1869)*, Julliard, 1961
58. E. Ollivier, *L'Empire libéral*, Garnier, 1895–1915, 14 vols.
59. C. de Rémusat, *Mémoires de ma vie*, vols. IV–V, introduction by C. H. Pouthas, Plon, 1967
60. A. de Tocqueville, *Oeuvres complètes*, Gallimard 1951– (in progress), especially:
    Vol. VIII. *Correspondance d'A. de Tocqueville et de G. de Beaumont*
    Vol. IX. *Correspondance d'A. de Tocqueville avec P.-P. Royer-Collard et avec J.-J. Ampère* annotated and introduced by A. Jardin
61. J. Vier, *Daniel Stern: lettres républicaines du second Empire*, Editions du Cèdre, 1951

## Regional studies

Journals of regional history, such as *Revue du Nord, Cahiers d'histoire, Annales du Midi* and *Annales de l'Est*, are well worth consulting.

Valuable information may also be found in master's theses such as, in addition to those listed by Dansette (**1**):

62. A. Lecointre, 'Un quartier de Paris sous le second Empire: les Halles dans *Le Ventre de Paris* de Zola', Diplôme d'Etudes Supérieures, Paris, 1971
63. A. Sabatier, *Religion et politique dans le canton de Vernoux (Ardèche)*, research project, Grenoble, 1971

The works below have been grouped under three separate headings.


*1. Studies in regional (in most cases rural) history*

64. J. Anglade, *La Vie quotidienne dans le Massif central au XIXe siècle*, Hachette, 1971
65. A. Armengaud, *Les Populations de l'Est-Aquitain au début de l'époque contemporaine: recherches sur une région moins développée (vers 1845–vers 1871)*, Paris and The Hague, Mouton, 1961
66. P. Barral, 'Les Forces politiques sous le second Empire dans l'Isère', *Actes du 77e Congrès des Sociétés savantes*, Grenoble, 1952
67. P. Bernard, *Economie et sociologie de la Seine-et-Marne, 1850–1950*, A. Colin, 1962
68. Y. Brékilien, *La Vie quotidienne des paysans en Bretagne au XIXe siècle*, Hachette, 1966
69. H. Carel, 'La Haute-Saône de 1850 à 1914', typewritten dissertation, Paris, 1970
70. H. Contamine, *Metz et la Moselle de 1814 à 1870*, Nancy, Société d'Impressions Typographiques, 1932
71. G. Dupeux, *Aspects de l'histoire sociale et politique du Loir-et-Cher, 1848–1914*, Paris and The Hague, Mouton, 1962
72. R. Laurent, *Les Vignerons de la Côte-d'Or au XIXe siècle*, Les Belles Lettres, 1958
73. J. Lovie, *La Savoie dans la vie française de 1860 à 1875*, PUF, 1963
74. C. Marcilhacy, *Le Diocèse d'Orléans sous l'épiscopat de Mgr Dupanloup, 1849–1878*, Plon, 1962
75. R. Thabault, *1848–1914: l'ascension d'un peuple: mon village: ses hommes, ses routes, son école*, Delagrave, 1945
76. G. Thuillier, *Aspects de l'économie nivernaise au XIXe siècle*, A. Colin, 1966
77. V. Wright, 'Religion et politique dans les Basses-Pyrénées pendant la IIe République et le second Empire', *Annales du Midi*, 1969


*2. Studies on the larger provincial towns*

78. F. Codaccioni, *Lille, 1848–1914: contribution à une étude des structures sociales*, Lille, Service de Reproduction des Thèses de l'Université, 1971
79. L. Desgraves and G. Dupeux, *Histoire de Bordeaux*, vol. VI, Bordeaux, Fédération Historique du Sud-Ouest, 1969
80. P. Guillaume, *La Population de Bordeaux au XIXe siècle*, A. Colin, 1972
81. J. P. Kintz, 'Journaux politiques et journalistes strasbourgeois sous la IIe République et à la fin du second Empire', mimeographed Thèse de 3e Cycle, Strasbourg, 1970
82. P. Léon, *La Naissance de la grande industrie en Dauphiné*, vol. II, Gap, Louis-Jean, 1954
83. C. M. Leonard, *Lyon Transformed: Public Works of the Second Empire, 1853–1864*, Berkeley, University of California Press, 1961
84. *Marseille sous le second Empire*, conference held in 1960, Plon, 1961

*3. Studies on Paris*

85. J. Bastié, *La Croissance de la banlieue parisienne*, PUF, 1964
86. L. Chevalier, *La Formation de la population parisienne au XIXe siècle*, A. Colin, 1950
87. L. Chevalier, *Classes laborieuses et classes dangereuses à Paris pendant la première moitié du XIXe siècle*, Plon, 1958
88. M. Cornu, *La Conquête de Paris*, Mercure de France, 1972
89. Y. Magadur, 'L'évolution du faubourg Saint-Antoine sous le second Empire', *Information Historique*, 1964
90. A. Morizet, *Du vieux Paris au Paris moderne: Haussmann et ses prédécesseurs*, Hachette, 1932
91. D. H. Pinkney, *Napoleon III and the Rebuilding of Paris*, Princeton University Press, 1958
92. G. Massa-Gille, *Histoire des emprunts de la ville de Paris (1814–1875)*, Commission Historique des Travaux de la Ville de Paris, 1973

**Studies relating to various episodes or aspects of the period**

*1. For chapter 1 (apart from the preceding volume in this series)*

Studies about the emperor:

93. A. Dansette, *Louis-Napoléon à la conquête du pouvoir*, Hachette, 1961
94. S. Desternes and H. Chandey, *Napoleon III, homme du XXe siècle*, Hachette, 1961
95. G. E. Boilet, *La Doctrine sociale de Napoléon III*, Tequi, 1969
96. Brison G. Gooch, ed., *Napoleon III, Man of Destiny: Enlightened Statesman or Protofascist*, New York, Holt, Rinehart and Winston, 1962
97. G. Roux, *Napoléon III*, Flammarion, 1969

On the regime:

98. M. Flory, 'L'Appel au peuple napoléonien', *Revue Internationale d'Histoire Politique et Constitutionnelle*, July–September, 1952
99. M. Prélot, 'La Signification constitutionnelle du second Empire', *Revue Française de Science Politique*, January–March 1953
100. V. Wright, *Le Conseil d'Etat sous le second Empire*, A. Colin, 1972
101. T. Zeldin, *The Political System of Napoleon III*, London, Macmillan, 1958

*2. For chapter 2*

On the imperial personnel:

102. E. Beau de Loménie, *Les Responsabilités des dynasties bourgeoises*, vol. I, Denoël, 1943
103. J. Lhomme, *La Grande Bourgeoisie au pouvoir (1830–1880)*, PUF, 1960
104. J. Maurain, *Un bourgeois français au XIXe siècle: Baroche, ministre de Napoléon III*, Alcan, 1936
105. N. Blayau, *Billault, ministre de Napoléon III d'après ses papiers personnels, 1805–1863*, C. Klincksieck, 1969
106. J. Rohr, *Victor Duruy, ministre de Napoléon III: essai sur la politique de l'instruction publique au temps de l'Empire libéral*, Librairie Générale de Droit et de Jurisprudence, 1967
107. G. N. Lameyre, *Haussmann, préfet de Paris*, Flammarion, 1958

108. J. Durieux, *Le Ministre Pierre Magne d'après ses lettres et ses souvenirs*, H. Champion, 1929
109. G. Grothe, *Le Duc de Morny*, Fayard, 1968
110. M. Parturier, *Morny et son temps*, Hachette, 1969
111. H. Farat, *Persigny, un ministre de Napoléon III*, Hachette, 1957
112. R. Schnerb, *Rouher et le Second Empire*, A. Colin, 1949
113. P. Raphaël and M. Gontard, *Un ministre de l'Instruction publique sous l'Empire autoritaire: Hippolyte Fortoul (1851–1856)*, PUF, 1976

On administrative problems, see, in addition to (**6**):

114. L. Girard, A. Prost and R. Gossez, *Les Conseillers généraux en 1870*, PUF, 1967

### 3. For chapter 3

On demography:

115. A. Armengaud, *La Population française du XIXe siècle*, PUF, 1971
116. Mme Cahen, 'Evolution de la population active en France', *Etudes et Conjoncture*, June 1953
117. J. C. Toutain, *La Population de la France de 1700 à 1959*, Cahier de l'ISEA (Institut de Science Economique Appliquée), 1963

On the economy:

118. M. Barbance, *La Compagnie générale transatlantique*, Arts et Métiers Graphiques, 1955
119. J. Bouvier, 'Le Mouvement d'une civilisation nouvelle', in G. Duby, ed., *Histoire de la France* (see **5**)
120. J. Bouvier, *Les Rothschild*, Fayard, 1967; new, expanded edn, 1983
121. J. Bouvier, *Le Crédit lyonnais de 1863 à 1882*, Société d'Edition et de Vente des Publications de l'Education Nationale (SEVPEN), 1961
122. J. Bouvier, F. Furet and M. Gillet, *Le Mouvement du profit en France au XIXe siècle*, Paris and The Hague, Mouton, 1965
123. R. Cameron, *La France et le développement économique de l'Europe*, Le Seuil, 1971
124. R. Cameron, 'Profit, croissance et stagnation en France au XIXe siècle', *Economie Appliquée*, 1957
125. F. Caron, *Histoire de l'exploitation d'un grand réseau français: la Compagnie des chemins de fer du Nord de 1846 à 1936*, Paris and The Hague, Mouton, 1972
126. F. Crouzet, Essai de construction d'un indice annuel de la production industrielle française du XIXe siècle', *Annales: Economies, Sociétés, Civilisations (ESC)*, January–February 1970
127. P. Dupont-Ferrier, *Le Marché financier de Paris sous le second Empire*, Alcan, 1925
128. C. Fohlen, *L'Industrie textile au temps du second Empire*, Plon, 1956
129. B. Gille, *Histoire de la maison Rothschild*, vol. II, Geneva, Droz, 1967
130. M. Gillet, *Les Charbonnages du Nord de la France au XIXe siècle*, Paris and The Hague, Mouton, 1973
131. L. Girard, 'L'Affaire Mirès', *Bulletin de la Société d'Histoire Moderne et Contemporaine*, 1951
132. L. Girard, *La Politique des travaux publics du second Empire*, A. Colin, 1952
133. P. Guillaume, *La Compagnie des mines de la Loire (1846–1854): essai sur l'apparition de la grande industrie capitaliste en France*, PUF, 1966
134. C. Juglar, *Des crises commerciales et de leur retour périodique*, 1860; reprinted Farnborough, Hants., Gregg Press, 1968

135. E. Labrousse, *Aspects de l'évolution économique et sociale de la France et du Royaume-Uni de 1815 à 1880*, CDU, 1949

136. D. S. Landes, 'Vieille banque et banque nouvelle: la révolution financière du XIXe siècle', *Revue d'Histoire Moderne et Contemporaine*, 1956

137. J. Marczewski, *Le Produit physique de l'économie française de 1789 à 1913*, Cahier de l'ISEA, 1965

138. T. J. Markovitch, *L'Industrie française de 1789 à 1964*, 4 Cahiers de l'ISEA, 1965–6

139. T. J. Markovitch, *Salaires et profits industriels en France sous la monarchie de Juillet et le Second Empire*, Cahier de l'ISEA, 1967

140. J. Merley, *L'Industrie en Haute-Loire de la fin de la monarchie de Juillet aux débuts de la IIIe République*, Lyons, Centre d'Histoire Economique et Sociale de la Région Lyonnaise, 1972

141. G. P. Palmade, *Capitalisme et capitalistes français au XIXe siècle*, A. Colin, 1961

142. F. Rivet, *La Navigation à vapeur sur la Saône et le Rhône, 1783–1863*, PUF, 1962

143. J. C. Toutain, *Les Transports en France de 1830 à 1965*, Cahier de l'ISEA, 1967

144. R. Trempé, *Les Mineurs de Carmaux, 1848–1914*, Editions Ouvrières, 1971

145. J. Vial, *L'Industrialisation de la sidérurgie française, 1814–1864*, Paris and The Hague, Mouton, 1967


*4. For chapter 4*

146. N. Delefortrie and J. Morice, *Les Revenus départementaux en 1864 et en 1954*, preface by J. M. Jeanneney and M. Flamant, 'Recherches sur l'économie française' series, Fondation Nationale des Sciences Politiques, A. Colin, 1959

147. J. C. Toutain, *La Consommation alimentaire en France de 1789 à 1964*, Cahier de l'ISEA, 1971

148. A. Prost, *L'Enseignement en France, 1800–1967*, A. Colin, 1968

On the rural world:

149. J. J. Darmon, *Le Colportage de librairie en France sous le second Empire*, Plon, 1972

150. G. Kuhnholtz-Lordat, *Napoléon III et la paysannerie française*, Monte Carlo, Regain, 1962

151. J. C. Toutain, *Le Produit de l'agriculture française de 1700 à 1958*, Cahier de l'ISEA, 1961

152. P. Vigier, *Essai sur la répartition foncière dans la région alpine: son évolution des origines du cadastre à la fin du second Empire*, SEVPEN, 1963

On the working-class world:

153. G. Duveau, *La Vie ouvrière sous le second Empire*, Gallimard, 1946

154. J. Lhomme, 'Le Pouvoir d'achat de l'ouvrier français au cours d'un siècle, 1840–1940', *Le Mouvement Social*, April–June 1968

155. J. Rougerie, 'Remarques sur l'histoire des salaires à Paris', *ibid.*

156. P. Pierrard, *La Vie ouvrière à Lille sous le second Empire*, Bloud et Gay, 1965

157. H. Vanier, *La Mode et ses métiers: frivolités et luttes des classes, 1830–1870*, A. Colin, 1960

On the 'enlightened classes':

158. P. Barral, *Les Perier de l'Isère au XIXe siècle d'après leur correspondance familiale*, PUF, 1964

159. J. Lethève, *Impressionnistes et symbolistes devant la presse*, A. Colin, 1959

5. *For chapters 5 and 6*

On religious issues:

160. J. Maurain, *La Politique ecclésiastique du second Empire*, Alcan, 1930
161. J. Gadille, 'Autour de Louis Veuillot et de *L'Univers*', *Cahiers d'Histoire*, 1969
162. J. Gadille, *Albert du Boÿs, ses 'Souvenirs du concile du Vatican', 1869–1870: l'intervention du gouvernement impérial à Vatican I*, Louvain, Bibliothèque de la *Revue d'Histoire Ecclésiastique*, 1968
163. G. Weill, *Histoire de l'idée laïque en France*, Alcan, 1925

On anti-opposition measures and the revival of the republican 'party':

164. H. C. Payne, *The Police State of Louis Napoleon Bonaparte, 1851–1860*, Seattle, University of Washington Press, 1966
165. R. W. Reichert, 'Antibonapartist elections to the Académie française (1852–1870)', *Journal of Modern History*, March 1963
166. V. Wright, 'La Loi de sûreté générale de 1858', *Revue d'Histoire Moderne et Contemporaine*, July–September 1969
167. M. Sorre, 'Les Pères du radicalisme, expression de la doctrine républicaine à la fin du second Empire', *Revue Française de Science Politique*, October–December 1951
168. G. Weill, *Histoire du parti républicain (1814–1870)*, Alcan, 1928
169. I. Tchernoff, *Le Parti républicain au coup d'Etat et sous le second Empire*, Pedone, 1906
170. J. Chastenet, *Gambetta*, Fayard, 1969
171. M. Dommanget, *Blanqui et l'opposition républicaine à la fin du second Empire*, A. Colin, 1960
172. R. L. Williams, *Henri Rochefort*, Editions de Trévise, 1970

On military and foreign problems:

173. B. Schnapper, *Le Remplacement militaire au XIXe siècle*, SEVPEN, 1968
174. L. M. Case, *French Opinion on War and Diplomacy during the Second Empire*, Philadelphia, University of Pennsylvania Press, 1954
175. L. Girard, 'Révolution ou conservatisme en Europe (1856): une polémique de la presse parisienne après la guerre de Crimée', *Mélanges P. Renouvin: études d'histoire des relations internationales*, PUF, 1966
176. S. Bobr-Tylingo, *Napoléon III, l'Europe et la Pologne, 1863–1864*, Rome, Institutum Historicum Polonicum, 1963
177. L. M. Case and W. Spencer, *The United States and France: Civil War Diplomacy*, Philadelphia, University of Pennsylvania Press, 1970
178. J. G. Larregola, *Le Gouvernement français face à la guerre de Sécession*, Pedone, 1970
179. G. Delamare, *La Tragédie méxicaine, une faute de Napoléon III*, Liège, Thone, 1963
180. C. Schefer, *La Grande Pensée de Napoléon III: les origines de l'expédition du Mexique, 1858–1862*, Rivière, 1939
181. M. Emerit, 'L'Opinion de Napoléon III sur la question du trône d'Espagne en 1869', *Revue d'Histoire Moderne et Contemporaine*, July 1969

On the new trade policy:

182. P. Bairoch, 'Commerce extérieur et développement économique: quelques enseignements de l'expérience libre-échangiste de la France au XIXe siècle', *Revue Economique*, January 1970

183. A. L. Dunham, *The Anglo-French Treaty of Commerce of 1860 and the Progress of the Industrial Revolution in France*, Detroit, University of Michigan Press, 1930
184. C. Fohlen, 'Bourgeoisie française, libre-échange et intervention de l'Etat', *Revue Economique*, 1956

On colonial policy:

185. C. R. Ageron, 'La Vie politique en Algérie sous le second Empire' and 'Abd-el-Kader, souverain d'un "Royaume arabe d'Orient"', in *Politiques coloniales du Maghreb*, PUF, 1972
186. C. A. Julien, *Histoire de l'Algérie contemporaine*, vol. I, PUF, 1964
187. J. Valette, 'Origines et enseignements de l'expédition du Mékong, 1866–1868', *Bulletin de la Société d'Histoire Moderne*, 1968

On the social problem:

188. *La Première Internationale*, Centre National de la Recherche Scientifique (CNRS), 1964
189. J. Dubois, *Le Vocabulaire politique et social en France de 1869 à 1872*, Larousse, 1962
190. *L'Actualité de Proudhon*, Editions de l'Institut de Sociologie de l'Université Libre de Bruxelles, 1967
191. P. Léon, 'Les Grèves de 1867–1870 dans le département de l'Isère', *Revue d'Histoire Moderne et Contemporaine*, 1954
192. F. L'Huillier, *La Lutte ouvrière à la fin du second Empire*, A. Colin, 1957

On the elections of 1869 and the liberal Empire:

193. L. Girard et al., *Les Elections de 1869*, Rivière, 1960. (On these elections see also *Cahiers d'Histoire*, 1961 and 1962, *Revue d'Alsace*, 1960 and *Revue d'Histoire Economique et Sociale*, 1963)
194. T. Zeldin, *Emile Ollivier and the Liberal Empire of Napoleon III*, Oxford: Clarendon Press, 1963
195. V. Wright, 'Les Préfets d'Emile Ollivier', *Revue Historique*, July–September 1968
·196. J. P. Azéma and M. Winock, *Naissance et mort de la IIIe République*, Calmann-Lévy, 1970

On the war and the Commune:*

197. M. Baumont, *L'Echiquier de Metz*, Hachette, 1971
198. M. Chanal, *La Guerre de 1870*, Bordas, 1972
199. A. Guérin, *La Folle Guerre de 1870*, Hachette, 1970
200. J. Jaurès, *La Guerre de 1870–1871*, Flammarion, reprinted 1970
201. 'La Commune de 1871' (conference), *Le Mouvement Social*, April–June 1972
202. K. Marx, *La Guerre civile en France (1871)*, Editions Sociales, 1952
203. J. P. Azéma and M. Winock, *Les Communards*, Le Seuil, 1964
204. J. Bruhat, J. Dautry and E. Tersen, *La Commune de 1871*, Editions Sociales, reprinted 1971
205. H. Lefebvre, *La Proclamation de la Commune*, Gallimard, 1965
206. C. Rihs, *La Commune de Paris: sa structure et ses doctrines*, Le Seuil, 1973
207. J. Rougerie, *Procès des communards*, Julliard, 1964

* The history of the Commune has been dealt with in numerous studies. I have listed here only some of the more recent works, which include fuller bibliographies (in particular **204**, **207** and **208**).

208. J. Rougerie, *Paris libre, 1871*, Le Seuil, 1971
209. W. Serman, *La Commune*, PUF, 1971

### Supplementary bibliography

210. C. R. Ageron, *L'Algérie algérienne de Napoléon III à de Gaulle*, Sindbad, 1980
211. J. Autin, *Les Frères Pereire: le bonheur d'entreprendre*, Librairie Académique Perrin, 1984
212. P. Bairoch, *Commerce extérieur et développement économique de l'Europe au XIXe siècle*, Paris and The Hague, Mouton, 1976
213. L. Bergeron, *Les Capitalistes en France (1789–1914)*, Gallimard, 1978
214. L. Bergeron, *L'Industrialisation de la France au XIXe siècle*, Hatier, 1979
215. F. Braudel and E. Labrousse, *Histoire économique et sociale de la France*, pt 3, vols. I and II, PUF, 1976 and 1979
216. J. P. Chaline, *Les Bourgeois de Rouen: une élite urbaine au XIXe siècle*, Presses de la Fondation Nationale des Sciences Politiques, 1982
217. A. Corbin, *Archaïsme et modernité en Limousin au XIXe siècle, 1845–1880*, Rivière, 1975
218. C. Dufresne, *Morny, l'homme du Second Empire*, Librairie Académique Perrin, 1983
219. J. Gaillard, *Paris, la ville (1852–1870)*, H. Champion, 1977
220. J. Gaillard, 'Le Baron Haussmann', *L'Histoire*, no. 37, September 1981
221. G. Garrier, *Paysans du Beaujolais et du Lyonnais, 1800–1870*, Grenoble, Presses Universitaires de Grenoble, 1973
222. L. Girard, *Nouvelle Histoire de Paris: la Deuxième République et le Second Empire*, Hachette, 1981
223. P. J. Harrigan, *Mobility, Elites and Education in French Society of the Second Empire*, Waterloo (Ontario), Wilfred Laurier University Press, 1980
224. Y. Lequin, *Les Ouvriers de la région lyonnaise, 1848–1914*, Lyons, Presses Universitaires de Lyon, 1977
225. A. Plessis, *La Banque de France et ses deux cents actionnaires sous le Second Empire*, Geneva, Droz, 1982
226. A. Plessis, *Régents et gouverneurs de la Banque de France sous le Second Empire*, Geneva, Droz, 1984
227. A. Rey-Goldzeiguer, *Le Royaume arabe: la politique algérienne de Napoléon III, 1861–1870*, Algiers, Société Nationale d'Edition et de Diffusion, 1977
228. William H. C. Smith, *Napoléon III*, Hachette, 1982
229. W. Serman, *Les Officiers français dans la nation, 1848–1914*, Aubier, 1982
230. T. Zeldin, *France, 1848–1945*, Oxford, Oxford University Press, 1973 and 1977, 2 vols.

# Index of names